The Auto-Biography of Edward Gibbon, Esq: Illustrated from His Letters, with Occasional Notes and Narratives

Edward Gibbon, John Holroyd Sheffield

THE

AUTO-BIOGRAPHY

OF

EDWARD GIBBON, ESQ.,

ILLUSTRATED FROM HIS LETTERS, WITH OCCASIONAL
NOTES AND NARRATIVES.

BY JOHN, LORD SHEFFIELD.

COMPLETE IN ONE VOLUME:

NEW YORK:

BUCKLAND & SUMNER,
NO. 79 JOHN STREET.

Bennet & Warner, Printers, No. 142 Nassau street.

1846

INTRODUCTORY REMARKS

THE melancholy duty of examining the papers of my deceased friend devolved upon me at a time when I was depressed by severe afflictions.

In that state of mind, I hesitated to undertake the task of selecting and preparing his manuscripts for the press. The warmth of my early and long attachment to Mr Gibbon made me conscious of a partiality, which it was not proper to indulge, especially in revising many of his juvenile and unfinished compositions. I had to guard, not only against a sentiment like my own, which I found extensively diffused, but also against the eagerness occasioned by a very general curiosity to see in print every literary relic, however imperfect, of so distinguished a writer.

Being aware how disgracefully authors of eminence have been often treated, by an indiscreet posthumous publication of fragments and careless effusions; when I had selected those papers which to myself appeared the fittest for the public eye, I consulted some of our common friends, whom I knew to be equally anxious with myself for Mr. Gibbon's fame, and fully competent, from their judgment, to protect it.

Under such a sanction it is, that, no longer suspecting myself to view through too favorable a medium the compositions of my friend, I now venture to publish them; and it may, here be proper to give some information to the reader, respecting the Memoirs of Mr. Gibbon's life and writings, a work which he seems to have projected with peculiar solicitude and attention, and of which he left six different sketches, all in his own hand-writing. One of these sketches, the most diffuse and circumstantial, so far as it proceeds, ends at the time when he quitted Oxford. Another at the year 1764, when he travelled to Italy. A third, at his father's death, in 1770. A fourth, which he continued to a short time after his return to Lausanne in 1788, appears in the form of Annals, much less detailed than the others. The two remaining sketches are still more imperfect. It is difficult to discover the order in which these several pieces were written, but there is reason to believe that the most copious was the last. From all these the following Memoirs have been carefully selected, and put together.

My hesitation in giving these Memoirs to the world, arose principally from the circumstance of Mr. Gibbon's appearing, in some respect, not to have been satisfied with them, as he had so frequently varied their form: yet, notwithstanding this diffidence, the compositions, though unfinished, are so excellent, that they may justly entitle my friend to appear as his own biographer, rather than to have that task undertaken by any other person less qualified for it.

This opinion has rendered me anxious to publish the present Memoirs, without any unnecessary delay; for I am persuaded that the author of them cannot be made to appear in a truer light than he does in the following pages. In them, and in his different Letters which I have added, will be found a complete picture of his talents, his disposition, his studies, and his attainments.

Those slight variations of character, which naturally arose in the progress of his life, will be unfolded in a series of Letters, selected from a correspondence between him and myself, which continued full thirty years, and ended with his death.

It is to be lamented, that the sketches of the Memoirs, except that composed in the form of Annals, and which seems rather designed as heads for a future work, cease about twenty years before Mr. Gibbon's death; and consequently, that we have the least detailed account of the most interesting part of his life. His correspondence during that period, will, in great measure, supply the deficiency. By many, the Letters will be found a very interesting part of the present publication. They will prove how pleasant, friendly, and amiable Mr. Gibbon was in private life; and if, in publishing letters so flattering to myself, I incur the imputation of vanity, I shall meet the charge with a frank confession that I am indeed highly vain of having enjoyed, for so many years, the esteem, the confidence, and the affection of a man, whose social qualities endeared him to the most accomplished society, and whose talents, great as they were, must be acknowledged to have been fully equalled by the sincerity of his friendship.

Whatever censure may be pointed against the editor, the public will set a due value on the Letters for their intrinsic merit. I must, indeed, be blinded, either by vanity or affection, if they do not display the heart and mind of their author, in such a manner as justly to increase the number of his admirers.

I have not been solicitous to garble or expunge passages which, to some, may appear trifling. Such passages will often, in the opinion of the deserving reader, mark the character of the writer, and the omission of them would materially take from the ease and familiarity of authentic letters.

Few men, I believe, have ever so fully unveiled their own character, by a minute narrative of their sentiments and pursuits, as Mr. Gibbon will here be found to have done; not with study and labor—not with an affected frankness, but with a genuine confession of his little foibles and peculiarities, and a good-humored and natural display of his own conduct and opinions.

I will close all I mean to say, as the editor of these Memoirs, by assuring the reader, that, although I have in some measure newly arranged those interesting papers, by forming one regular narrative from the six different sketches, I have nevertheless adhered with scrupulous fidelity to the very words of their author; and I use the letter S. to mark such notes of my own, as it seemed necessary to add.

It remains only to express a wish, that in discharging this latest office of affection, my regard to the memory of my friend may appear, as I trust it will do, proportioned to the high satisfaction which I enjoyed for many years in possessing his entire confidence, and very partial attachment.

SHEFFIELD.

Sheffield Place, 6th Aug., 1795.

CONTENTS.

CONTENTS.

CHAPTER XII.

AUTO-BIOGRAPHY

OF

EDWARD GIBBON, ESQ.

MEMOIRS

OF

MY LIFE AND WRITINGS.

~~~~~~~~~~~~~~~~~

THE AUTHOR'S INTRODUCTION.

In the fifty-second year of my age, after the completion of an arduous and successful work, I now propose to
employ some moments of my leisure in reviewing the
simple transactions of a private and literary life. Truth,
naked, unblushing truth, the first virtue of more serious
history, must be the sole recommendation of this personal
narrative. The style shall be simple and familiar; but
style is the image of character; and the habits of correct
writing may produce, without labor or design, the appearance of art and study. My own amusement is my
motive, and will be my reward; and if these sheets are
communicated to some discreet and indulgent friends, they
will be secreted from the public eye till the author shall
be removed beyond the reach of criticism or ridicule.*

* This passage is found in one only of the six sketches, and in that which
seems to have been the first written, and which was laid aside among loose

A lively desire of knowing and of recording our ancestors so generally prevails, that it must depend on the influence of some common principle in the minds of men. We seem to have lived in the persons of our forefathers; it is the labor and reward of vanity to extend the term of this ideal longevity. Our imagination is always active to enlarge the narrow circle in which nature has confined us. Fifty or a hundred years may be allotted to an individual, but we step forwards beyond death with such hopes as religion and philosophy will suggest; and we fill up the silent vacancy that precedes our birth, by associating ourselves to the authors of our existence. Our calmer judgment will rather tend to moderate, than to suppress, the pride of an ancient and worthy race. The satirist may laugh, the philosopher may preach; but Reason herself will respect the prejudices and habits, which have been consecrated by the experience of mankind.

Wherever the distinction of birth is allowed to form a superior order in the state, education and example should always, and will often, produce among them a dignity of

papers. Mr. Gibbon, in his communications with me on the subject of his Memoirs, a subject which he had never mentioned to any other person, expressed a determination of publishing them in his lifetime; and never appears to have departed from that resolution, excepting in one of his letters annexed, in which he intimates a doubt, though rather carelessly, whether in his time, or at any time, they would meet the eye of the public. In a conversation, however, not long before his death, it was suggested to him, that, if he should make them a full image of his mind, he would not have nerves to publish them in his lifetime, and therefore that they should be posthumous. He answered, rather eagerly, that he was determined to publish them *in his lifetime.*—S.

sentiment, and propriety of conduct, which is guarded from dishonour by their own and the public esteem. If we read of some illustrious line so ancient that it has no beginning, so worthy that it ought to have no end, we sympathise in its various fortunes; nor can we blame the generous enthusiasm, or even the harmless vanity, of those who are allied to the honours of its name. For my own part, could I draw my pedigree from a general, a statesman, or a celebrated author, I should study their lives with the diligence of filial love. In the investigation of past events, our curiosity is stimulated by the immediate or indirect reference to ourselves; but in the estimate of honour we should learn to value the gifts of Nature above those of Fortune; to esteem in our ancestors the qualities that best promote the interests of society; and to pronounce the descendant of a king less truly noble than the offspring of a man of genius, whose writings will instruct or delight the latest posterity. The family of Confucius is, in my opinion, the most illustrious in the world. After a painful ascent of eight or ten centuries, our barons and princes of Europe are lost in the darkness of the middle ages; but, in the vast equality of the empire of China, the posterity of Confucius have maintained, above two thousand two hundred years, their peaceful honours and perpetual succession. The chief of the family is still revered, by the sovereign and the people, as the lively image of the wisest of mankind. The nobility of the Spencers has been illustrated and enriched by the trophies of Marlborough; but I exhort them to consider the Fairy Queen as the most precious jewel of their coronet. I have exposed my private feelings, as I shall always do, without scruple or reserve. That these sentiments are just, or at least natural, I am inclined to believe, since I do not feel myself interested in the cause; for I can derive from my ancestors neither glory nor shame.

Yet a sincere and simple narrative of my own life may amuse some of my leisure hours; but it will subject me, and perhaps with justice, to the imputation of vanity. I may judge, however, from the experience both of past and of the present times, that the public are always curious to know the men, who have left behind them any image of their minds: the most scanty accounts of such men are compiled with diligence, and perused with eagerness; and the student of every class may derive a lesson, or an example, from the lives most similar to his own. My name may hereafter be placed among the thousand articles of a Biographia Britannica; and I must be conscious, that no one is so well qualified, as myself, to describe the series of my thoughts and actions. The authority of my masters, of the grave Thaunus, and the philosophic Hume, might be sufficient to justify my design; but it would not be difficult to produce a long list of ancients and moderns, who, in various forms, have exhibited their own portraits. Such portraits are often the most interesting, and sometimes the only interesting parts of their writings; and, if they be sincere, we seldom complain of the minuteness or proximity of these personal memorials. The lives of the younger Pliny, of Petrarch, and of Erasmus, are expressed in the epistles, which they themselves have given to the world. The essays of Montaigne and Sir William Temple brings us home to the houses and bosoms of the authors: we smile without contempt at the headstrong passions of Benevenuto Cellini, and the gay follies of Colley Cibber.   The confessions of St. Austin and Rousseau disclose the secrets of the human heart: the commentaries of the learned Huet have survived his evangelical demonstration; and the memoirs of Goldoni are more truly dramatic than his Italian comedies.   The heretic and the churchman are strongly marked in the characters and fortunes of Whiston and Bishop Newton; and even the dulness of Michael de Marolles and Anthony Wood acquires some value from the faithful representation of men and manners.   That I am equal or superior to some of these, the effects of modesty or affectation cannot force me to dissemble.

CHAP. I.

ACCOUNT AND ANECDOTES OF HIS FAMILY.

My family is originally derived from the county of Kent. The southern district, which borders on Sussex and the sea, was formerly overspread with the great forest Anderida, and even now retains the denomination of the *Weald*, or Woodland. In this district, and in the hundred and parish of Rolvenden, the Gibbons were possessed of lands in the year one thousand three hundred and twenty-six; and the elder branch of the family, without much increase or diminution of property, still adheres to its native soil. Fourteen years after the first appearance of his name, John Gibbon is recorded as the Marmorarius or architect of King Edward the Third: the strong and stately castle of Queensborough, which guarded the entrance of the Medway, was a monument of his skill; and the grant of an hereditary toll on the passage from Sandwich to Stonar, in the Isle of Thanet, is the reward of no vulgar artist. In the visitations of the heralds, the Gibbons are frequently mentioned; they held the rank of esquire in an age, when that title was less promiscuously assumed: one of them, under the reign of Queen Elizabeth, was captain of the militia of Kent; and a free school, in the neighboring town of Benenden, proclaims the charity and opulence of its founder. But

time, or their own obscurity, has cast a veil of oblivion
over the virtues and vices of my Kentsh ancestors; their
character or station confined them to the labours and
pleasures of a rural life: nor is it in my power to follow
the advice of the poet, in an enquiry after a name—

> "Go search it there, where to be born, and die,
> Of rich and poor makes all the history."

So recent is the institution of our parish registers. In
the beginning of the seventeenth century, a younger
branch of the Gibbons, of Rolvenden, migrated from the
country to the city; and from this branch I do not blush
to descend. The law requires some abilities; the church
imposes some restraints; and before our army and navy,
our civil establishments, and Indian empire, had opened so
many paths to fortune, the mercantile profession was
more frequently chosen by youth of a liberal race and
education, who aspired to create their own independence.
Our most respectable families have not disdained the
counting-house, or even the shop; their names are
enrolled in the livery and companies of London; and in
England, as well as in the Italian commonwealths, heralds
have been compelled to declare, that gentility is not degraded by the exercise of trade.

The armorial ensigns which, in the times of chivalry,
adorned the crest and shield of the soldier, are now become an empty decoration, which every man, who has
money to build a carriage, may paint according to his
fancy on the panels. My family arms are the same which
were borne by the Gibbons of Kent in an age, when the
College of Heralds religiously guarded the distinctions of

blood and name: a lion rampant gardant, between three
scallop-shells argent, on a field azure.* I should not however have been tempted to blazon my coat of arms, were
it not connected with a whimsical anecdote.—About the
reign of James the First, the three harmless scallop-shells
were changed by Edmund Gibbon, Esq., into three *ogreses,*
or female cannibals, with a design of stigmatizing three
ladies, his kinswomen, who had provoked him by an unjust lawsuit. But this singular mode of revenge, for which
he obtained the sanction of Sir William Seager, king-at-
arms, soon expired with its author; and, on his own
monument in the Temple Church, the monsters vanish,
and the three scallop-shells resume their proper and
hereditary place.

Our alliances by marriage it is not disgraceful to mention. The chief honour of my ancestry is James Fiens,
Baron Say and Seale, and Lord High Treasurer of England, in the reign of Henry the Sixth; from whom by the
Phelips, the Whetnalls, and the Cromers, I am lineally
descended in the eleventh degree. His dismission and
imprisonment in the Tower were insufficient to appease
the popular clamor; and the treasurer, with his son-in-law
Cromer, was beheaded (1450), after a mock trial by the
Kentish insurgents. The black list of his offences, as it
is exhibited in Shakespeare, displays the ignorance and
envy of a plebian tyrant. Besides the vague reproaches
of selling Maine and Normandy to the Dauphin, the trea-

* The father of Lord Chancellor Hardwicke married an heiress of this
family of Gibbon. The chancellor's escutcheon in the Temple Hall, quarters the arms of Gibbon, as does also that in Lincoln's Inn Hall, of Charles
York, Chancellor in 1770.—S.

surer is specially accused of luxury, for riding on a foot-cloth; and of treason, for speaking French, the language of our enemies :—" Thou hast most traitorously corrupted the youth of the realm," says Jack Cade to the unfortu-nate lord, "in erecting a grammar-school; and whereas before our forefathers had no other books than the score and the tally, thou hast caused printing to be used; and, contrary to the king, his crown, and dignity, thou hast built a paper-mill. It will be proved in thy face, that thou hast men about thee who usually talk of a noun and a verb, and such abominable words, as no christian ear can endure to hear." Our dramatic poet is generally more attentive to character than to history; and I much fear that the art of printing was not introduced into Eng-land till several years after Lord Say's death; but of some of these meritorious crimes I should hope to find my ancestor guilty; and a man of letters may be proud of his descent from a patron and martyr of learning.

In the beginning of the last century, Robert Gibbon, Esq., of Rolvenden, in Kent, (who died in 1618,) had a son of the same name of Robert, who settled in London, and became a member of the Cloth-workers' Company. His wife was a daughter of the Edgars, who flourished about four hundred years in the county of Suf-folk, and produced an eminent and wealthy sergeant-at-law, Sir Gregory Edgar, in the reign of Henry the Sev-enth. Of the sons of Robert Gibbon, (who died in 1643,) Matthew did not aspire above the station of a linen-draper in Leadenhall-street; but John has given to the public some curious memorials of his existence, his cha-racter, and his family. He was born on the 3d of Novem-

ber in the year 1629; his education was liberal, at a
grammar school, and afterwards in Jesus College at Cambridge; and he celebrates the retired content which he
enjoyed at Allesborough in Worcestershire, in the house
of Thomas Lord Coventry, where John Gibbon was employed as a domestic tutor, the same office which Mr.
Hobbes exercised in the Devonshire family. But the
spirit of my kinsman soon immerged into more active
life; he visited foreign countries as a soldier and a traveller, acquired the knowledge of the French and Spanish
languages, passed some time in the Isle of Jersey, crossed
the Atlantic, and resided upwards of a twelvemonth
(1659) in the rising colony of Virginia. In this remote
province, his taste, or rather passion, for heraldry, found
a singular gratification at a war-dance of the native In-
dians. As they moved in measured steps, brandishing
their tomahawks, his curious eye contemplated their little
shields of bark, and their naked bodies, which were
painted with the colours and symbols of his favourite science. "At which I exceedingly wondered; and concluded that heraldry was ingrafted *naturally* into the
sense of human race. If so, it deserves a greater esteem
than now-a-days is put upon it." His return to England
after the Restoration was soon followed by his marriage
—his settlement in a house in St. Catharine's Cloister,
near the Tower, which devolved to my grandfather—and
his introduction into the Heralds' College (in 1671) by the
style and title of Blue-mantle Pursuivant at Arms. In this
office he enjoyed near fifty years the rare felicity of
uniting, in the same pursuit, his study and inclination: his
name is remembered in the College, and many of his let-

ters are still preserved.   Several of the most respectable
characters of the age, Sir William Dugdale, Mr. Ashmole,
Dr. John Betts, and Dr. Nehemiah Grew, were his friends;
and in the society of such men, John Gibbon may be
recorded without disgrace as the member of an astrologi-
cal club.   The study of hereditary honours is favourable
to the royal prerogative; and my kinsman, like most of
his family, was a high Tory both in church and state.
In the latter end of the reign of Charles the Second, his
pen was exercised in the cause of the Duke of York: the
Republican faction he most cordially detested; and as
each animal is conscious of its proper arms, the heralds'
revenge was emblazoned on a most diabolical escutcheon.
But the triumph of the Whig government checked the
preferment of Blue-mantle; and he was even suspended
from his office till his tongue could learn to pronounce the
oath of abjuration.   His life was prolonged to the age of
ninety; and, in the expectation of the inevitable though
uncertain hour, he wished to preserve the blessings of
health, competence, and virtue.   In the year 1682 he
published at London his Introductio ad Latinam Blaso-
niam, an original attempt, which Camden had desiderated,
to define, in a Roman idiom, the terms and attributes of a
Gothic institution.   It is not two years since I acquired
in a foreign land, some domestic intelligence of my own
family; and this intelligence was conveyed to Switzerland from the heart of Germany.   I had formed an acquaintance with Mr. Langer, a lively and ingenious
scholar, while he resided at Lausanne as preceptor to the
hereditary Prince of Brunswick.   On his return to his
proper station of librarian to the ducal library of Wolfen-

buttel, he accidentally found among some literary rubbish a small old English volume of heraldry, inscribed with the name of John Gibbon. From the title only Mr. Langer judged that it might be an acceptable present to his friend; and he judged rightly. His manner is quaint and affected; his order is confused: but he displays some wit, more reading, and still more enthusiasm; and if an enthusiast be often absurd, he is never languid. An English text is perpetually interspersed with Latin sentences in prose and verse; but in his own poetry he claims an exemption from the laws of prosedy. Amidst a profusion of geneological knowledge, my kinsman could not be forgetful of his own name; and to him I am indebted for almost the whole of my information concerning the Gibbon family. From this small work (a duodecimo of one hundred and sixty-five pages) the author expected immortal fame: and at the conclusion of his labour he sings, in a strain of self-exultation:

> " Usque huc corrigitur Romana Blasonia per me
>   Verborumque dehinc barbara forma cadat.
> Hic liber, in meritum si forsitan incidet usum,
>   Testis rite meæ sedulitatis erit.
> Quicquid agat Zoilns, ventura fatebitur, ætas
>   Artis quod fueram non Clypearis inops."

Such are the hopes of authors! In the failure of those hopes John Gibbon has not been the first of his profession, and very possib y may not be the last of his name. His brother Matthew Gibbon, the draper, had one daughter and two sons—my grandfather Edward, who was born in the year 1666, and Thomas, afterwards Dean of Carlisle. According to the mercantile creed, that the

best book is a profitable ledger, the writings of John the
herald would be much less precious than than those of
his nephew Edward: but an author professes at least to
write for the public benefit; and the slow balance of trade
can be pleasing to those persons only, to whom it is
advantageous. The successful industry of my granfather
raised him above the level of his immediate ancestors;
he appears to have launched into various and extensive
dealings: even his opinions were subordinate to his interest; and I find him in Flanders clothing King William's troops, while he would have contracted with more
pleasure, though not perhaps at a cheaper rate, for the
service of King James. During his residence abroad,
his concerns at home were managed by his mother
Hester, an active and notable woman. Her second
husband was a widower, of the name of Acton: they
united the children of their first nuptials. After his marriage with the daughter of Richard Acton, goldsmith in
Leadenhall-street, he gave his own sister to Sir Whitmore
Acton, of Aldenham; and I am thus connected, by a triple alliance, with that ancient and loyal family of Shrop-
shire baronets. It consisted about that time of seven
brothers, all of gigantic stature; one of whom,.a pigmy
of six feet two inches, confessed himself the last and least
of the seven; adding, in the true spirit of party, that such
men were not born since the Revolution. Under the
Tory administration of the four last years of Queen Ann
(1710—1714), Mr. Edward Gibbon was appointed one of
the Commissioners of the Customs; he sat at that board
with Prior: but the merchant was better qualified for his
station than the poet; since Lord Bolingbroke has been

heard to declare, that he had never conversed with a man, who more clearly understood the commerce and finances of England. In the year 1716 he was elected one of the directors of the South Sea Company; and his books exhibited the proof that, before his acceptance of this fatal office, he had acquired an independent fortune of sixty thousand pounds.

CHAP. II.

THE SOUTH SEA SCHEME.

But his fortune was overwhelmed in the shipwreck of the year twenty, and the labours of thirty years were blasted in a single day. Of the use or abuse of the South Sea scheme, of the guilt or innocence of my grandfather and his brother directors, I am neither a competent nor a disinterested judge. Yet the equity of modern times must condemn the violent and arbitrary proceedings, which would have disgraced the cause of justice, and would render injustice still more odious. No sooner had the nation awakened from its golden dream, than a popular and even a parliamentary clamour demanded their victims: but it was acknowledged on all sides that the South Sea directors, however guilty, could not be touched by any known laws of the land. The speech of Lord Molesworth, the author of the State of Denmark, may show the temper, or rather the intemperance, of the House of Commons. "Extraordinary crimes," exclaimed that ardent Whig, "call aloud for extraordinary remedies. The Roman lawgivers had not foreseen the possible existence of a parricide: but as soon as the first monster appeared, he was sewn in a sack, and thrown headlong into the river; and I shall be content to inflict the same treatment on the authors of our present ruin." His motion was not

literally adopted; but a bill of pains and penalties was introduced, a retroactive statute, to punish the offences, which
did not exist at the time they were committed.   Such a
pernicious violation of liberty and law can be excused
only by the most imperious necessity; nor could it be
defended on this occasion by the plea of impending danger or useful example.   The legislature restrained the
persons of the directors, imposed an exorbitant security
for their appearance, and marked their characters with a
previous note of ignominy: they were compelled to deliver, upon oath, the strict value of their estates; and were
disabled for making any transfer or alienation of any part
of their property.   Against a bill of pains and penalties it
is the common right of every subject to be heard by his
counsel at the bar: they prayed to be heard; their prayer
was refused; and their oppressors, who required no
evidence, would listen to no defence.   It had been at first
proposed that one-eighth of their respective estates should
be allowed for the future support of the directors; but it was
specially urged, that in the various shades of opulence
and guilt such an unequal proportion would be too light
for some, and for some might possible be too heavy. The
character and conduct of each man were separately
weighed; but instead of the calm solemnity of a judicial
inquiry, the fortune and honour of three and thirty Englishmen were made the topic of hasty conversation, the
sport of a lawless majority; and the basest member of
the committee, by a malicious word or a silent vote, might
indulge his general spleen or personal animosity. Injury
was aggravated by insult, and insult was embittered by
pleasantry, Allowances of twenty pounds, or one shil-

ling, were facetiously moved. A vague report that a
director had formerly been concerned in *another* project,
by which some unknown persons had lost their money,
was admitted as a proof of his actual guilt. One man
was ruined because he had dropped a foolish speech, that
his horses should feed upon gold; another because he
was grown so proud, that, one day at the Treasury, he
had refused a civil answer to persons much above him.
All were condemned, absent and unheard, in arbitrary
fines and forfeitures, which swept away the greatest part
of their substance. Such bold oppression can scarcely be
shielded by the omnipotence of parliament; and yet it
may be seriously questioned, whether the judges of the
South Sea directors were the true and legal representatives of the country. The first parliament of George the
First had been chosen (1715) for three years: the term
had elapsed, their trust was expired; and the four additional years (1718—1722), during which they continued to
sit, were derived not from the people, but from themselves; from the strong measures of the septennial bill,
which can only be paralleled by *il serar di consiglio* of
the Venetian history. Yet candor will own that to the
same parliament every Englishman is deeply indebted:
the septennial act, so vicious in its origin, has been sanc-
tioned by time, experience, and the national consent. Its
first operation secured the House of Hanover on the
throne, and its permanent influence maintains the peace
and stability of government. As often as a repeal has
been moved in the House of Commons, I have given in
its defence a clear and conscientious vote.

My grandfather could not expect to be treated with

more lenity than his companions. His Tory principles
and connections rendered him obnoxious to the ruling
powers : his name is reported in a suspicious secret ; and
his well-known abilities could not plead the excuse of
ignorance or error, In the first proceedings against the
South Sea directors, Mr. Gibbon is one of the few who
were taken into custody ; and, in the final sentence, the
measures of his fine proclaims him eminently guilty
The total estimate which he delivered on oath to the
House of Commons amounted to one hundred and six
thousand five hundred and forty-three pounds five shillings and sixpence, exclusive of antecedent settlements.

Two different allowances of fifteen and of ten thousand
pounds were moved for Mr. Gibbon : but, on the question
being put, it was carried without a division for the
smaller sum. On these ruins, with the skill and credit of
which parliament had not been able to despoil him, my
grandfather at a mature age erected the edifice of a new
fortune : the labours of sixteen years were amply rewarded ; and I have reason to believe that the second
structure was not much inferior to the first. He had
realized a very considerable property in Sussex, Hampshire, Buckinghamshire and the New River Company :
and had acquired a spacious house,* with gardens and
lands, at Putney, in Surrey, where he resided in decent
hospitality. He died in December, 1736, at the age of
seventy : and by his last will, at the expense of Edward,
his only son, (with whose marriage he was not perfectly
reconciled,) enriched his two daughters, Catharine and

---

* Since inhabited by Mr. Wood, Sir John Shelly, Duke of Norfolk, &c.

Hester. The former became the wife of Mr. Edward Elliston, an East India captain: their daughter and heiress Catharine was married in the year 1756 to Edward Elliot, Esq. (now Lord Elliot), of Port Elliot in the county of Cornwall; and their three sons are my nearest male relations on the father's side.

CHAP. III.

CHARACTER OF MR. WILLIAM LAW.

A life of devotion and celibacy was the choice of my aunt, Mrs. Hester Gibbon, who, at the age of eighty-five, still resides at a hermitage at Cliffe, in Northamptonshire; having long survived her spiritual guide and faithful companion, Mr. William Law, who at an advanced age, about the year 1761, died in her house. In our family he had left the reputation of a worthy and pious man, who believed all that he professed, and practised all that he enjoined. The character of a non-juror, which he maintained to the last, is a sufficient evidence of his principles in church and state; and the sacrifice of interest to conscience will be always respectable. His theological writings, which our domestic connexion has tempted me to peruse, preserve an imperfect sort of life, and I can pronounce with more confidence and knowledge on the merits of the author. His last compositions are darkly tinctured by the incomprehensible visions of Jacob Behmen; and his discourse on the absolute unlawfulness of stage-entertainments is sometimes quoted for a ridiculous intemperance of sentiment and language.—" The actors and spectators must all be damned: the playhouse is the porch of Hell, the place of the Devil's abode, where he holds his filthy court of evil spirits; a play is the

Devil's triumph, a sacrifice performed to his glory, as much as in the heathen temples of Bachus or Venus, &c. &c." But these sallies of religious frenzy must not extinguish the praise which is due to Mr. William Law as a wit and a scholar. His argument on topics of less absurdity is specious and acute, his manner is lively, his style forcible and clear; and, had not his vigorous mind been clouded by enthusiasm, he might be ranked with the most agreeable and ingenious writers of the times. While the Bangorian controversy was a fashionable theme, he entered the lists on the subject of Christ's kingdom, and the authority of the priesthood: against the plain account of the sacrament of the Lord's Supper he resumed the combat with Bishop Hoadley, the object of Whig idolatry, and Tory abhorrence; and at every weapon of attack and defence the non-juror, on the ground which is common to both, approves himself at least equal to the prelate. On the appearance of the Fable of the Bees, he drew his pen against the licentious doctrine that private vices are public benefits; and morality as well as religion must join in his applause. Mr. Law's master-work, the "Serious Call," is still read as a popular and powerful book of devotion. His precepts are rigid, but they are founded on the gospel: his satire is sharp, but it is drawn from the knowledge of human life; and many of his portraits are not unworthy of the pen of La Bruyere. If he finds a spark of piety in his reader's mind, he will soon kindle it to a flame; and a philosopher must allow that he exposes, with equal severity and truth, the strange contradiction between the faith and practice of the Christian world. Under the names of Flavia and Miranda he has admirably described my two aunts—the heathen and the Christian sister.

My father, Edward Gibbon, was born in October, 1707: at the age of thirteen he could scarcely feel that he was disinherited by act of parliament; and, as he advanced towards manhood, new prospects of fortune opened to his view. A parent is most attentive to supply in his children the deficiencies of which he is conscious in himself: my grandfather's knowledge was derived from a strong understanding, and the experience of the ways of men; but my father enjoyed the benefits of a liberal education as a scholar and a gentleman. At Westminster School, and afterwards at Emanuel College in Cambridge, he passed through a regular course of academical discipline; and the care of his learning and morals was entrusted to his private tutor, the same Mr. William Law. But the mind of a saint is above or below the present world; and while the pupil proceeded on his travels, the tutor remained at Putney, the much-honoured friend and spiritual director of the whole family. My father resided some time at Paris, to acquire the fashionable exercises; and as his temper was warm and social, he indulged in those pleasures, for which the strictness of his former education had given him a keener relish. He afterwards visited several provinces of France: but his excursions were neither long nor remote; and the slender knowledge which he had gained of the French language, was gradually obliterated. His passage through Besançon is marked by a singular consequence in the chain of human events. In a dangerous illness Mr. Gibbon was attended, at his own request by

one of his kinsmen of the name of Acton, the younger
brother of a younger brother, who had applied himself to
the study of physic.   During the slow recovery of his
patient, the physician himself was attacked by the malady of love : he married his mistress, renounced his country and religion, settled at Besançon, and became the
father of three sons ; the eldest of whom, General Acton,
is conspicuous in Europe as the principal minister of the
King of the Two Sicilies.   By an uncle whom another
stroke of fortune had transplanted to Leghorn, he was
educated in the naval service of the Emperor; and his
valour and conduct in the command of the Tuscan fri-
gates protected the retreat of the Spaniards from Algiers.
On my father's return to England he was chosen, in the
general election of 1734, to serve in parliament for the
borough of Petersfield; a burgage tenure, of which my
grandfather possessed a weighty share, till he alienated
(I know not why) such important property.   In the opposition to Sir Robert Walpole and the Pelhams, prejudice and society connected his son with the Tories,—
shall I say Jacobites? or as they were pleased to style
themselves, the country gentlemen?   With them he gave
many a vote ; with them he drank many a bottle.   Without acquiring the fame of an orator or a statesman, he
eagerly joined in the great opposition which, after a
seven years' chase, hunted down Sir Robert Walpole:
and in the pursuit of an unpopular minister, he gratified
a private revenge against the oppressor of his family in
the South Sea persecution.

CHAP. IV.

MR. GIBBON'S BIRTH, &c.

I was born at Putney, in the county of Surrey, the 27th of April, O. S., in the year one thousand seven hundred and thirty-seven; the first child of the marriage of Edward Gibbon, Esq. and of Judith Porten.* My lot might have been that of a slave, a savage, or a peasant: nor can I reflect without pleasure on the bounty of Nature, which cast my birth in a free and civilised country, in an age of science and philosophy, in a family of honourable rank, and decently endowed with the gifts of fortune. From my birth I have enjoyed the right of primogeniture; but I was succeeded by five brothers and one sister, all of whom were snatched away in their infancy. My five brothers, whose names may be found in the parish register of Putney, I shall not pretend to lament: but from my childhood to the present hour, I have deeply and sincerely regretted my sister, whose life

* The union to which I owe my birth was a marriage of inclination and esteem. Mr. James Porten, a merchant of London, resided with his family at Putney, in a house adjoining to the bridge and churchyard, where I have passed many happy hours of my childhood. He left one son (the late Sir Stanier Porten) and three daughters; Catharine, who preserved her maiden name, and of whom I shall hereafter speak; another daughter married Mr. Darell of Richmond, and left two sons, Edward and Robert; the youngest of the three sisters was Judith, my mother.

was somewhat prolonged, and whom I remember to have
seen an amiable infant.   The relation of a brother and a
sister, especially if they do not marry, appears to me of
a very singular nature.   It is a familiar and tender
friendship with a female, much about our own age; an
affection perhaps softened by the secret influence of sex,
but pure from any mixture of sensual desire, the sole
·species of Platonic love that can be indulged with truth
and without danger.

At the general election of 1741, Mr. Gibbon and Mr.
Delme stood an expensive and successful contest at
Southampton, against Mr. Dummer and Mr. Henly, afterwards Lord Chancellor and Earl of Northington.   The
Whig candidates had a majority of the resident voters;
but the corporation was firm in the Tory interest: a sudden creation of one hundred and seventy new freemen
turned the scale; and a supply was readily obtained of
respectable volunteers, who flocked from all parts of
England to support the cause of their political friends.
The new parliament opened with the victory of an opposition, which was fortified by strong clamor and strange
coalitions.   From the event of the first divisions, Sir
Robert Walpole perceived that he could no longer lead a
majority in the House of Commons, and prudently resigned (after a dominion of one and twenty years) the
guidance of the state (1742).   But the fall of an unpopular minister was not succeeded, according to general
expectation, by a millenium of happiness and virtue:
some courtiers lost their places, some patriots lost their
characters, Lord Orford's offences vanished with his
power; and after a short vibration, the Pelham govern-

ment was fixed on the old basis of Whig aristocracy. In the year 1745, the throne and the constitution were attacked by a rebellion, which does not inflict much honour on the national spirit: since the English friends of the Pretender wanted courage to join his standard, and his enemies (the bulk of the people) allowed him to advance into the heart of the kingdom. Without daring, perhaps without desiring, to aid the rebels, my father invariably adhered to the Tory opposition. In the most critical season he accepted, for the service of the party, the office of alderman in the city of London: but the duties were so repugnant to his inclination and habits, that he resigned his gown at the end of a few months. The second parliament in which he sat was prematurely dissolved (1747) : and as he was unable or unwilling to maintain a second contest for Southampton, the life of the senator expired in that dissolution.

The death of a new-born child before that of its parents may seem an unnatural, but it is strictly a probable, event: since of any given number the greater part are extinguished before their ninth year, before they possess the faculties of the mind or body. Without accusing the profuse waste or imperfect workmanship of Nature, I shall only observe, that this unfavourable chance was multiplied against my infant existence. So feeble was my constitution, so precarious my life, that, in the baptism of each of my brothers, my father's prudence successively repeated my christian name of Edward, that, in case of the departure of the eldest son, this patronymic appellation might be still perpetuated in the family.

————Uno avulso non deficit alter.

To preserve and to rear so frail a being, the most tender assiduity was scarcely sufficient; and my mother's
attention was somewhat diverted by her frequent preg-
nancies, by an exclusive passion for her husband, and by
the dissipation of the world, in which his taste and
authority obliged her to mingle.   But the maternal office
was supplied by my aunt, Mrs. Catharine Porten; at
whose name I feel a tear of gratitude trickling down my
cheek.   A life of celibacy transferred her vacant affection
to her sister's first child: my weakness excited her pity;
her attachment was fortified by labour and success: and
if there be any, as I trust there are some, who rejoice that
I live, to that dear and excellent woman they must hold
themselves indebted.   Many anxious and solitary days
did she consume in the patient trial of every mode of
relief and amusement.   Many wakeful nights did she sit
by my bed-side in trembling expectation that each hour
would be my last.   Of the various and frequent disorders
of my childhood my own recollection is dark; nor do I
wish to expatiate on so disgusting a topic.   Suffice it to
say, that while every practitioner, from Sloane and Ward
to the Chevalier Taylor, was successively summoned to
torture or relieve me, the care of my mind was too frequently neglected for that of my health: compassion
always suggested an excuse for the indulgence of the
master, or the idleness of the pupil; and the chain of my
education was broken, as often as I was recalled from the
school of learning to the bed of sickness.

As soon as the use of speech had prepared my infant
reason for the admission of knowledge, I was taught the
arts of reading, writing, and arithmetic.   So remote is

the date, so vague is the memory of their origin in myself, that, were not the error corrected by analogy, I
should be tempted to conceive them as innate. In my
childhood'I was praised for the readiness with which I
could multiply and divide, by memory alone, two sums
of several figures: such praise encouraged my growing
talent; and had I persevered in this line of application, I
might have acquired some fame in mathematical studies.

After this previous institution at home, or at a day-
school at Putney, I was delivered at the age of seven into
the hands of Mr. John Kirkby, who exercised about
eighteen months the office of my domestic tutor. His
own words, which I shall here transcribe, inspire in his
favour a sentiment of pity and esteem.—" During my
abode in my native county of Cumberland, in quality of
an indigent curate, I used now and then in a summer,
when the pleasantness of the season invited, to take a solitary walk to the sea-shore, which lies about two miles
from the town where I lived. Here I would amuse myself, one while in viewing at large the agreeable prospect
which surrounded me, and another while (confining my
sight to nearer objects) in admiring the vast variety of
beautiful shells, thrown upon the beach; some of the
choicest of which I always picked up, to divert my little
ones upon my return. One time among the rest, taking
such a journey in my head, I sat down upon the declivity
of the beach with my face to the sea, which was now
come up within a few yards of my feet; when immediately the sad thought of the wretched condition of my
family, and the unsuccessfulness of all endeavours to
amend it, came crowding into my mind, which drove me

into a deep melancholy, and ever and anon forced tears
from my eyes." Distress at last forced him to leave the
country. His learning and virtue introduced him to my
father; and at Putney he might have found at least a
temporary shelter, had not an act of indiscretion again
driven him into the world. One day reading prayers in
the parish church, he most unluckily forgot the name of
King George: his patron, a loyal subject, dismissed him with
some reluctance, and a decent reward: and *how* the poor
man ended his days I have never been able to learn. Mr.
John Kirkby is the author of two small volumes; the Life
of Automathes (London, 1745), and an English and Latin
Grammar (London, 1746); which, as a testimony of
gratitude, he dedicated (November 5th, 1745) to my
father. The books are before me: from them the pupil
may judge the preceptor; and, upon the whole, his judgment will not be unfavourable. The grammar is executed with accuracy and skill, and I know not whether
any better existed at the time in our language: but the
life of Automathes aspires to the honours of a philosophical fiction. It is the story of a youth, the son of a
shipwrecked exile who lives alone on a desert island from
infancy to the age of manhood. A hind is his nurse; he
inherits a cottage, with many useful and curious instru-
ments; some ideas remain of the education of his two
first years; some arts are borrowed from the beavers of
a neighboring lake; some truths are revealed in superna-
tural visions. With these helps, and his own industry,
Automathes becomes a self-taught though speechless
philosopher, who had investigated with success his own
mind, the natural world, the abstract sciences, and the

great principles of morality and religion. The author is
not entitled to the merit of invention, since he has blended
the English story of Robinson Crusoe with the Arabian
romance of Hai Ebn Yokhdam, which he might have read
in the Latin version of Pocock. In the Automathes I
cannot praise either the depth of thought or elegance of
style; but the book is not devoid of entertainment or
instruction; and among several interesting passages, I
would select the discovery of fire, which produces by accidental mischief the discovery of conscience. A man
who had thought so much on the subjects of language and
education was surely no ordinary preceptor; my childish
years, and his hasty departure, prevented me from enjoying the full benefit of his lessons; but they enlarged my
knowledge of arithmetic, and left me a clear impression
of the English and Latin rudiments.

CHAP. V.

THE AUTHOR IS SENT TO DR. WOODDESON'S SCHOOL.

In my ninth year (January, 1746), in a lucid interval of comparative health, my father adopted the convenient and customery mode of English education; and I was sent to Kingston-upon-Thames, to a school of about seventy boys, which was kept by Dr. Wooddeson and his assistants. Every time I have since passed over Putney Common, I have always noticed the spot where my mother, as we drove along in the coach, admonished me that I was now going into the world, and must learn to think and act for myself. The expression may appear ludicrous: yet there is not, in the course of life, a more remarkable change than the removal of a child from the luxury and freedom of a wealthy house, to the frugal diet and strict subordination of a school; from the tenderness of parents, and the obsequiousness of servants, to the rude familiarity of his equals, the insolent tyranny of his seniors, and the rod, perhaps, of a cruel and capricious pedagogue. Such hardships may steel the mind and body against the injuries of fortune; but my timid reserve was astonished by the crowd and tumult of the school; the want of strength and activity disqualified me for the sports of the play-field; nor have I forgotten how often in the year forty-six, I was reviled and buffeted for the sins of my Tory ancestors. By the common methods of discipline, at the expense of many tears and some blood, I purchased the knowledge of the Latin syntax; and not long since, I was possessed of the dirty volumes of Phædrus and Cornelius Nepos, which I painfully construed and darkly understood. The choice of these authors is not injudicious. The *lives* of Cornelius Nepos, the friend of Attucus and Cicero, are composed in the style of the purest age: his simplicity is elegant, his brevity copious: he exhibits a series of men and manners; and with such illustrations, as every pedant is not indeed qualified to give, this classic biographer may initiate a young student in the history of Greece and Rome. The use of fables or apologues has been approved in every age from ancient India to modern Europe. They convey in familiar images the truths of morality and prudence; and the most childish understanding (I advert to the scruples of Rousseau) will not suppose either that beasts *do* speak, or that men *may* lie. A fable represents the genuine characters of animals; and a skilful master might extract from Pliny and Buffon some pleasing lessons of natural history, a science well adapted to the taste and capacity of children. The Latinity of Phædrus is not exempt from an alloy of the silver age; but his manner is concise, terse, and sententious: the Thracian slave discreetly breathes the spirit of a freeman; and when the text is found, the style is perspicuous. But his fables, after a long oblivion, were first published by Peter Pithou, from a corrupt manuscript. The labours of fifty editors confess the defects of the copy as well as the value of the original; and the school-boy may have been whipped for misapprehending a passage, which Bentley could not restore, and which Burman could not explain.

My studies were too frequently interrupted by sickness; and after a real or nominal residence at Kingston school for near two years, I was finally recalled (December, 1747) by my mother's death, which was occasioned, in her thirty-eighth year, by the consequences of her last labour. I was too young to feel the importance of my loss; and the image of her person and conversation is faintly imprinted in my memory. The affectionate heart of my aunt, Catharine Porten, bewailed a sister and a friend; but my poor father was inconsolable, and the transport of grief seemed to threaten his life or his reason. I can never forget the scene of our first interview, some weeks after the fatal event; the awful silence, the room hung with black, the mid-day tapers, his sighs and tears; his praises of my mother, a saint in heaven; his solemn adjuration that I would cherish her memory and imitate her virtues; and the fervour with which he kissed and blessed me as the sole surviving pledge of their loves. The storm of passion insensibly subsided into calmer melancholy. At a convivial meeting of his friends, Mr. Gibbon might affect or enjoy a gleam of cheerfulness; but his plan of happiness was for ever destroyed: and after the loss of his companion he was left alone in a world, of which the business and pleasures were to him irksome or insipid. After some unsuccessful trials he renounced the tumult of London and the hospitality of Putney, and buried himself in the rural or rather rustic solitude of Buriton; from which, during several years, he seldom emerged.

As far back as I can remember, the house, near Putney-bridge and churchyard, of my maternal grandfather, appears in the light of my proper and native home. It was there that I was allowed to spend the greatest part of my time, in sickness or in health, during my school vacations and my parents' residence in London, and finally after my mother's death. Three months after that event, in the spring of 1748, the commercial ruin of her father, Mr. James Porten, was accomplished and declared. He suddenly absconded: but as his effects were not sold, nor the house evacuated, till the Christmas following, I enjoyed during the whole year the society of my aunt, without much consciousness of her impending fate. I feel a melancholy pleasure in repeating my obligations to that excellent woman, Mrs. Catharine Porten, the true mother of my mind as well as of my health. Her natural good sense was improved by the perusal of the best books in the English language, and if her reason was sometimes clouded by prejudice, her sentiments were never disguised by hypocrisy or affectation. Her indulgent tenderness, the frankness of her temper, and my innate rising curiosity, soon removed all distance between us: like friends of an equal age, we freely conversed on every topic, familiar or abstruse; and it was her delight and reward to observe the first shoots of my young ideas. Pain and languor were often soothed by the voice of instruction and amusement; and to her kind lessons I ascribe my early and invincible love of reading, which I would not exchange for the treasures of India. I should perhaps be astonished, were it possible to ascertain the date, at which a favourite tale was engraved, by frequent repetition, in my memory: the Cavern of the Winds; the Palace of Felicity; and the fatal moment, at the end of three months or centuries, when Prince Adolphus is overtaken by Time, who had worn out so many pair of wings in the pursuit. Before I left Kingston school I was well acquainted with Pope's Homer and the Arabian Nights Entertainments, two books which will always please by the moving picture of human manners and specious miracles: nor was I then capable of discerning that Pope's translation is a portrait endowed with every merit, excepting that of likeness to the original. The verses of Pope accustomed my ear to the sound of poetic harmony; in the death of Hector, and the shipwreck of Ulysses, I tasted the new emotions of terror and pity; and seriously disputed with my aunt on the vices and virtues of the heroes of the Trojan war. From Pope's Homer to Dryden's Virgil was an easy transition; but I know not how, from some fault in the author, the translator, or the reader, the pious Æneas did not so forcibly seize on my imagination; and I derived more pleasure from Ovid's Metamorphoses, especially in the fall of Phaeton and the speeches of Ajax and Ulysses. My grandfather's flight unlocked the door of a tolerable library; and I turned over many English pages of poetry and Romance, of history and travels. Where a title attracted my eye, without fear or awe I snatched the volume from the shelf; and Mrs. Porten, who indulged herself in moral and religious speculations, was more prone to encourage than to check a curiosity above the strength of a boy. This year (1748), the twelfth of my age, I shall note as the most propitious to the growth of my intellectual stature.

CHAP. VI.

MR. GIBBON IS ENTERED AT WESTMINSTER SCHOOL.

THE relics of my grandfather's fortune afforded a bare annuity for his own maintenance; and his daughter, my worthy aunt, who had already passed her fortieth year, was left destitute. Her noble spirit scorned a life of obligation and dependence; and after revolving several schemes, she preferred the humble industry of keeping a boarding-house for Westminster School,* where she laboriously earned a competence for her old age. This singular opportunity of blending the advantages of private and public education decided my father. After the Christmas holidays in January, 1749, I accompanied Mrs. Porten to her new house in College-street; and was immediately entered in the school, of which Dr. John Nicoll was at that time head master. At first I was alone; but my aunt's resolution was praised; her character was esteemed; her friends were numerous and active: in the course of some years she became the mother of forty or fifty boys, for the most part of family and fortune; and as her primitive habitation was too narrow, she built and occupied a spacious mansion in Dean's Yard. I shall

* It is said in the family, that she was principally induced to this undertaking by her affection for her nephew, whose weak constitution required her constant and unremitted attention.—S.

always be ready to join in the common opinion, that our
public schools, which have produced so many eminent
characters, are the best adapted to the genius and constitution of the English people.   A boy of spirit may acquire a
previous and practical experience of the world ; and his
playfellows may be the future friends of his heart or his interest.   In a free intercourse with his equals, the habits of
truth, fortitude, and prudence will insensibly be matured.
Birth and riches are measured by the standard of personal
merit ; and the mimic scene of a rebellion has displayed,
in their true colours, the ministers and patriots of the
rising generation.   Our seminaries of learning do not ex-
actly correspond with the precept of a Spartan king,
" that the child should be instructed in the arts, which
will be useful to the man ;" since a finished scholar may
emerge from the head of Westminster or Eton, in total
ignorance of the business and conversation of English gentlemen in the latter end of the eighteenth century.   But
these schools may assume the merit of teaching all that
they pretend to teach, the Latin and Greek languages:
they deposit in the hands of a disciple the keys of two
valuable chests ; nor can he complain, if they are afterwards lost or neglected by his own fault.   The necessity of leading in equal ranks so many unequal powers of
capacity and application, will prolong to eight or ten
years the juvenile studies, which might be despatched in
half that time by the skilful master of a single pupil.   Yet
even the repetition of exercise and discipline contributes
to fix in a vacant mind the verbal science of grammar
and prosody : and the private or voluntary student, who
possesses the sense and spirit of the classics, may offend,

by a false quantity, the scrupulous ear of a well-flogged critic. For myself, I must be content with a very small share of the civil and literary fruits of a public school. In the space of two years (1749, 1750), interrupted by danger and debility, I painfully climbed into the third form; and my riper age was left to acquire the beauties of the Latin and the rudiments of the Greek tongue. Instead of audaciously mingling in the sports, the quarrels, and the connexions of our little world, I was still cherished at home under the maternal wing of my aunt; and my removal from Westminster long preceded the approach of manhood.

The violence and variety of my complaints, which had excused my frequent absence from Westminster School, at length engaged Mrs. Porten, with the advice of physicians, to conduct me to Bath: at the end of Michaelmas vacation (1750) she quitted me with reluctance, and I remained several months under the care of a trusty maid-servant. A strange nervous affection, which alternately contracted my legs, and produced, without any visible symptoms, the most excruciating pain, was ineffectually opposed by the various methods of bathing and pumping. From Bath I was transported to Winchester, to the house of a physician; and after the failure of his medical skill, we had again recourse to the virtues of the Bath waters. During the intervals of these fits, I moved with my father to Buriton and Putney; and a short unsuccessful trial was attempted to renew my attendance at Westminster School. But my infirmities could not be reconciled with the hours and discipline of a public seminary: and instead of a domestic tutor, who might have watched the favourable moments, and gently advanced the progress of my learning, my father was too easily content with such occasional teachers as the different places of my residence could supply. I was never forced, and seldom was I persuaded, to admit these lessons : yet I read with a clergyman at Bath some odes of Horace, and several episodes of Virgil, which gave me an imperfect and transient enjoyment of the Latin poets. It might now be apprehended that I should continue for life an illiterate cripple : but, as I approached my sixteenth year, nature displayed in my favour her mysterious energies; my constitution was fortified and fixed; and my disorders, instead of growing with my growth and strengthening with my strength, most wonderfully vanished. I have never possessed or abused the insolence of health; but since that time few persons have been more exempt from real or imaginary ills ; and, till I am admonished by the gout, the reader will no more be troubled with the history of my bodily complaints. My unexpected recovery again encouraged the hope of my education; and I was placed at Esher, in Surrey, in the house of the Reverend Mr. Philip Francis, in a pleasant spot, which promised to unite the various benefits of air, exercise, and study (January, 1752). The translator of Horace might have taught me to relish the Latin poets, had not my friends discovered in a few weeks, that he preferred the pleasures of London to the instruction of his pupils.

CHAP. VII.

THE AUTHOR ENTERS MAGDALEN COLLEGE, OXFORD.

My father's perplexity at this time, rather than his prudence, was urged to embrace a singular and desperate measure. Without preparation or delay he carried me to Oxford; and I was matriculated in the university as a gentleman commoner of Magdalen College, before I had accomplished the fifteenth year of my age (April 3, 1752).

The curiosity, which had been implanted in my infant mind, was still alive and active; but my reason was not sufficiently informed to understand the value, or to lament the loss, of three precious years from my entrance at Westminster to my admission at Oxford. Instead of repining at my long and frequent confinement to the chamber or the couch, I secretly rejoiced in those infirmities, which delivered me from the exercises of the school, and the society of my equals. As often as I was tolerably exempt from danger and pain, reading, free desultory reading, was the employment and comfort of my solitary hours. At Westminster, my aunt sought only to amuse and indulge me; in my stations at Bath and Winchester, at Buriton and Putney, a false compassion respected my sufferings; and I was allowed, without control or advice, to gratify the wanderings of an unripe taste. My indiscriminate appetite subsided by degrees in the *historic* line: and since philosophy has exploded all innate ideas and natural propensities, I must ascribe this choice to the assiduous perusal of the Universal History, as the octavo volumes successively appeared. This unequal work, and a treatise of Hearne, the *Ductor historicus*, referred and introduced me to the Greek and Roman historians, to as many at least as were accessible to an English reader. All that I could find were greedily devoured, from Littlebury's lame Herodotus, and Spelman's valuable Xenophon, to the pompous folios of Gordon's Tacitus, and a ragged Procopius of the beginning of the last century. The cheap acquisition of so much knowledge confirmed my dislike to the study of languages; and I argued with Mrs. Porten, that, were I master of Greek and Latin, I must interpret to myself in English the thoughts of the original, and that such extemporary versions must be inferior to the elaborate translations of professed scholars; a silly sophism, which could not easily be confuted by a person ignorant of any other language than her own. From the ancient I leaped to the modern world: many crude lumps of Speed, Rapin, Mezeray, Davila, Machiavel, Father Paul, Bower, &c. I devoured like so many novels; and I swallowed with the same voracious appetite the descriptions of India and China, of Mexico and Peru.

My first introduction to the historic scenes, which have since engaged so many years of my life, must be ascribed to an accident. In the summer of 1751, I accompanied my father on a visit to Mr. Hoare's, in Wiltshire; but I was less delighted with the beauties of Stourhead, than with discovering in the library a common book, the continuation of Echard's Roman History, which is indeed executed with more skill and taste than the previous work. To me the reigns of the successors of Constantine were absolutely new; and I was immersed in the passage of the Goths over the Danube, when the summons of the dinner-bell reluctantly dragged me from my intellectual feast. This transient glance served rather to irritate than to appease my curiosity; and as soon as I returned to Bath I procured the second and third volumes of Howell's History of the World, which exhibit the Byzantine period on a larger scale. Mahomet and his Saracens soon fixed my attention; and some instinct of criticism directed me to the genuine sources. Simon Ockley, an original in every sense, first opened my eyes; and I was led from one book to another, till I had ranged round the circle of oriental history. Before I was sixteen, I had exhausted all that could be learned in English of the Arabs and Persians, the Tartars and Turks; and the same ardour urged me to guess at the French of D'Herbelot, and to construe the barbarous Latin of Pocock's Abulfaragius. Such vague and multifarious reading could not teach me to think, to write, or to act; and the only principle that darted a ray of light into the indigested chaos, was an early and rational application to the order of time and place. The maps of Cellarius and Wells imprinted in my mind the picture of ancient geography: from Stranchius I imbibed the elements of chronology: the Tables of Helvicus and Anderson, the Annals of Usher and Prideaux, distinguished the connexion of events, and engraved the multitude of names and dates in a clear and indelible series. But in the discussion of the first ages I overleaped the bounds of modesty and use. In my childish balance I presumed to weigh the systems of Scaliger and Petavius, of Marsham and Newton, which I could seldom study in the originals: and my sleep has been disturbed by the difficulty of reconciling the Septuagint with the Hebrew computation. I arrived at Oxford with a stock of erudition that might have puzzled a doctor, and a degree of ignorance, of which a school-boy might have been ashamed.

At the conclusion of this first period of my life, I am tempted to enter a protest against the trite and lavish praise of the happiness of our boyish years, which is echoed with so much affectation in the world. That happiness I have never known, that time I have never regretted; and were my poor aunt still alive, she would bear testimony to the early and constant uniformity of my sentiments. It will indeed be replied, that *I* am not a competent judge; that pleasure is incompatible with pain; that joy is excluded from sickness; and that the felicity of a school-boy consists in the perpetual motion of thoughtless and playful agility, in which I was never qualified to excel. My name, it is most true, could never be enrolled among the sprightly race, the idle progeny of Eton or Westminster,

> " Who foremost may delight to cleave,
>   With pliant arm the glassy wave,
>   Or urge the flying ball."

The poet may gayly describe the short hours of recreation; but he forgets the daily tedious labours of the school, which is approached each morning with anxious and reluctant steps.

A traveller who visits Oxford or Cambridge, is surprised and edified by the apparent order and tranquillity that prevail in the seats of the English muses. In the most celebrated universities of Holland, Germany, and Italy, the students, who swarm from different countries, are loosely dispersed in private lodgings at the houses of the burghers: they dress according to their fancy and fortune; and in the intemperate quarrels of youth and wine, their *swords*, though less frequently than of old, are sometimes stained with each other's blood. The use of arms is banished from our English universities; the uniform habit of the academies, the square cap and black gown, is adapted to the civil and even clerical profession; and from the doctor in divinity to the under-graduate, the degrees of learning and age are externally distinguished. Instead of being scattered in a town, the students of Oxford and Cambridge are united in colleges; their maintenance is provided at their own expense, or that of the founders; and the stated hours of the hall and chapel represent the discipline of a regular, and, as it were, a religious community. The eyes of the traveller are attracted by the size or beauty of the public edifices; and the principal colleges appear to be so many palaces, which a liberal nation has erected and endowed for the habitation of science. My own introduction to the university of Oxford forms a new æra in my life; and at the distance of forty years I still remember my first emotions of surprise and satisfaction. In my fifteenth year I felt myself suddenly raised from a boy to a man: the per-

sons, whom I respected as my superiors in age and academical rank, entertained me with every mark of attention and civility, and my vanity was flattered by the
velvet cap and silk gown, which distinguished a gentleman commoner from a plebian student. A decent allowance, more money than a school-boy had ever seen, was
at my own disposal; and I might command, among the
tradesmen of Oxford, an indefinite and dangerous latitude
of credit. A key was delivered into my hands, which
gave me the free use of a numerous and learned library;
my apartment consisted of three elegant and well-fur-
nished rooms in the new building, a stately pile, of Magdalen College; and the adjacent walks, had they been
frequented by Plato's disciples, might have been compared to the Attic shade on the banks of the Ilissus.
Such was the fair prospect of my entrance (April 3,
1752), into the university of Oxford.

A venerable prelate, whose taste and erudition must
reflect honour on the society in which they were formed,
has drawn a very interesting picture of his academical
life.—"I was educated (says Bishop Lowth) in the University of Oxford. I enjoyed all the advantages, both
public and private, which that famous seat of learning so
largely affords. I spent many years in that illustrious
society, in a well-regulated course of useful discipline
and studies, and in the agreeable and improving commerce of gentlemen and scholars; in a society where
emulation without envy, ambition without jealousy, con-
tention without animosity, incited industry, and awakened
genius; where a liberal pursuit of knowledge, and a genuine freedom of thought, was raised, encouraged, and

pushed forward by example, by commendation, and by authority. I breathed the same atmosphere that the Hookers, the Chillingworths, and the Lockes had breathed before ; whose benevolence and humanity were as extensive as their vast genius and comprehensive knowledge ; who always treated their adversaries with civility and respect ; who made candour, moderation, and liberal judgment as much the rule and law as the subject of their discourse. And do you reproach me with my education in this place, and with my relation to this most respectable body, which I shall always esteem my greatest advantage and my highest honour?" I transcribe with pleasure this eloquent passage, without examining what benefits or what rewards were derived by Hooker, or Chillingworth, or Locke, from their academical institution ; without inquiring, whether in this angry controversy the spirit of Lowth himself is purified from the intolerant zeal, which Warburton had ascribed to the genius of the place. It may indeed be observed, that the atmosphere of Oxford did not agree with Mr. Locke's constitution, and that the philosopher justly despised the academical bigots, who expelled his person and condemned his principles. The expression of gratitude is a virtue and a pleasure: a liberal mind will delight to cherish and celebrate the memory of its parents ; and the teachers of science are the parents of the mind. I applaud the filial piety, which it is impossible for me to imitate ; since I must not confess an imaginary debt, to assume the merit of a just or generous retribution. To the university of Oxford *I* acknowledge no obligation ; and she will as cheerfully renounce me for a son, as I am willing to disclaim her for a mother. I spent fourteen months at Magdalen College; they proved the fourteen months the most idle and unprofitable of my whole life: and the reader will pronounce between the school and the scholar; but I cannot affect to believe that Nature had disqualified me for all literary pursuits. The specious and ready excuse of my tender age, imperfect preparation, and hasty departure, may doubtless be alleged; nor do I wish to defraud such excuses of their proper weight. Yet in my sixteenth year I was not devoid of capacity or application; even my childish reading had displayed an early though blind propensity for books; and the shallow flood might have been taught to flow in a deep channel and a clear stream. In the discipline of a well-constituted academy, under the guidance of skilful and vigilant professors, I should gradually have risen from translations to originals, from the Latin to the Greek classics, from dead languages to living science: my hours would have been occupied by useful and agreeable studies, the wanderings of fancy would have been restrained, and I should have escaped the temptations of idleness, which finally precipitated my departure from Oxford.

Perhaps in a separate annotation I may coolly examine the fabulous and real antiquities of our sister universities, a question which has kindled such fierce and foolish disputes among their fanatic sons. In the mean while, it will be acknowledged that these venerable bodies are sufficiently old to partake of all the prejudices and infirmities of age. The schools of Oxford and Cambridge were founded in a dark age of false and barbarous science; and they are still tainted with the vices of their origin.

Their primitive discipline was adapted to the education of priests and monks; and the government still remains in the hands of the clergy, an order of men whose manners are remote from the present world, and whose eyes are dazzled by the light of philosophy. The legal incorporation of these societies by the charters of popes and kings had given them a monopoly of the public instruction; and the spirit of monopolists is narrow, lazy, and oppressive: their work is more costly and less productive than that of independent artists; and the new improvements so eagerly grasped by the competition of freedom, are admitted with slow and sullen reluctance in those proud corporations, above the fear of a rival, and below the confession of an error. We may scarcely hope that any reformation will be a voluntary act; and so deeply are they rooted in law and prejudice, that even the omnipotence of parliament would shrink from an inquiry into the state and abuses of the two universities.

The use of academical degrees, as old as the thirteenth century, is visibly borrowed from the mechanic corporations; in which an apprentice, after serving his time, obtains a testimonial of his skill, and a license to practice his trade and mystery. It is not my design to depreciate those honours, which could never gratify or disappoint my ambition; and I should applaud the institution, if the degrees of bachelor or licentiate were bestowed as the reward of manly and successful study: if the name and rank of doctor or master were strictly reserved for the professors of science, who have approved their title to the public esteem.

In all the universities of Europe, excepting our own,

the languages and sciences are distributed among a numerous list of effective professors: the students, according to their taste, their calling, and their diligence, apply themselves to the proper masters: and in the annual repetition of public and private lectures, these masters are assiduously employed. Our curiosity may inquire what number of professors has been instituted at Oxford? (for I shall now confine myself to my own university;) by whom they are appointed, and what may be the probable chances of merit or incapacity; how many are stationed to the three faculties, and how many are left for the liberal arts; what is the form, and what the substance of their lessons? But all these questions are silenced by one short and singular answer, "That in the University of Oxford, the greater part of the public professors have for these many years given up altogether even the pretence of teaching." Incredible as the fact may appear, I must rest my belief on the positive and impartial evidence of a master of moral and political wisdom, who had himself resided at Oxford. Dr. Adam Smith assigns as the cause of their indolence, that, instead of being paid by voluntary contributions, which would urge them to increase the number, and to deserve the gratitude of their pupils, the Oxford professors are secure in the enjoyment of a fixed stipend, without the necessity of labour, or the apprehension of control. It has indeed been observed, nor is the observation absurd, that excepting in experimental sciences, which demand a costly apparatus and a dexterous hand, the many valuable treatises, that have been published on every subject of learning, may now supesede the ancient mode of oral

instruction. Were this principle true in its utmost latitude, I should only infer that the offices and salaries,
which are become useless, ought without delay to be
abolished. But there still remains a material difference
between a book and a professor; the hour of the lec-
turer enforces attendance; attention is fixed by the presence, the voice, and the occasional questions of the
teacher: the most idle will carry something away; and
the more diligent will compare the instructions, which
they have heard in the school, with the volumes, which
they peruse in their chamber. The advice of a skilful
professor will adapt a course of reading to every mind
and every situation; his authority will discover, admonish,
and at last chastise the negligence of his disciples; and
his vigilant inquiries will ascertain the steps of their literary progress. Whatever science he professes, he may
illustrate in a series of discourses, composed in the leisure
of his closet, pronounced on public occasions, and finally
delivered to the press. I observe with pleasure, that, in
the University of Oxford, Dr. Lowth, with equal eloquence and erudition, has executed this task in his incomparable *Prælections* on the Poetry of the Hebrews.

The college of St. Mary Magdalen was founded in
the fifteenth century by Wainfleet, Bishop of Winchester;
and now consists of a president, forty fellows, and a number of inferior students. It is esteemed one of the largest
and most wealthy of our academical corporations, which
may be compared to the Benedictine abbeys of catholic
countries; and I have loosely heard that the estates be-
longing to Magdalen College, which are leased by those
indulgent landlords at small quit-rents and occasional fines,

might be raised in the hands of private avarice to an annual revenue of nearly thirty thousand pounds. Our colleges are supposed to be schools of science as well as of education; nor is it unreasonable to expect that a body of literary men, devoted to a life of celibacy, exempt from the care of their own subsistence, and amply provided with books, should devote their leisure to the prosecution of study, and that some effects of their studies should be manifested to the world. The shelves of their library groan under the weight of the Benedictine folios, of the editions of the fathers, and the collections of the middle ages, which have issued from the single abbey of St. Germain des Prés at Paris. A composition of genius must be the offspring of one mind; but such works of industry as may be divided among many hands, and must be continued during many years, are the peculiar province of a laborious community. If I inquire into the manufactures of the monks of Magdalen, if I extend the inquiry to the other colleges of Oxford and Cambridge, a silent blush, or a scornful frown, will be the only reply. The fellows or monks of my time were decent easy men, who supinely enjoyed the gifts of the founder; their days were filled by a series of uniform employments; the chapel and the hall, the coffee-house and the common room, till they retired, weary and well satisfied, to a long slumber. From the toil of reading, or thinking, or writing, they had absolved their conscience; and the first shoots of learning and ingenuity withered on the ground, without yielding any fruits to the owners or the public. As a gentleman commoner, I was admitted to the society of the fellows, and fondly expected that some questions

of literature would be the amusing and instructive topics
of their discourse. Their conversation stagnated in a
round of college business, Tory politics, personal anecdotes, and private scandal: their dull and deep potations
excused the brisk intemperance of youth; and their constitutional toasts were not expressive of the most lively
loyalty for the house of Hanover. A general election
was now approaching: the great Oxfordshire contest
already blazed with all the malevolence of party zeal.
Magdalen College was devoutly attached to the old interest; and the names of Wenman and Dashwood were
more frequently pronounced than those of Cicero and Chry-
sostom. The example of the senior fellows could not inspire the under-graduates with a liberal spirit or studious
emulation; and I cannot describe, as I never knew, the
discipline of college. Some duties may possibly have
been imposed on the poor scholars, whose ambition aspired to the peaceful honours of a fellowship (*ascribi
quietis ordinibus——deorum*); but no independent members were admitted below the rank of a gentleman commoner, and our velvet cap was the cap of liberty. A
tradition prevailed that some of our predecessors had
spoken Latin declamations in the hall; but of this ancient
custom no vestige remained: the obvious methods of
public exercises and examinations were totally unknown;
and I have never heard that either the president or the
society interfered in the private economy of the tutors
and their pupils.

The silence of the Oxford professors, which deprives
the youth of public instruction, is imperfectly supplied by
the tutors, as they are styled, of the several colleges.

Instead of confining themselves to a single science which
had satisfied the ambition of Burman or Bernoulli, they
teach, or promise to teach, either history or mathematics,
or ancient literature, or moral philosophy: and as it is
possible that they may be defective in all, it is highly
probable that of some they will be ignorant. They are
paid, indeed, by private contributions; but their appointment depends on the head of the house: their diligence
is voluntary, and will consequently be languid, while the
pupils themselves, or their parents, are not indulged in the
liberty of choice or change. The first tutor into whose
hands I was resigned, appears to have been one of the
best of the tribe; Dr. Waldegrave was a learned and pious
man, of a mild disposition, strict morals, and abstemious
life, who seldom mingled in the politics or the jollity of
the college. But his knowledge of the world was confined to the university; his learning was of the last,
rather than of the present age; his temper was indolent;
his faculties, which were not of the first rate, had been
relaxed by the climate, and he was satisfied, like his fellows, with the slight and superficial discharge of an
important trust. As soon as my tutor had sounded the
insufficiency of his disciple in school learning, he proposed
that we should read every morning from ten to eleven the
comedies of Terence. The sum of my improvement in
the University of Oxford is confined to three or four
Latin plays; and even the study of an elegant classic,
which might have been illustrated by a comparison of
ancient and modern theatres, was reduced to a dry and
literal interpretation of the author's text. During the
first weeks I constantly attended these lessons in my

tutor's room; but as they appeared equally devoid of profit or pleasure, I was once tempted to try the experiment of a formal apology. The apology was accepted with a smile. I repeated the offence with less ceremony; the excuse was admitted with the same indulgence: the slightest motive of laziness or indisposition, the most trifling avocation at home or abroad, was allowed as a worthy impediment; nor did my tutor appear conscious of my absense or neglect. Had the hour of lecture been constantly filled, a single hour was a small portion of my academical leisure. No plan of study was recommended for my use; no exercises were prescribed for his inspection; and, at the most precious season of youth, whole days and weeks were suffered to elapse without labour or amusement, without advice or account. I should have listened to the voice of reason and of my tutor; his mild behaviour had gained my confidence. I preferred his society to that of the younger students; and in our evening walks to the top of Heddington Hill, we freely conversed on a variety of subjects. Since the days of Pocock and Hyde, oriental learning has always been the pride of Oxford, and I once expressed an inclination to study Arabic. His prudence discouraged this childish fancy; but he neglected the fair occasion of directing the ardour of a curious mind. During my absence in the summer vacation, Dr. Waldegrave accepted a college living at Washington, in Sussex, and on my return I no longer found him at Oxford. From that time I have lost sight of my first tutor; but at the end of thirty years (1781) he was still alive; and the practice of exercise and temperance had entitled him to a healthy old age.

CHAP. VIII.

THE AUTHOR'S FIRST ATTEMPT AT WRITING HISTORY.

THE long recess between the Trinity and Michaelmas terms empties the College of Oxford, as well as the courts of Westminster. I spent, at my father's house at Burlton, in Hampshire, the two months of August and September. It is whimsical enough, that as soon as I left Magdalen College, my taste for books began to revive; but it was the same blind and boyish taste for the pursuit of exotic history. Unprovided with original learning, uninformed in the habit of thinking, unskilled in the arts of composition, I resolved—to write a book. The title of this first essay, the Age of Sesostris was perhaps suggested by Voltaire's Age of Louis XIV. which was new and popular; but my sole object was to investigate the probable date of the life and reign of the conqueror of Asia. I was then enamoured of Sir John Marsham's Canon Chronicus; an elaborate work, of whose merits and defects I was not yet qualified to judge. According to his specious, though narrow plan, I settled my hero about the time of Solomon, in the tenth century before the Christian æra. It was therefore incumbent on me, unless I would adopt Sir Isaac Newton's shorter chronology, to remove a formidable objection; and my solution, for a

youth of fifteen, is not devoid of ingenuity.   In his version
of the Sacred Books, Manetho, the high priest, has iden-
tified Sethosis, or Sesostris, with the elder brother of
Danaus, who landed in Greece, according to the Parian
Marble, 1510 years before Christ.   But in my supposition
the high priest is guilty of a voluntary error; flattery is
the prolific parent of falsehood.   Manetho's History of
Egypt is dedicated to Ptolemy Philadelphus, who derived
a fabulous or illegitimate pedigree from the Macedonian
kings of the race of Hercules.   Danaus is the ancestor of
Hercules; and after the failure of the elder branch, his
descendants, the Ptolemies, are the sole representatives
of the royal family, and may claim by inheritance the
kingdom which they hold by conquest.   Such were my
juvenile discoveries; at a riper age, I no longer presume
to connect the Greek, the Jewish, and the Egyptian antiquities, which are lost in a distant cloud.   Nor is this
the only instance, in which the belief and knowledge of
the child are superseded by the more rational ignorance
of the man.   During my stay at Buriton, my infant labour
was diligently prosecuted, without much interruption from
company or country diversions; and I already heard the
music of public applause.   The discovery of my own
weakness was the first symptom of taste.   On my return
to Oxford, the Age of Sesostris was wisely relinquished;
but the imperfect sheets remained twenty years at the
bottom of a drawer, till, in a general clearance of papers,
(November, 1772,) they were committed to the flames.

   After the departure of Dr. Waldegrave, I was transferred, with his other pupils, to his academical heir, whose
literary character did not command the respect of the

college. Dr. **** well remembered that he had a salary
to receive, and only forgot that he had a duty to perform.
Instead of guiding the studies, and watching over the behaviour of his disciple, 1 was never summoned to attend
even the ceremony of a lecture; and, excepting one
voluntary visit to his rooms, during the eight months of
his titular office, the tutor and pupil lived in the same
college as strangers to each other. The want of experience, of advice, and of occupation, soon betrayed me into
some improprieties of conduct, ill-chosen company, late
hours, and inconsiderate expense. My growing debts
might be secret; but my frequent absence was visible
and scandalous; and a tour to Bath, a visit into Buckinghamshire, and four excursions to London in the same
winter, were costly and dangerous frolics. They were,
indeed, without a meaning, as without an excuse. The
irksomeness of a cloistered life repeatedly tempted me to
wander; but my chief pleasure was that of travelling;
and I was too young and bashful to enjoy, like a manly
Oxonian in town, the pleasures of London. In all these
excursions I eloped from Oxford; I returned to college;
in a few days I eloped again, just as if I had been an independent stranger in a hired lodging, without once hearing the voice of admonition, without once feeling the hand
of control. Yet my time was lost, my expenses were
multiplied, my behaviour abroad was unknown; folly as
well as vice should have awakened the attention of my
superiors, and my tender years would have justified a
more than ordinary degree of restraint and discipline.

It might, at least, be expected that an ecclesiastical
school should inculcate the orthodox principles of religion.

But our venerable mother had contrived to unite the opposite extremes of bigotry and indifference ; a heretic, or
unbeliever, was a monster in her eyes; but she was always, or often, or sometimes, remiss in the spiritual education of her own children. According to the statutes of
the university, every student before he is matriculated,
must subscribe his assent to the thirty-nine articles of the
church of England, which are signed by more than read,
and read by more than believe them. My insufficient
age excused me, however, from the immediate performance of this legal ceremony ; and the vice-chancellor
directed me to return, as soon as I should have accomplished my fifteenth year; recommending me, in the
mean while, to the instruction of my college. My college
forgot to instruct : I forgot to return, and was myself forgotten by the first magistrate of the university. Without a single lecture, either public or private, either christian or protestant, without any academical subscription,
without any episcopal confirmation; I was left by the
dim light of my catechism to grope my way to the chapel
and communion table, where I was admitted, without a
question how far, or by what means, I might be qualified
to receive the sacrament. Such almost incredible neglect
was productive of the worst mischiefs. From my childhood I have been fond of religious disputation: my poor
aunt has been often puzzled by the mysteries which she
strove to believe ; nor had the elastic spring been totally
broken by the weight of the atmosphere of Oxford. The
blind activity of idleness urged me to advance without
armour into the dangerous mazes of controversy ; and,
at the age of sixteen, I bewildered myself in the errors of

the church of Rome. The progress of my conversion
may tend to illustrate, at least, the history of my own
mind. It was not long since Dr. Middleton's Free Inquiry had sounded an alarm in the theological world:
much ink and much gall had been spilled in the defence
of the primitive miracles; and the two dullest of their
champions were crowned with academic honours by the
University of Oxford. The name of Middleton was unpopular; and his proscription very naturally led me to
peruse his writings, and those of his antagonists. His
bold criticism, which approaches the precipice of infide-
lity, produced on my mind a singular effect; and had I
persevered in the communion of Rome, I should now
apply to my own fortune the prediction of the Sybil,

————Via prima salutis,
Quod minimè reris, Graiâ, pandetur ab urbe.

The elegance of style and freedom of argument were repelled by a shield of prejudice. I still revered the character, or rather the names, of the saints and fathers
whom Dr. Middleton exposes; nor could he destroy my
implicit belief, that the gift of miraculous powers was
continued in the church, during the first four or five centuries of Christianity. But I was unable to resist the
weight of historical evidence, that within the same period
most of the leading doctrines of popery were already introduced in theory and practice: nor was my conclusion
absurd, that miracles are the test of truth, and that the
church must be orthodox and pure, which was so often approved by the visible interposition of the Deity. The
marvellous tales which are so boldy attested by the Basils

Chrysostoms, the Austins and Jeromes, compelled me to
embrace the superior merits of celibacy, the institution
of the monastic life, the use of the sign of the cross, of
holy oil, and even of images, the invocation of saints, the
worship of relics, the rudiments of purgatory in prayers
for the dead, and the tremendous mystery of the sacrifice of
the body and blood of Christ, which insensibly swelled
into the prodigy of transubstantiation. In these dispo-
sitions, and already more than half a convert, I formed
an unlucky intimacy with a young gentleman of our
college, whose name I shall spare. With a character
less resolute, Mr. **** had imbibed the same religious
opinions; and some popish books, I know not through
what channel, were conveyed into his possession. I read,
I applauded, I believed; the English translations of two
famous works of Bossuet, Bishop of Meaux, the Exposition of the Catholic Doctrine, and the History of the Protestant Variations, achieved my conversion, and I surely
fell by a noble hand.* I have since examined the originals
with a more discerning eye, and shall not hesitate to pronounce, that Bossuet is indeed a master of all the weapons
of controversy. In the exposition, a specious apology,
the orator assumes, with consummate art, the tone of
candour and simplicity: and the ten-horned monster is
transformed, at his magic touch, into the milk-white hind,
who must be loved as soon as she is seen. In the History,
a bold and well-aimed attack, he displays, with a happy

---

* Mr. Gibbon never talked with me on the subject of his conversion to
popery but once; and then he imputed his change to the works of Parsons
the jesuit, who lived in the reign of Elizabeth, and who, he said, had
urged all the best arguments in favour of the Roman Catholic religion.—S.

mixture of narrative and argument, the faults and follies, the changes and contradictions of our first reformers; whose variations (as he dexterously contends) are the mark of historical error, while the perpetual unity of the catholic church is the sign and test of infallible truth. To my present feelings it seems incredible that I should ever believe that I believed in transubstantiation. But my conqueror oppressed me with the sacramental words, "Hoc est corpus meum," and dashed against each other the figurative half-meanings of the Protestant sects: every objection was resolved into omnipotence; and after repeating at St. Mary's the Athanasian creed, I humbly acquiesced in the mystery of the real presence.

> " To take up half on trust, and half to try,
> Name it not faith, but bungling bigotry.
> Both knave and fool, the merchant we may call,
> To pay great sums, and to compound the small.
> For who would break with Heaven, and would not break for all ?"

No sooner had I settled my new religion than I resolved to profess myself a Catholic. Youth is sincere and impetuous; and a momentary glow of enthusiasm had raised me above all temporal considerations.*

By the keen Protestants, who would gladly retaliate the example of persecution, a clamour is raised of the increase of popery: and they are always loud to declaim against the toleration of priests and jesuits, who pervert so many of his Majesty's subjects from their religion and allegiance. On the present occasion, the fall of one or more of her sons directed this clamour against the uni-

---

* He described the letter to his father, announcing his conversion, as written with all the pomp, the dignity, and self-satisfaction of a martyr.—S.

versity; and it was confidently affirmed that popish
missionaries were suffered, under various disguises, to
introduce themselves into the colleges of Oxford. But
justice obliges me to declare, that, as far as relates to
myself, this assertion is false; and that I never conversed
with a priest, or even with a papist, till my resolution
from books was absolutely fixed. In my last excursion
to London, I addressed myself to Mr. Lewis, a Roman
Catholic bookseller, in Russell-street, Covent-garden, who
recommended me to a priest, of whose name and order I
am at present ignorant. In our first interview he soon
discovered that persuasion was needless. After sound-
ing the motives and merits of my conversion, he consented
to admit me into the pale of the church; and at his feet,
on the eighth of June 1753, I solemnly, though privately,
abjured the errors of heresy. The seduction of an English youth of family and fortune was an act of as much
danger as glory; but he bravely overlooked the danger,
of which I was not then sufficiently informed. " Where
a person is reconciled to the see of Rome, or procures
others to be reconciled, the offence (says Blackstone)
amounts to high treason." And if the humanity of the
age would prevent the execution of this sanguinary
statute, there were other laws of a less odious cast, which
condemned the priest to perpetual imprisonment, and
transferred the proselyte's estate to his nearest relation.
An elaborate controversial epistle, approved by my director and addressed to my father, announced and justified
the step which I had taken. My father was neither a bigot
nor a philosopher; but his affection deplored the loss of
an only son; and his good sense was astonished at my

strange departure from the religion of my country. In the first sally of passion he divulged a secret which prudence might have suppressed, and the gates of Magdalen College were for ever shut against my return. Many years afterwards, when the name of Gibbon was become as notorious as that of Middleton, it was industriously whispered at Oxford, that the historian had formerly "turned papist:" my character stood exposed to the reproach of inconstancy; and this invidious topic would have been handled without mercy by my opponents, could they have separated my cause from that of the university. For my own part, I am proud of an honest sacrifice of interest to conscience. I can never blush, if my tender mind was entangled in the sophistry that seduced the acute and manly understandings of Chillingworth and Bayle, who afterwards emerged from superstition to scepticism.

While Charles the First governed England, and was himself governed by a catholic queen, it cannot be denied that the missionaries of Rome laboured with impunity and success in the court, the country and even the universities. One of the sheep,

> ———Whom the grim wolfe with privy paw
> Daily devours apace, and nothing said,

is Mr. William Chillingworth, Master of Arts, and Fellow of Trinity College, Oxford; who, at the ripe age of twenty-eight years, was persuaded to elope from Oxford to the English seminary at Douay in Flanders. Some disputes with Fisher, a subtle jesuit, might first awaken him from the prejudices of education: but he yielded to

his own victorious argument, " that there must be somewhere an infallible judge ; and that the church of Rome
is the only christian society which either does or can
pretend to that character." After a short trial of a few
months, Mr. Chillingworth was again tormented by religious scruples: he returned home, resumed his studies,
unravelled his mistakes, and delivered his mind from the
yoke of authority and superstition. His new creed was
built on the principle, that the Bible is our sole judge,
and private reason our sole interpreter: and he ably
maintains this principle in the Religion of a Protestant, a
book which, after startling the doctors of Oxford, is still
esteemed the most solid defence of the Reformation.
The learning, the virtue, the recent merits of the author
entitled him to fair preferment: but the slave had now
broken his fetters; and the more he weighed, the less
was he disposed to subscribe to the thirty-nine articles of
the church of England. In a private letter he declares,
with all the energy of language, that he could not subscribe
to them without subscribing to his own damnation; and
that if ever he should depart from this immovable resolution, he would allow his friends to think him a madman
or an atheist. As the letter is without a date, we cannot
ascertain the number of weeks or months that elapsed
between this passionate abhorrence and the Salisbury
Register, which is still extant. " Ego Gulielmus Chillingworth, . . . omnibus hisce articulis, ... et singulis
in iisdem contentis volens, et ex animo subscribo, et con-
sensum meum iisdem præbeo. 20 die Julii 1638." But,
alas ! the chancellor and prebendary of Sarum soon deviated from his own subscription: as he more deeply scru-

tinized the article of the Trinity, neither scripture nor the primitive fathers could long uphold his orthodox belief; and he could not but confess, "that the doctrine of Arius is either a truth, or at least no damnable heresy." From this middle region of the air, the descent of his reason would naturally rest on the firmer ground of the Socinians : and if we may credit a doubtful story, and the popular opinion, his anxious inquiries at last subsided in philosophic indifference. So conspicuous, however, were the candour of his nature and the innocence of his heart, that this apparent levity did not affect the reputation of Chillingworth. His frequent changes proceeded from too nice an inquisition into truth. His doubts grew out of himself: he assisted them with all the strength of his reason: he was then too hard for himself: but finding as little quiet and repose in those victories, he quickly recovered, by a new appeal to his own judgment : so that in all his sallies and retreats, he was in fact his own convert.

Bayle was the son of a Calvinist minister in a remote province of France, at the foot of the Pyrenees. For the benefit of education, the Protestants were tempted to risk their children in the catholic universities; and in the twenty-second year of his age, young Bayle was seduced by the arts and arguments of the jesuits of Toulouse. He remained about seventeen months (9th March, 1669 —19th August, 1670,) in their hands, a voluntary captive; and a letter to his parents, which the new convert composed or subscribed '(15th April, 1670), is darkly tinged with the spirit of popery. But nature had designed him to think as he pleased, and to speak as he thought:

his piety was offended by the excessive worship of crea-
tures; and the study of physics convinced him of the
impossibility of transubstantiation, which is abundantly
refuted by the testimony of our senses.   His return to the
communion of a falling sect was a bold and disinterested
step, that exposed him to the rigour of the laws; and a
speedy flight to Geneva protected him from the resentment of his spiritual tyrants, unconscious as they were of
the full value of the prize which they had lost.   Had
Bayle adhered to the catholic church, had he embraced
the ecclesiastical profession, the genius and favour of
such a proselyte might have inspired wealth and honours
in his native country; but the hypocrite would have
found less happiness in the comforts of a benefice, or the
dignity of a mitre, than he enjoyed at Rotterdam in a private state of exile, indigence, and freedom.   Without a
country, or a patron, or a prejudice, he claimed the liberty,
and subsisted by the labours, of his pen: the inequality of
his volumnious works is explained and excused by his
alternately writing for himself, for the booksellers, and
for posterity; and if a severe critic would reduce him to
a single folio, that relic, like the books of the Sybil, would
become still more valuable.   A calm and lofty spectator
of the religious tempest, the philosopher of Rotterdam
condemned with equal firmness the persecution of Louis
the Fourteenth, and the republican maxims of the Cal-
vinists; their vain prophecies, and the intolerant bigotry
which sometimes vexed his solitary retreat.   In reviewing
the controversies of the times, he turned against each
other the arguments of the disputants; successively
wielded the arms of the Catholics and Protestants, he

proves that neither the way of authority nor the way of examination can afford the multitude any test of religious truth; and dexterously concludes that custom and education must be the sole grounds of popular belief. The ancient paradox of Plutarch, that atheism is less pernicious than superstition, acquires a tenfold vigour, when it is adorned with the colours of his wit, and pointed with the acuteness of his logic. His Critical Dictionary is a vast repository of facts and opinions; and he balances the *false* religions in his sceptical scales, till the opposite quantities (if I may use the language of algebra) annihilate each other. The wonderful power which he so boldly exercised, of assembling doubts and objections, had tempted him jocosely to assume the title of the νεφεληγερετα Ζευς, the cloud-compelling Jove; and in a conversation with the ingenious Abbé (afterwards Cardinal) de Polignac, he freely disclosed his universal Pyrrhonism. " I am most truly (said Bayle) a Protestant; for I protest indifferently against all systems and all sects."

The academical resentment, which I may possibly have provoked, will prudently spare this plain narrative of my studies, or rather of my idleness, and of the unfortunate event which shortened the term of my residence at Oxford. But it may be suggested, that my father was unlucky in the choice of a society, and the chance of a tutor. It will perhaps be asserted, that, in the lapse of forty years, many improvements have taken place in the college and in the university. I am not unwilling to believe, that some tutors might have been found more active than Dr. Waldegrave, and less contemptible than Dr.* * * *. About the same time, and in the same walk, a Bentham was still treading in the footsteps of a Burton, whose maxims he had adopted, and whose life he had published. The biographer indeed preferred the school logic to the new philosophy, Burgursdicius to Locke; and the hero appears, in his own writings, a stiff and conceited pedant. Yet even these men, according to the measure of their capacity, might be diligent and useful; and it is recorded of Burton, that he taught his pupils what he knew; some Latin, some Greek, some ethics and metaphysics; referring them to proper masters for the languages and sciences of which he was ignorant. At a more recent period, many students have been attracted by the merit and reputation of Sir William Scott, then a tutor in University College, and now conspicuous in the profession of the civil law; my personal acquaintance with that gentleman has inspired me with a just esteem for his abilities and knowledge; and I am assured that his lectures on history would compose, were they given to the public, a most valuable treatise. Under the auspices of the present Archbishop of York, Dr. Markham, himself an eminent scholar, a more regular discipline has been introduced, as I am told, at Christ Church;* a

---

* This was written on the information Mr. Gibbon had received, and the observation he had made, previous to his late residence at Lausanne. During his last visit to England, he had an opportunity of seeing at Sheffield Place some young men of the college above alluded to; he had great satisfaction in conversing with them, made many enquiries respecting their course of study, applauded the discipline of Christ Church, and the liberal attention shown by the Dean, to those whose only recommendation was their merit. Had Mr. Gibbon lived to revise this work, I am sure he would have mentioned the name of Dr. Jackson with the highest commendation, and also that of Dr. Bagot, Bishop of St. Asaph, whose attention to the

course of classical and philosophical studies is proposed, and even pursued, in that numerous seminary; learning has been made a duty, a pleasure, and even a fashion; and several young gentlemen do honour to the college in which they have been educated. According to the will of the donor, the profit of the second part of Lord Clarendon's History has been applied to the establishment of a riding-school, that the polite exercises might be taught, I know not with what success, in the university. The Vinerian professorship is of far more serious impor-

duties of his office while he was Dean of Christ Church College were unremitted. There are other colleges at Oxford, with whose discipline my friend was unacquainted, to which, without doubt, he would willingly have allowed their due praise, particularly Brazen Nose and Oriel Colleges: the former under the care of Dr. Cleaver, Bishop of Chester, the latter under that of Dr. Eveleigh. It is still greatly to be wished that the general expense, or rather extravagance, of young men at our English universities, may be more effectually restrained. The expense, in which they are permitted to indulge, is inconsistent not only with a necessary degree of study, but with those habits of morality which should be promoted, by all means possible, at an early period of life. An academical education in England is at present an object of alarm and terror to every thinking parent of moderate fortune. It is the apprehension of the expense, of the dissipation, and other evil consequences, which arise from the want of proper restraint at our own universities, that forces a number of our English youths to those of Scotland, and utterly excludes many from any sort of academical instruction. If a charge be true, which I have heard insisted on, that the heads of our colleges in Oxford and Cambridge are vain of having under their care chiefly men of opulence, who may be supposed exempt from the necessity of economical control, they are indeed highly censurable: since the mischief of allowing early habits of expense and dissipation is great, in various respects, even to those possessed of large property; and the most serious evil from this indulgence must happen to youths of humbler fortune, who certainly form the majority of students both at Oxford and Cambridge.—S.

tance; the laws of his country are the first science of an Englishman of rank and fortune, who is called to be a magistrate, and may hope to be a legislator.   This judicious institution was coldly entertained by the graver doctors, who complained (I have heard the complaint) that it would take the young people from their books: but Mr. Viner's benefaction is not unprofitable, since it has at least produced the excellent Commentaries of Sir William Blackstone.

CHAP. IX.

THE AUTHOR REMOVES TO LAUSANNE.

AFTER carrying me to Putney, to the house of his friend, Mr. Mallet,* by whose philosophy I was rather scandalized than reclaimed, it was necessary for my father to form a new plan of education, and to devise some method which, if possible, might effect the cure of my spiritual malady. After much debate it was determined, from the advice and personal experience of Mr. Elliot (now Lord Elliot), to fix me, during some years, at Lausanne, in Switzerland. Mr. Frey, a Swiss gentleman of Basle, undertook the conduct of the journey: we left London the 19th of June, crossed the sea from Dover to Calais, travelled post through several provinces of France, by the direct road of St. Quentin, Rheims, Langres, and Besançon, and arrived the 30th of June at Lausanne, where I was immediately settled under the roof and tuition of Mr. Pavilliard, a calvinist minister.

The first marks of my father's displeasure rather astonished than afflicted me: when he threatened to banish, and disown, and disinherit a rebellious son, I cherished a secret hope that he would not be able or willing to effect

* The author of a life of Bacon, which has been rated above its value; of some forgotten poems and plays; and of the pathetic ballad of William and Margaret.—S.

his menaces; and the pride of conscience encouraged me to sustain the honourable and important part which I was now acting. My spirits were raised and kept alive by the rapid motion of my journey, the new and various scenes of the Continent, and the civility of Mr. Frey, a man of sense, who was not ignorant of books or the world. But after he had resigned me into Pavilliard's hands, and I was fixed in my new habitation, I had leisure to contemplate the strange and melancholy prospect before me. My first complaint arose from my ignorance of the language. In my childhood I had once studied the French grammar, and I could imperfectly understand the easy prose of a familiar subject. But when I was thus suddenly cast on a foreign land, I found myself deprived of the use of speech and of hearing; and, during some weeks, incapable not only of enjoying the pleasures of conversation, but even of asking or answering a question in the common intercourse of life. To a home-bred Englishman every object, every custom was offensive; but the native of any country might have been disgusted with the general aspect of his lodging and entertainment. I had now exchanged my elegant apartment in Magdalen College for a narrow, gloomy street, the most unfrequented of an unhandsome town, for an old inconvenient house, and for a small chamber ill-contrived and ill-furnished, which, on the approach of winter, instead of a companionable fire, must be warmed by the dull and invisible heat of a stove. From a man I was again degraded to the dependence of a school-boy. Mr. Pavilliard managed my expenses, which had been reduced to a diminitive state: I received a small monthly allowance for my pocket-money; and helpless and awkward as I have ever been, I no longer enjoyed the indispensable comfort of a servant. My condition seemed as destitute of hope, as it was devoid of pleasure : I was separated for an indefinite, which appeared an infinite, term from my native country ; and I had lost all connexion with my catholic friends. I have since reflected with surprise, that as the Romish clergy of every part of Europe maintain a close correspondence with each other, they never attempted, by letters or messages, to rescue me from the hands of the heretics, or at least to confirm my zeal and constancy in the profession of the faith. Such was my first introduction to Lausanne; a place where I spent nearly five years with pleasure and profit, which I afterwards revisited without compulsion, and which I have finally selected as the most grateful retreat for the decline of my life.

But it is the peculiar felicity of youth that the most unpleasing objects and events seldom make a deep or lasting impression; it forgets the past, enjoys the present, and anticipates the future. At the flexible age of sixteen I soon learned to endure, and gradually to adopt, the new forms of arbitrary manners : the real hardships of my situation were alienated by time. Had I been sent abroad in a more splendid style, such as the fortune and bounty of my father might have supplied, I might have returned home with the same stock of language and science, which our countrymen usually import from the continent. An exile and a prisoner as I was, their example betrayed me into some irregularites of wine, of play, and of idle excursions: but I soon felt the impossibility of associating with them on equal terms ; and

after the departure of my first acquaintance, I held a cold
and civil correspondence with their successors.   This
seclusion from English society was attended with the
most solid·benefits. ˙In the Pays de Vaud, the French
language is used with less imperfection than in most of
the distant provinces of France: in Pavilliard's family,
necessity compelled me to listen and to speak; and if I
was at first disheartened by the apparent slowness, in a
few months I was astonished by the rapidity of my progress.   My pronunciation was formed by the constant
repetition of the same sounds; the variety of words and
idioms, the rules of grammar, and distinctions of genders,
were impressed in my memory: ease and freedom were
obtained by practice; correctness and elegance by labour; and before I was recalled home, French, in which
I spontaneously thought, was more familiar than English
to my ear, my tongue, and my pen.   The first effect of
this opening knowledge was the revival of my love of
reading, which had been chilled at Oxford; and I soon
turned over, without much choice, almost all the French
books in my tutor's library.   Even these amusements
were productive of real advantage: my taste and judgment were now somewhat riper.   I was introduced to a
new mode of style and literature: by the comparison of
manners and opinions, my views were enlarged, my
prejudices were corrected, and a copious voluntary abstract of the Histoire de l'Eglise et de l'Empire, by Le
Sueur, may be placed in·a middle line between my
childish and my manly studies.   As soon as I was able
to converse with the natives, I began to feel some satisfaction in their company: my awkward timidity was

polished and emboldened; and I frequented, for the first time, assemblies of men and women. The acquaintance of the Pavilliards prepared me by degrees for more elegant society. I was received with kindness and indulgence in the best families of Lausanne; and it was in one of these that I formed an intimate and lasting connexion with Mr. Deyverdun, a young man of an amiable temper and excellent understanding. In the arts of fencing and dancing, small indeed was my proficiency; and some months were idly wasted in the riding-school. My unfitness to bodily exercise reconciled me to a sedentary life, and the horse, the favourite of my countrymen, never contributed to the pleasures of my youth.

My obligations to the lessons of Mr. Pavilliard, gratitude will not suffer me to forget: he was endowed with a clear head and a warm heart; his innate benevolence had assuaged the spirit of the Church; he was rational, because he was moderate: in the course of his studies he had acquired a just though superficial knowledge of most branches of literature; by long practice, he was skilled in the arts of teaching; and he laboured with assiduous patience to know the character, gain the affection, and open the mind of his English pupil.* As

* *Translated Extract of a Letter from Mr. Pavilliard to Edward Gibbon, Esq.*
" Lausanne, July 25, 1753.

" Mr. Gibbon is, thank God, very well; and appears to me to be very comfortable at our house; I have even reason to think that he feels some attachment to myself, of which I am very glad, and which I shall strenuously endeavour to increase; because then he will have more confidence in me, and in what I intend to say to him.

" I have not yet ventured to speak to him upon religious topics, for I am not sufficiently acquainted with the English language to support a long

soon as we began to understand each other, he gently led me, from a blind and undistinguished love of reading, into the path of instruction. I consented with pleasure that a portion of the morning hours should be consecrated to a plan of modern history and geography, and to the critical perusal of the French and Latin classics; and at each step I felt myself invigorated by the habits of application and method. His prudence repressed and dissembled some youthful sallies; and as soon as I was confirmed in the habits of industry and temperance, he gave the reins into my own hands. His favourable report of my behaviour and progress gradually obtained some latitude of action and expense; and he wished to alleviate the hardships of my lodging and entertainment. The principles of philosophy were associated with the examples of taste; and by a singular chance, the book,

conversation in it, though I can read English authors with considerable facilitiy; and Mr. Gibbon does not understand enough French, though he is making rapid progress in it.

" I am much pleased with the politeness and suavity of your son's disposition, and I flatter myself I shall always be able to speak favourably of him to you. He applies closely to reading."

From the Same to the Same.

Lausanne, August, 13, 1753.

" Mr. Gibbon is, thank God, in good health; I feel an affection for him, and am exceedingly attached to him, because he is mild and quiet. Respecting his religious sentiments, though I have not yet said anything to him on the subject, I have reason to hope he will open his eyes to the truth. I think so, because, when he was in my study, he made choice of two controversial books, and took them to peruse in his chamber. He has enjoined me to present you his most humble respects, and to ask you to allow him to learn riding; which exercise will, he thinks, contribute to his bodily health."

as well as the man, which contributed the most effectually to my education, has a stronger claim on my
gratitude than on my admiration. Mr. De Crousaz, the
adversary of Bayle and Pope, is not distinguished by
lively fancy or profound reflection; and even in his own
country, at the end of a few years, his name and writings
are almost obliterated. But his philosophy had been
formed in the school of Locke, his divinity in that of
Limborch and Le Clerc; in a long and laborious life,
several generations of pupils were taught to think, and
even to write; his lessons rescued the academy of Lausanne from Calvinistic prejudice; and he had the rare
merit of diffusing a more liberal spirit among the clergy
and people of the Pays de Vaud. His system of logic,
which in the last editions has swelled to six tedious and
prolix volumes, may be praised as a clear and methodical
abridgment of the art of reasoning, from our simple ideas
to the most complex operations of the human understanding. This system I studied, and meditated, and abstracted, till I have obtained the free command of an universal instrument, which I soon presumed to exercise on
my catholic opinions. Pavilliard was not unmindful that
his first task, his most important duty, was to reclaim me
from the errors of popery. The intermixture of sects
has rendered the swiss clergy acute and learned on the
topics of controversy; and I have some of his letters in
which he celebrates the dexterity of his attack, and my
gradual concessions, after a firm and well-managed defence.* I was willing, and I am now willing, to allow

* Mr. Pavilliard has described to me the astonishment with which he
gazed on Mr. Gibbon standing before him: a thin little figure, with a large

him a handsome share of the honour of my conversion: yet I must observe, that it was principally effected by my private reflections; and I still remember my solitary transport at the discovery of philosophical argument against the doctrine of transubstantiation; that the text of scripture which seems to inculcate the real presence, is attested only by a single sense—our sight; while the real presence itself is disproved by three of our senses —the sight, the touch and the taste. The various articles of the Romish creed disappeared like a dream; and after a full conviction, on Christmas-day, 1754, I received the sacrament in the church of Lausanne. It was here that I suspended my religious inquiries, acquiescing with implicit belief in the tenets and mysteries, which are adopted by the general consent of Catholics and Protestants.*

head, disputing and urging, with the greatest ability, all the best arguments that had ever been used in favour of popery. Mr. Gibbon many years ago became very fat and corpulent, but he had uncommonly small bones, and was very slightly made.—S.

*Letter from Mr. Pavilliard to Edward Gibbon, Esq.

" June 26th, 1754.

" Sir,

" I hope you will pardon my long silence, on account of the news which I now have to communicate to you. My delay has been owing neither to forgetfulness nor to negligence, but I have, from week to week, been expecting to be able to announce to you that your son had entirely renounced the false ideas that he had embraced; but it was necessary to dispute every inch of ground; and I have not found in him a man of fickle disposition, or one who passes rapidly from one opinion to another. Often when I had confuted all his reasonings upon any particular point, in such a manner as to leave him nothing to reply (which he has frankly acknowledged), he has told me that he did not believe there was no answer that might be made to me. Whereupon I did not deem it right to push it too far, and to extort an acknowledgment from him that his heart would disavow; I therefore gave him time for reflection; all my books were at his service; I returned to the charge when he had informed me that he had studied the matter as well as he possibly could; and thus at last I established a truth.

" I felt persuaded that, when I had overthrown the principal errors of the Romish church, I should only have to show him that the remainder are consequences from these, and that they are no longer tenable when the fundamental doctrines are overturned; but, as I have already said, I was deceived in this, and it was necessary to treat of each tenet in all its extent. By the grace of God, my time has not been lost, and now, if he may, perhaps, still retain some remains of his pernicious errors, yet he is no longer a member of the Romish church. This, then, is how we stand.

" I have overthrown the infallibility of the church; I have proved that St. Peter was never the prince of the apostles, and that, even if he was, the Pope is not his successor; that it is doubtful whether St. Peter ever was at Rome, and, supposing that he was, he never was bishop of that city; that transubstantiation is a human invention, and of recent introduction into the church; that the adoration of the host and the denial of the cup are contrary to the word of God; that there are saints but we know not who they are, and therefore we cannot pray to them; that the respect and worship paid to relics is improper; that there is no purgatory, and that the doctrine of indulgences is erroneous; that Lent and the Friday and Saturday fasts are ridiculous at the present day, and in the manner in which they are prescribed by the Romish church; and that the charges brought against us of diversity in our doctrine, and of having for reformers only persons of scandalous conduct and immoral life, are entirely false.

" You will easily perceive, sir, that these subjects require a long discussion, and that some time was necessary for your son to think over my arguments and to seek for answers. I have asked him several times whether my arguments and proofs appeared to him to be convincing; and he has always assured me that they were in such a manner that, as I told him himself a little while ago, I dare myself aver that he is no longer a Roman Catholic. I flatter myself that, after having obtained the victory on these points, I shall, with the help of God, be sure of him on the rest: so that I expect to tell you in a little time that the work is accomplished. I ought, however, to inform you that, though I have found your son very firm in his opinions, yet I have found him reasonable and open to conviction, and not what is called a quibbler. With respect to the subject of the Friday and Saturday fasts; a long time after I wrote you word that he had not mentioned that he wished to observe it, about the beginning of March, I observed one Friday that he did not eat any meat; I spoke to him privately to know the reason of it, fearing it might be through indisposition. He answered that he had done it purposely, and that he thought it incumbent upon him to conform to a practice of the church of which he was a member. We conversed some time upon the subject; he told me that he merely looked upon it as a good custom indeed, and worthy of observance, though not holy in itself nor of divine institution. I did not think proper to insist upon it at that time, or to force him to act against his conscience; I have since treated upon this point, which is certainly one of the least important and fundamental; and yet I have found a considerable time necessary to undeceive him, and to make him understand that he was wrong to subject himself to the practice of a church that he did not account to be infallible; that even if this custom had some utility at its institution, yet now it had none of any sort, since it did not in any way contribute to purity of morals; that thus there was no reason either in the institution of the practice or in the practice itself, that made it incumbent on him to observe it; that at the present time it was merely a matter of interest, since dispensations were to be bought with money for eating flesh, &c.; so that I have brought him back to christian liberty with great difficulty and only within a few weeks since.

"I have requested him to write to you, to apprize you of his sentiments and of his state of health; and I believe he has done so."

CHAP. X.

AUTHOR'S ACCOUNT OF THE BOOKS HE READ.

Such, from my arrival at Lausanne, during the first eighteen or twenty months (July, 1753—March, 1755,) were my useful studies, the foundation of all my future improvements.   But every man who rises above the common level has received two educations: the first from his teachers; the second, more personal and more important, from himself.   He will not, like the fanatics of the last age, define the moment of grace; but he cannot forget the æra of his life, in which his mind has expanded to its proper form and dimensions.   My worthy tutor had the good sense and modesty to discern how far he could be useful: as soon as he felt that I advanced beyond his speed and measure, he wisely left me to my genius; and the hours of lesson were soon lost in the voluntary labour of the whole morning, and sometimes of the whole day. The desire of prolonging my time, gradually confirmed the salutary habit of early rising; to which I have always adhered, with some regard to seasons and situations: but it is happy for my eyes and my health, that my temperate ardour has never been seduced to trespass on the hours of the night.   During the last three years of my residence in Lausanne, I may assume the merit of serious and solid application; but I am tempted to distinguish the last eight

months of the year 1755, as the period of the most extraordinary diligence and rapid progress.* In my French
and Latin translations I adopted an excellent method,
which, from my own success, I would recommend to the
imitation of students. I chose some classic writer, such
as Cicero and Vertot, the most approved for purity and
elegance of style. I translated, for instance, an epistle of
Cicero into French; and after throwing it aside, till the
words and phrases were obliterated from my memory, I
re-translated my French into such Latin as I could find;
and then compared each sentence of my imperfect version, with the ease, the grace, the propriety of the Roman
orator. A similar experiment was made on several
pages of the Revolutions of Vertot; I turned them into
Latin, re-turned them after a sufficient interval into my
own French, and again scrutinized the resemblance or
dissimilitude of the copy and the original. By degrees I
was less ashamed, by degrees I was more satisfied with

---

* JOURNAL, December, 1755.]—In finishing this year, I must remark
how favourable it was to my studies. In the space of eight months, from
the beginning of April, I learned the principles of drawing; made myself
complete master of the French and Latin languages, with which I was very
superficially acquainted before, and wrote and translated a great deal in
both; read Cicero's Epistles ad Familiares, his Brutus, all his Orations, his
Dialogues de Amicitiâ and de Senectute; Terence, twice; and Pliny's
Epistles. In French, Giannone's History of Naples, and the Abbé Banier's
Mythology, and M. de Boehat's Mémoires sur la Suisse, and wrote a very
ample relation of my tour. I likewise began to study Greek, and went
through the grammar. I began to make very large collections of what I
read. But what I esteem most of all, from the perusal and meditation of De
Crousaz's Logic, I not only understood the principles of that science, but
formed my mind to a habit of thinking and reasoning I had no idea of
before,

myself: and I persevered in the practice of these double translations, which filled several books, till I had acquired the knowledge of both idioms, and the command at least of a correct syle. This useful exercise of writing was accompanied and succeeded by the more pleasing occupation of reading the best authors. The perusal of the Roman classics was at once my exercise and reward. Dr. Middleton's History, which I then appreciated above its true value, naturally directed me to the writings of Cicero. The most perfect editions, that of Olivet, which may adorn the shelves of the rich, that of Ernesti, which should lie on the table of the learned, were not in my power. For the Familiar Epistles I used the text and English Commentary of Bishop Ross: but my general edition was that of Verburgius, published at Amsterdam, in two large volumes in folio, with an indifferent choice of various notes. I read, with application and pleasure, *all* the epistles, *all* the orations, and the most important trea· tises of rhetoric and philosophy; and as I read, I applauded the observation of Quintilian, that every student may judge of his own proficiency, by the satisfaction which he receives from the Roman orator. I tasted the beauties of language, I breathed the spirit of freedom, and I imbibed from his precepts and examples the public and private sense of a man. Cicero in Latin, and Xenophon in Greek, are indeed the two ancients whom I would first propose to a liberal scholar: not only for the merit of their style and sentiments, but for the admirable lessons, which may be applied almost to every situation of public and private life. Cicero's Epistles may in particular afford the models of every form of correspondence, from

the careless effusions of tenderness and friendship, to the
well-guarded declaration of discreet and dignified resentment. After finishing this great author, a library of eloquence and reason, I formed a more extensive plan of
reviewing the Latin classics,* under the four divisions of,
1. Historians, 2. Poets, 3. Orators, and 4. Philosophers,
in a chronological series, from the days of Plautus and
Sallust, to the decline of the language and empire of
Rome; and this plan, in the last twenty-seven months of
my residence at Lausanne (January, 1756—April, 1758),
I *nearly* accomplished. Nor was this review, however
rapid, either hasty or superficial. I indulged myself in a
second, and even a third perusal of Terence, Virgil,
Horace, Tacitus, &c., and studied to imbibe the sense and
spirit most congenial to my own. I never suffered a difficult or corrupt passage to escape, till I had viewed it in
every light of which it was susceptible: though often disappointed, I always consulted the most learned or ingenious commentators, Torrentius and Dacier on Horace,
Catrou and Servius on Virgil, Lipsius on Tacitus, Mezeriac on Ovid, &c.; and in the ardour of my inquiries, I
embraced a large circle of historical and critical erudition. My abstracts of each book were made in the
French language; my observations often branched into
particular essays; and I can still read, without contempt,
a dissertation of eight folio pages on eight lines (287—

---

* JOURNAL, January, 1756.]—I determined to read over the Latin
authors in order; and read this year, Virgil, Sallust, Livy, Velleius Paterculus, Valerius Maximus, Tacitus, Suetonius, Quintus Curtius, Justin,
Florus, Plautus, Terence, and Lucretius. I also read and meditated Locke
upon the Understanding.

294) of the fourth Georgic of Virgil. Mr. Deyverdun, my friend, whose name will be frequently repeated, had joined with equal zeal, though not with equal perseverance, in the same undertaking. To him every thought, every composition, was instantly communicated; with him I enjoyed the benefits of a free conversation on the topics of our common studies.

But it is scarcely possible for a mind endowed with any active curiosity to be long conversant with the Latin classics, without aspiring to know the Greek originals, whom they celebrate as their masters, and of whom they so warmly recommend the study and imitation;

———Vos exemplaria Græca
Nocturnâ versate manu, versate diurnâ.

Horace. Ep. ad Pisones, 268 line.

It was now that I regretted the early years which had been wasted in sickness or idleness, or mere idle reading; that I condemned the perverse method of our schoolmasters, who, by first teaching the mother-language, might descend with so much ease and perspecuity to the origin and etymology of a derivative idiom. In the nineteenth year of my age I determined to supply this defect; and the lessons of Pavilliard again contributed to smooth the entrance of the way, the Greek alphabet, the grammar, and the pronunciation according to the French accent. At my earnest request we presumed to open the Iliad; and I had the pleasure of beholding, though darkly and through a glass, the true image of Homer, whom I had long since admired in an English dress. After my tutor had left me to myself, I worked my way through about half the Iliad, and afterwards interpreted alone a large portion of Xenophon and Herodotus. But my ardour, destitute of aid and emulation, was gradually cooled, and, from the barren task of searching words in a lexicon, I withdrew to the free and familiar conversation of Virgil and Tacitus. Yet in my residence at Lausanne I had laid a solid foundation, which enabled me, in a more propitious season, to prosecute the study of Grecian literature.

From a blind idea of the usefulness of such abstract science, my father had been desirous, and even pressing, that I should devote some time to the mathematics ;* nor

Extract of a letter from Mr. Pavilliard to Edward Gibbon, Esq.

"January 12, 1757.

" Sir,

"You wished that your son should apply himself to Algebra; his taste for literature made him fearful lest it should injure his favourite studies; I have persuaded him that he formed a wrong idea of that province of Mathematics ; and the obedience he owes you, added to my arguments, has determined him to go through a course of it. I did not think that, with this repugnance, he would have made any great progress in it ; I was deceived; all that he does, he does well ; he is punctual at his lessons, applies himself to reading before them, and goes over them again carefully, so that he advances rapidly, and more than I should, myself, have expected. He is delighted at having begun, and I think he will go through a short course of geometry, which will not altogether occupy him above seven or eight months. While he is proceeding with these lessons, he has not at all remitted his other studies; he has made great progress in the Greek, and has read almost half the Iliad of Homer; I give him lessons regularly in that author. He has also finished the Latin historians, and is at present engaged upon the poets; he has read the whole of Plautus and Terence, and will soon have finished Lucretius. Moreover, he does not skim these authors over lightly, but wishes to make himself clear upon every thing ; so that with the genius he possesses, and his excellent memory and application, he will go deep into the sciences.

" I have already had the honour to inform you that, notwithstanding his

could I refuse to comply with so reasonable a wish. During two winters I attended the private lectures of Monsieur de Traytorrens, who explained the elements of algebra and geometry, as far as the comic sections of the Marquis de l'Hôpital, and appeared satisfied with my diligence and improvement.* But as my childish pro-

studies, he was in the habit of seeing company, and I may at the present time repeat what I then said."

From the Same to the Same.

" January, 14, 1758.

" Sir,

" I had the honour of writing to you on the 27th of July and the 26th of October last, and of giving you an account of the health, the studies, and conduct of your son. I have nothing to add to what I have already said to you about him; he is, thank God, perfectly well, and continues to study with close application; and I can assure you he makes considerable progress in different branches, makes himself highly esteemed by all who are acquinted with him, and I hope that, when he shows you in detail the extent of his acquirements, you will be very much pleased with him. Literature, which is his favourite study, does not occupy him entirely; he is proceeding with the mathematics, and his professor assures me that he never saw any one make so rapid a progress as he does, or have more ardour or application than he possesses. His happy and penetrating genius is assisted by one of the best of memories, so that he scarcely ever forgets anything he learns. I have not myself any less reason than before to be pleased with his conduct; though he studies a great deal, yet he sees company, but only those persons whose intercourse may be profitable to him."

* JOURNAL, January, 1757.]—I began to study algebra under M. de Traytorrens, went through the elements of algebra and geometry, and the three first books of the Marquis de l'Hôpital's Comic Sections. I also read Tibullus, Catullus, Propertius, Horace (with Dacier's and Torrentius's notes), Virgil, Ovid's Epistles and Mezeriac's Commentary, the Ars Amandi, and the Elegies; likewise the Augustus and Tiberius of Suetonius, and a Latin translation of Dion Cassius, from the death of Julius

pensity for numbers and calculations was totally extinct, I was content to receive the passive impression of my professor's lectures, without any active exercise of my own powers. As soon as I understood the principle, I relinquished for ever the pursuit of the mathematics; nor can I lament that I desisted, before my mind was hard ened by the habit of rigid demonstration, so destructive of the finer feelings of moral evidence, which must, how- ever, determine the actions and opinions of our lives. I listened with more pleasure to the proposal of studying the Law of Nature and Nations, which was taught in the Academy of Lausanne by Mr. Vicat, a professor of some learning and reputation. But, instead of attending his public or private course, I preferred in my closet the lessons of his masters, and my own reason. Without being disgusted by Grotius or Puffendorf, I studied in their writings the duties of a man, the rights of a citizen, the theory of justice (it is, alas! a theory), and the laws of peace and war, which have had some influence on the practice of modern Europe. My fatigues were alleviated by the good sense of their commentator Barbeyrac. Locke's Treatise of Government instructed me in the knowledge of Whig principles, which are rather founded in reason than experience; but my delight was in the frequent perusal of Montesquieu, whose energy of style

Cæsar to the death of Augustus. I also continued my correspondence begun last year with Mr. Allemand of Bex, and the Professor Breitinger of Zurich; and opened a new one with the Professor Gesner of Gottingen.

N. B. Last year and this I read St. John's Gospel, with part of Xeno- phon's Cyropædia; the Iliad and Herodotus: but, upon the whole, I rather neglected my Greek.

and boldness of hypothesis were powerful to awaken and stimulate the genius of the age. The logic of De Crousaz had prepared me to engage with his master Locke, and his antagonist Bayle; of whom the former may be used as a bridle, and the latter applied as a spur, to the curiosity of a young philosopher. According to the nature of their respective works, the schools of argument and objection, I carefully went through the Essay on Human Understanding, and occasionally consulted the most interesting articles of the Philosophic Dictionary. In the infancy of my reason I turned over, as an idle amusement, the most serious and important treatise: in its maturity, the most trifling performance could exercise my taste or judgment; and more than once I have been led by a novel into a deep and instructive train of thinking. But I cannot forbear to mention three particular books, since they have remotely contributed to form the historian of the Roman Empire. 1. From the Provincial Letters of Pascal, which almost every year I have perused with new pleasure, I learned to manage the weapon of grave and temperate irony, even on subjects of ecclesiastical solemnity. 2. The Life of Julian, by the Abbé de la Bleterie, first introduced me to the man and the times; and I should be glad to recover my first essay on the truth of the miracle which stopped the rebuilding of the Temple of Jerusalem. 3. In Giannone's Civil History of Naples, I observed with a critical eye the progress and abuse of sacerdotal power, and the revolutions of Italy in the darker ages. This various reading, which I now conducted with discretion, was digested according to the precept and model of Mr. Locke, into a large common-place book; a practice, however, which I do not strenuously recommend. The action of the pen will doubtless imprint an idea on the mind as well as on the paper: but I much question whether the benefits of this laborious method are adequate to the waste of time; and I must agree with Dr. Johnson, (Idler, No. 74,) "that what is twice read, is commonly better remembered than what is transcribed."

CHAP. XI.

AUTHOR'S TOUR IN SWITZERLAND.

DURING two years, if I forget some boyish excursions of a day or a week, I was fixed at Lausanne; but at the end of the third summer, my father consented that I should make the tour of Switzerland with Pavilliard: and our short absence of one month (September 21st—October 20th, 1755,) was a reward and relaxation of my assiduous studies,[*] The fashion of climbing the moun-

---

[*] *From Edward Gibbon to Mrs. Porten.*

* * * * * * * * * * * * * " Now for myself. As my father has given me leave to make a journey round Switzerland, we set out to-morrow. Buy a map of Switzerland, it will cost you but a shilling, and follow me. I go by Iverdun, Neufchâtel, Bienne or Biel, Soleure or Solothurn, Bâle or Basle, Baden, Zurich, Lucerne, and Berne. The voyage will be of about four weeks; so that *I hope to find a letter from you waiting for me.* As my father had given me leave to learn what I had a mind, I have learned to ride, and learn actually to dance and draw. Besides that, I often give ten or twelve hours a day to my studies. I find a great many agreeable people here, see them sometimes, and can say upon the whole, without vanity, that though I am the Englishman here who spends the least money, I am he who is the most generally liked. I told you that my father had promised to send me into France and Italy. I have thanked him for it; but if he would follow my plan, he won't do it yet a while. I never liked young travellers; they go too raw to make any great remarks, and they lose a time which is (in my opinion) the most precious part of a man's life. My scheme would be, to spend this winter at Lausanne (for though it is a very good place to acquire the air of good company and the French

tains and reviewing the glaciers, had not yet been introduced by foreign travellers, who seek the sublime beauties of nature.   But the political face of the country is
not less diversified by the forms and spirit of so many
various republics, from the jealous government of the
few to the licentious freedom of the *many*. I contem-.
plated with pleasure the new prospects of men and manners; though my conversation with the natives would
have been more free and instructive, had I possessed the
German, as well as the French, language. We passed
through most of the principal towns of Switzerland;
Neufchâtel, Bienne, Soleure, Arau, Baden, Zurich, Basle,
and Berne.   In every place we visited the churches, arsenals, libraries, and all the most eminent persons; and,
after my return, I digested my notes in fourteen or fifteen
sheets of a French journal, which I despatched to my
father, as a proof that my time and his money had not
been mis-spent. Had I found this journal among his

tongue, we have no good professors); to spend, I say, the winter at Lausanne ; go into England to see my friends a couple of months, and after
that, finish my studies, either at Cambridge (for after what has passed one
cannot think of Oxford), or at an university in Holland. If you liked the
scheme, *could you not propose it to my father by Metcalf, or somebody* who
has *a certain credit over him?* I forgot to ask you whether, in case my
father writes to tell me of his marriage, would you advise me to compliment
my mother-in-law? I think so. My health is so very regular that I have
nothing to say about it.

   " I have been¡ the whole day writing you this letter ; the preparation for
our voyage gave me a thousand interruptions. Besides that, I was obliged
to write in English. This last reason will seem a paradox to you, but I
assure you the French is much more familiar to me. I am. &c.

" E. Gibbon."

    "Lausanne, Sept. 20, 1755."

papers, I might be tempted to select some passages : but I will not transcribe the printed accounts, and it may be sufficient to notice a remarkable spot, which left a deep and lasting impression on my memory. From Zurich we proceeded to the Benedictine Abbey of Einfidlen, more commonly styled Our Lady of the Hermits. I was astonished by the profuse ostentation of riches in the poorest corner of Europe; amidst a savage scene of woods and mountains, a palace appears to have been erected by magic; and it was erected by the potent magic of religion. A crowd of palmers and votaries was prostrate before the altar. The title and worship of the Mother of God provoked my indignation; and the lively naked image of superstition suggested to me, as in the same place it had done to Zuinglius, the most pressing argument for the reformation of the church. About two years after this tour, I passed at Geneva a useful and agreeable month; but this excursion, and some short visits in the Pay de Vaud, did not materially interrupt my studious and sedentary life at Lausanne.

My thirst of improvement, and the languid state of science at Lausanne, soon prompted me to solicit a literary correspondence with several men of learning, whom I had not an opportunity of personally consulting. 1. In the perusal of Livy, (xxx. 44.) I had been stopped by a sentence in a speech of Hannibal, which cannot be reconciled by any torture with his character or argument. The commentators dissemble, or confess their perplexity. It occurred to me, that the change of a single letter, by substituting *otio* instead of *odio*, might restore a clear and consistent sense; but I wished to weigh my emendation in scales less partial than my own. I addressed myself to M. Crevier,* the successor of Rollin, and a professor in the university of Paris, who had published a large and valuable edition of Livy. His answer was speedy and polite; he praised my ingenuity, and adopted my conjecture. 2. I maintained a Latin correspondence, at first anonymous, and afterwards in my own name, with Professor Breitinger,† of Zurich, the learned editor of a Septuagint Bible. In our frequent letters we discussed questions of antiquity, many passages of the Latin classics. I proposed my interpretations and amendments. His censures (for he did not spare my boldness of conjecture) were sharp and strong; and I was encouraged by the consciousness of my strength, when I could stand in free debate against a critic of such eminence and erudition. 3. I corresponded on similiar topics with the celebrated Professor Matthew Gesner,‡ of the University of Gottingen; and he accepted, as courteously as the two former, the invitation of an unknown youth. But his abilities might possibly be decayed; his elaborate letters were feeble and prolix; and when I asked his proper direction, the vain old man covered half a sheet of paper with the foolish enumeration of his titles and offices. 4. These professors of Paris, Zurich, and Gottingen, were strangers, whom I presumed to address on the credit of their name; bnt Mr. Allemand,§ minister at Bex, was my personal friend, with whom I maintained a more free and interesting correspondence. He was a master of language, of science, and above all, of dispute; and his

---

* See Letters, No. I.   † See Letters, Nos. IV. and V.
‡ See Letters, Nos. VI. VII. and VIII.   § See Letters, Nos. II. and III.

acute and flexible logic could support, with equal address, and perhaps with equal indifference, the adverse
sides of every possible question. His spirit was active,
but his pen had been indolent. Mr. Allemand had exposed himself to much scandal and reproach, by an anonymous letter (1745) to the Protestants of France; in which
he labours to persuade them that *public* worship is the
exclusive right and duty of the state, and that their numerous assemblies of dissenters and rebels were not au-
thorized by the law or the gospel. His style is animated,
his arguments specious; and if the papist may seem to
lurk under the mask of a protestant, the philosopher is
concealed under the disguise of a papist. After some
trials in France and Holland, which were defeated by
his fortune or his character, a genius that might have
enlightened or deluded the world, was buried in a country
living, unknown to fame, and discontented with mankind.
Est sacrificulus in pago, et rusticos decipit. As often as
private or ecclesiastical business called him to Lausanne,
I enjoyed the pleasure and benefit of his conversation,
and we were mutually flattered by our attention to each
other. Our correspondence, in his absence chiefly turned
on Locke's metaphysics, which he attacked, and I defended; the origin of ideas, the principles of evidence,
and the doctrine of liberty;

And found no end, in wandering mazes lost.

By fencing with so skillful a master I acquired some dexterity in the use of my philosophic weapons; but I was
still the slave of education and prejudice. He had some

measures to keep; and I much suspect that he never showed me the true colours of his secret scepticism.

Before I was recalled from Switzerland, I had the satisfaction of seeing the most extraordinary man of the age; a poet, an historian, a philosopher, who has filled thirty quartos, of prose and verse, with his various productions, often excellent, and always entertaining. Need I add the name of Voltaire? After forfeiting, by his own misconduct, the friendship of the first of kings, he retired at the age of sixty, with a plentiful fortune, to a free and beautiful country, and resided two winters (1757 and 1758) in the town or neighbourhood of Lausanne. My desire of beholding Voltaire, whom I then rated above his real magnitude, was easily gratified. He received me with civility as an English youth; but I cannot boast of any peculiar notice or distinction; *Virgilium vidi tantùm.*

The ode which he composed on his first arrival on the banks of the Leman Lake, "O maison d'Aristippe! O jarden d'Epicure," &c., had been imparted as a secret to the gentleman by whom I was introduced. He allowed me to read it twice; I knew it by heart; and as my discretion was not equal to my memory, the author was soon displeased by the circulation of a copy. In writing this trivial anecdote, I wished to observe whether my memory was impaired, and I have the comfort of finding that every line of the poem is still engraved in fresh and indelible characters. The highest gratification which I derived from Voltaire's residence at Lausanne, was the uncommon circumstance of hearing a great poet declaim his own productions on the stage. He had formed a company of gentlemen and ladies some of whom were not destitute of talents. A decent theatre was framed at Monrepos, a country-house at the end of a suburb; dresses and scenes were provided at the expense of the actors; and the author directed the rehearsals with the zeal and attention of paternal love. In two successive winters his tragedies of Zaïre, Alzire, Zulime, and his sentimental comedy of the Enfant Prodigue, were played at the theatre of Monrepos. Voltaire represented the characters best adapted to his years, Lusignan, Alvarez, Benasser, Euphemon. His declamation was fashioned to the pomp and cadence of the old stage; and he expressed the enthusiasm of poetry, rather than the feelings of nature. My ardour which soon became conspicuous, seldom failed of procuring me a ticket. The habits of pleasure fortified my taste for the French theatre, and that taste has perhaps abated my idolatry for the gigantic genuis of Shakespear, which is inculcated from our infancy as the first duty of an Englishman. The wit and philosophy of Voltaire, his table ánd theatre, refined, in a visible degree, the manners of Lausanne; and, however addicted to study, I enjoyed my share of the amusements of society. After the representation of Monrepos, I sometimes supped with the actors. I was now familiar in some, and acquainted in many, houses; and my evenings were generally devoted to cards and conversation, either in private parties or numerous assemblies.

CHAP. XII.

MADEMOISELLE CURCHOD—AFTERWARDS MADAME NECKER.

I hesitate, from the apprehension of ridicule, when I approach the delicate subject of my early love. By this word I do not mean the polite attention, the gallantry, without hope or design, which has originated in the spirit of chivalry, and is interwoven with the texture of French manners. I understand by this passion the union of desire, friendship, and tenderness, which is inflamed by a single female, which prefers her to the rest of her sex, and which seeks her possession as the supreme or the sole happiness of our being. I need not blush at recollecting the object of my choice; and though my love was disappointed of success, I am rather proud that I was once capable of feeling such a pure and exalted sentiment. The personal attractions of Mademoiselle Susan Curchod were embellished by the virtues and talents of the mind. Her fortune was humble, but her family was respectable. Her mother, a native of France, had preferred her religion to her country. The profession of her father did not extinguish the moderation and philosophy of his temper, and he lived, content with a small salary and laborious duty, in the obscure lot of minister of Crassy, in the mountains that separate the Pays de Vaud

from the county of Burgundy.*   In the solitude of a
sequestered village he bestowed a liberal, and even
learned, education on his only daughter.   She surpassed
his hopes by her proficiency in the sciences and languages; and in her short visits to some relations at Lausanne, the wit, the beauty, and erudition of Mademoiselle
Curchod were the theme of universal applause.   The
report of such á prodigy awakened my curiosity; I saw
and loved.   I found her learned without pedantry, lively
in conversation, pure in sentiment, and elegant in manners; and the first sudden emotion was fortified by the
habits and knowledge of a more familiar acquaintance.
She permitted me to make her two or three visits at her

Extracts from the Journal.

March, 1757.	I wrote some critical observations upon Plautus.
March 8th.	I wrote a long dissertation on some lines of Virgil.
June.	I saw Mademoiselle Curchod—*Omnia Vincit amor, et nos cedamus amori.*
August.	I went to Crassy, and staid two days.
Sept. 15th.	I went to Geneva.
Oct. 15th.	I came back to Lausanne, having passed through Crassy.
Nov. 1st.	I went to visit M. de Watteville at Loin, and saw Made-moiselle Curchod in my way through Rolle.
Nov. 17th	I went to Crassy, and staid there six days.
Jan. 1758.	In the three first months of this year I read Ovid's Metamor-phoses, finished the conic sections with M. de Tray-torrens, and went as far as the infinite series; I like-wise read Sir Isaac Newton's Chronology, and wrote my critical observations upon it.
Jan. 23rd.	I saw Alzire acted by the society at Monrepos. Voltaire acted Alvarez; D'Hermanches, Zamore; De St. Cierge, Guzman; M. de Gentil, Monteze; and Ma-dame Denys, Alzire.

ther's house. I passed some happy days there, in the mountains of Bergundy, and her parents honourably encouraged the connexion. In a calm retirement the gay vanity of youth no longer fluttered in her bosom; she listened to the voice of truth and passion, and I might presume to hope that I had made some impression on a virtuous heart. At Crassey and Lausanne I indulged my dream of felicity: but on my return to England, I soon discovered that my father would not hear of this strange alliance, and that without his consent I was myself destitute and helpless. After a painful struggle I yielded to my fate: I sighed as a lover, I obeyed as a son;* my wound was insensibly healed by time, absence, and the habits of a new life. My cure was accelerated by a faithful report of tranquillity and cheerfulness of the lady herself, and my love subsided in friendship and esteem. The minister of Crassey soon afterwards died; his stipend died with him: his daughter retired to Geneva, where, by teaching young ladies, she earned a hard subsistence for herself and her mother; but in her lowest distress she maintained a spotless reputation, and a dignified behaviour. A rich banker of Paris, a citizen of Geneva, had the good fortune and good sense to discover and possess this inestimable treasure; and in the capital of taste and luxury she resisted the temptations of wealth, as she had sustained the hardships of indigence. The

* See Œuvres de Rousseau, tom. xxxiii. p. 88, 89, octavo edition. As an author I shall not appeal from the judgment, or taste, or caprice of Jean Jacques: but that extraorninary man, whom I admire and pity, should have been less precipitate in condemning the moral character and conduct of a strange.

genius of her husband has exalted him to the most con-spicuous station in Europe. In every change of prosperity and disgrace he has reclined on the bosom of a faithful friend; and Mademoiselle Curchod is now the wife of M. Necker, the minister, and perhaps the legislator, of the French monarchy.

Whatsoever have been the fruits of my educatien, they must be ascribed to the fortunate banishment which placed me at Lausanne. I have sometimes applied to my own fate the verses of Pindar, which remind an Olympic champion that his victory was the consequence of his exile; and that at home, like a domestic fowl, his days might have rolled away inactive and inglorious.

> . . . ἤτοι και τεα κευ,
> Ἐνδομαχας ἀπ' ἀλεκτωρ,
> Συγγονω παρ' ἑρτιο,
> Ἀκλεης τιμα κατεφυλλοροησε ποδων.
> Εἰ μη στασις ἀντιανειρα
> Κνωσιας ἀμερσε πατρας.*   *Olymp.* XII.

If my childish revolt against the religion of my country had not stripped me in time of my academical gown, the five important years so liberally improved in the studies and conversation of Lausanne, would have been steeped

---

* Thus like the crested bird of Mars, at home
    Engaged in foul domestic jars,
    And wasted with intestine wars,
  Inglorious hadst thou spent thy vig'rous bloom:
    Had not sedition's civil broils
    Expelled thee from thy native Crete,
    And driven thee with more glorious toils,
  The Olympic crown in Pisa's plain to meet. *West's Pindar.*

in port and prejudice among the monks of Oxford. Had
the fatigue of idleness compelled me to read, the path of
learning would not have been enlighted by a ray of
philosophic freedom. I should have grown to manhood
ignorant of the life and language of Europe, and my
knowledge of the world would have been confined to an
English cloister. But my religious error fixed me at
Lausanne in a state of banishment and disgrace. The
rigid course of discipline and abstinence, to which I was
condemned, invigorated the constitution of my mind and
body; poverty and pride restrained me from my countrymen. One mischief, however, and in their eyes a serious and irreparable mischief was derived from the success of my Swiss education: I had ceased to be an Englishman. At the flexible period of youth, from the age
of sixteen to twenty-one, my opinions, habits, and sentiments were cast in a foreign mould; the faint and distant
remembrance of England was almost obliterated; my
native language was grown less familiar; and I should have
cheerfully accepted the offer of a moderate independence
on the terms of perpetual exile. By the good sense and
temper of Pavilliard my yoke was insensibly lightened:
he left me master of my time and actions; but he could
neither change my situation, nor increase my allowance;
and with the progress of my years and reason I impatiently sighed for the moment of my deliverance. At
length, in the spring of the year 1758, my father signified
his permission and his pleasure that I should immediately
return home. We were then in the midst of a war: the
resentment of the French at our taking their ships without a declaration, had rendered that polite nation some-

what peevish and difficult. They denied a passage to
English travellers, and the road through Germany was
circuitous, toilsome, and perhaps, in the neighborhood of
the armies, exposed to some danger. In this perplexity,
two Swiss officers of my acquaintance, in the Dutch service, who were returning to their garrisons, offered to
conduct me through France as one of their companions;
nor did we sufficiently reflect that my borrowed name
and regimentals might have been considered, in case of
discovery, in a very serious light. I took my leave of
Lausanne on the 11th of April, 1758, with a mixture of
joy and regret, in the firm resolution of revisiting, as a
man, the persons and places which had been so dear to
my youth. We travelled slowly, but pleasantly, in a
hired coach, over the hills of Franche-Compté and the
fertile province of Lorraine; and passed, without accident or inquiry, through several fortified towns of the
French frontier: from thence we entered the wild Ar-
dennes of the Austrian duchy of Luxembourg; and after
crossing the Meuse at Leige, we traversed the heaths of
Brabant, and reached, on the 15th day, our Dutch garrison of Blois le Duc. In our passage through Nanc, my
eye was gratified by the aspect of a regular and beautiful
city, the work of Stanislaus, who, after the storms of
Polish royalty, reposed in the love and gratitude of his
new subjects of Lorraine. In our halt at Maestricht I
visited M. de Beaufort, a learned critic, who was known
to me by his specious arguments against the five first centuries of the Roman history. After dropping my regimental companions, I stepped aside to visit Rotterdam
and the Hague. I wished to have observed a country,

the monument of freedom and industry; but my days were numbered, and a longer delay would have been ungraceful. I hastened to embark at the Brill, landed the next day at Hardwich, and proceeded to London, where my father awaited my arrival. The whole term of my first absence from England was four years, ten months, and fifteen days.

In the prayers of the church our personal concerns are judiciously reduced to the threefold distinction of *mind, body,* and *estate.* The sentiments of the mind excite and exercise our social sympathy. The review of my moral and literary character is the most interesting to myself and to the public; and I may expatiate without reproach on my private studies; since they have produced the public writings, which can alone entitle me to the esteem and friendship of my readers. The experience of the world inculcates a discreet reserve on the subject of our person and estate, and we soon learn that a free disclosure of our riches or poverty would provoke the malice of envy, or encourage the insolence of contempt.

The only person in England whom I was impatient to see, was my aunt Porten, the affectionate guardian of my tender years. I hastened to her house in College-street, Westminister; and the evening was spent in the effusions of joy and confidence. It was not without some awe and apprehension that I approached the presence of my father. My infancy, to speak the truth, had been neglected at home; the severity of his look and language at our last parting still dwelt on my memory; nor could I form any notion of his character, or my probable reception. They were both more agreeable than I could expect. The domestic discipline of our ancestors has been relaxed by the philosophy and softness of the age; and if my father remembered that he had trembled before a stern parent, it was only to adopt with his own son an opposite mode of behaviour. He received me as a man and a friend; all constraint was banished at our first interview, and we ever afterwards continued on the same terms of easy and equal politeness. He applauded the success of my education; every word and action was expressive of the most cordial affection; and our lives would have passed without a cloud, if his economy had been equal to his fortune, or if his fortune had been equal to his desires. During my absence he had married his second wife, Miss Dorothea Patton, who was introduced to me with the most unfavourable prejudice. I considered his second marriage as an act of displeasure, and I was disposed to hate the rival of my mother. But the injustice was in my own fancy, and the imaginary monster was an amiable and deserving woman. I could not be mistaken in the first view of her understanding, her knowledge, and the elegant spirit of her conversation: her polite welcome, and her assiduous care to study and gratify my wishes, announced at least that the surface would be smooth; and my suspicions of art and falsehood were gradually dispelled by the full discovery of her warm and exquisite sensibility. After some reserve on my side, our minds associated in confidence and friendship; and as Mrs. Gibbon had neither children nor the hopes of children, we more easily adopted the tender names and genuine characters of mother and of son. By the indulgence of these parents, I was left at liberty to consult my taste or reason in the choice of place, of company, and of amusements; and my excursions were bounded only by the limits of the island, and the measure of my income. Some faint efforts were made to procure me the employment of a secretary to a foreign embassy; and I listened to a scheme which would again have transported me to the Continent. Mrs. Gibbon, with seeming wisdom, exhorted me to take chambers in the Temple, and devote my leisure to the study of the law. I cannot repent of having neglected her advice. Few men, without the spur of necessity, have resolution to force their way through the thorns and thickets of that gloomy labyrinth. Nature had not endowed me with the bold and ready eloquence which makes itself heard amidst the tumult of the bar; and I should probably have been diverted from the labours of literature, without acquiring the fame or fortune of a successful pleader. I had no need to call to my aid the regular duties of a profession; every day, every hour was agreeably filled; nor have I known, like so many of my countrymen, the tediousness of an idle life.

Of the two years (May, 1758—May, 1760,) between my return to England, and the embodying of the Hampshire militia, I passed about nine months in London, and the remainder in the country. The metropolis affords many amusements which are open to all. It is itself an astonishing and perpetual spectacle to the curious eye; and each taste, each sense may be gratified by the variety of objects which will occur in the long circuit of a morning walk. I assiduously frequented the theatres at a very propitious æra of the stage, when a constellation of excellent actors, both in tragedy and comedy, was eclipsed by the meridian brightness of Garrick, in the maturity of his judgment and vigour of his performance. The pleasures of a town life are within the reach of every man who is regardless of his health, his money, and his company. By the contagion of example I was sometimes seduced; but the better habits which I had formed at Lausanne, induced me to seek a more elegant and rational society; and if my search was less easy and successful than I might have hoped, I shall at present impute the failure to the disadvantages of my situation and character. Had the rank and fortune of my parents given them an annual establishment in London, their own house would have introduced me to a numerous and polite circle of acquaintance. But my father's taste had always preferred the highest and the lowest company, for which he was equally qualified; and after twelve years' retirement, he was no longer in the memory of the great with whom he had associated. I found myself a stranger in the midst of a vast and unknown city; and at my entrance into life I was reduced to some dull family parties, and some scattered connexions, which were not such as I should have chosen for myself. The most useful friends of my father were the Mallets: they received me with civility and kindness, at first on his account, and afterwards on my own; and (if I may use Lord Chesterfield's words) I was soon *domesticated* in their house. Mr. Mallet, a name among the English poets, is praised, by an unforgiving enemy, for the ease and elegance of his conversation, and his wife was not destitute of wit or learning. By his assistance I was introduced to Lady Hervey, the mother of the present

Earl of Bristol. Her age and infirmities confined her at home : her dinners were select ; in the evening her house was open to the best company of both sexes, and all nations ; nor was I displeased at her preference and affectation of the manners, the language and the literature of France. But my progress in the English world was in general left to my own efforts, and those efforts were languid and slow. I had not been endowed by art or nature with those happy gifts of confidence and address, which unlock every door and every bosom ; nor would it be reasonable to complain of the just consequences of my sickly childhood, foreign education, and reserved temper. While coaches were rattling through Bond-street, I have passed many a solitary evening in my lodging with my books. My studies were sometimes interrupted by a sigh, which I breathed towards Lausanne ; and on the approach of spring, I withdrew without reluctance from the noisy and extensive scene of crowds without company and dissipation without pleasure. In each of the twenty-five years of my acquaintance with London (1758—1783) the prospect gradually brightened ; and this unfavourable picture most properly belongs to the first period after my return from Switzerland.

My father's residence in Hampshire, where I have passed many light, and some heavy hours, was at Buriton, near Petersfield, one mile from the Portsmouth road, and at the easy distance of fifty-eight miles from London.* An old mansion, in a state of decay, had been converted

* The estate and manor of Beriton, otherwise Buriton, were considerable, and were sold a few years ago to Lord Stowell.—S.

into the fashion and convenience of a modern house: and if strangers had nothing to see, the inhabitants had little to desire. The spot was not happily chosen, at the end of the village and the bottom of the hill: but the aspect of the adjacent grounds was various and cheerful; the downs commanded a noble prospect, and the long hanging woods in sight of the house could not perhaps have been improved by art or expense. My father kept in his own hands the whole of the estate, and even rented some additional land; and whatsoever might be the balance of profit and loss, the farm supplied him with amusement and plenty. The produce maintained a number of men and horses, which were multiplied by the intermixture of domestic and rural servants; and in the intervals of labour the favourite team, a handsome set of bays or greys, was harnessed to the coach. The economy of the house was regulated by the taste and prudence of Mrs. Gibbon. She prided herself in the elegance of her occasional dinners; and from the uncleanly avarice of Madame Pavilliard, I was suddenly transported to the daily neatness and luxury of an English table. Our immediate neighbourhood was rare and rustic; but from the verge of our hills, as far as Chichester and Goodwood, the western district of Sussex was interspersed with noble seats and hospitable families, with whom we cultivated a friendly, and might have enjoyed a very frequent, intercourse. As my stay at Buriton was always voluntary, I was received and dismissed with smiles; but the comforts of my retirement did not depend on the ordinary pleasures of the country. My father could never inspire me with his love and knowledge of farming. I never handled a gun, I seldom mounted a horse; and my philosophic walks were soon terminated by a shady bench, where I was long detained by the sedentary amusement of reading or meditation. At home I occupied a pleasant and spacious apartment; the library on the same floor was soon considered as my peculiar domain; and I might say with truth, that I was never less alone than when by myself. My sole complaint, which I piously suppressed, arose from the kind restraint imposed on the freedom of my time. By the habit of early rising I always secured a sacred portion of the day, and many scattered moments were stolen and employed by my studious industry. But the family hours of breakfast, of dinner, of tea, and of supper, were regular and long: after breakfast Mrs. Gibbon expected my company in her dressing-room; after tea, my father claimed my conversation and the perusal of the newspapers; and in the midst of an interesting work I was often called down to receive the visit of some idle neighbours. Their dinners and visits required, in due season, a similar return; and I dreaded the period of the full moon, which was usually reserved for our more distant excursions. I could not refuse attending my father, in the summer of 1759, to the races at Stockbridge, Reading, and Odiham, where he had entered a horse for the hunters plate; and I was not displeased with the sight of our Olympic games, the beauty of the spot, the fleetness of the horses, and the gay tumult of the numerous spectators. As soon as the militia business was agitated, many days were tediously consumed in meetings of deputy lieutenants at Petersfield, Alton and Winchester. In the close of the same year, 1759, Sir Simeon (then Mr.) Stewart attempted an unsuccessful contest for the county of Southampton, against Mr. Legge, Chancellor of the Exchequer: a well-known contest, in which Lord Bute's influence was first exerted and censured. Our canvass at Portsmouth and Gosport lasted several days; but the interruption of my studies was compensated in some degree by the spectacle of English manners, and the acquisition of some practical knowledge.

If in a more domestic or more dissipated scene my application was somewhat relaxed, the love of knowledge was inflamed and gratified by the command of books; and I compared the poverty of Lausanne with the plenty of London. My father's study at Buriton was stuffed with much trash of the last age, with much high church divinity and politics, which have long since gone to their proper place; yet it contained some valuable editions of the classics and the fathers, the choice, as it would seem, of Mr. Law; and many English publications of the times had been occasionally added. From this slender beginning I have gradually formed a numerous and select library, the foundation of my works, and the best comfort of my life, both at home and abroad. On the receipt of the first quarter, a large share of my allowance was appropriated to my literary wants. I cannot forget the joy with which I exchanged a bank-note of twenty pounds for the twenty volumes of the Memoirs of the Académy of Inscriptions; nor would it have been easy, by any other expenditure of the same sum, to have procured so large and lasting a fund of rational amusement. At a time when I most assiduously frequented this school of ancient literature, I thus expressed my opinion of a learned and various collection, which since the year 1759 has been doubled in magnitude, though not in merit—"Une de ces sociétés, qui ont mieux immortalisé Louis XIV. qu'une ambition souvent pernicieuse aux hommes, commençait dejà ces recherches qui réunissent la justesse de l'esprit, l'aménité et l'erudition: où l'on voit tant des decouvertes, et quelquefois, ce qui ne cede qu'à peine aux decouvertes, une *ignorance* modeste et *savante*." The review of my library must be reserved for the period of its maturity; but in this place I may allow myself to observe, that I am not conscious of having ever bought a book from a motive of ostentation, that every volume, before it was deposited on the shelf, was either read or sufficiently examined, and that I soon adopted the tolerating maxim of the elder Pliny, "nullum esse librum tam malum ut non ex aliquâ parte prodesset." I could not yet find leisure or courage to renew the pursuit of the Greek language, excepting by reading the lessons of the Old and New Testament every Sunday, when I attended the family to church. The series of my Latin authors were less strenuously completed; but the acquisition, by inheritance or purchase, of the best editions of Cicero, Quintilian, Livy, Tacitus, Ovid, &c. afforded a fair prospect, which I seldom neglected. I persevered in the useful method of abstracts and observations; and a single example may suffice, of a note which had almost swelled into a work. The solution of a passage of Livy (xxviii. 38.) involved me in the dry and dark treatises of Greaves, Arburthnot, Hooper, Bernard, Eisenschmidt, Gronovius, La Barré, Freret, &c; and in my French essay (chap.

20.) I ridiculously send the reader to my own *manuscript* remarks on the weights, coins, and measures of the ancients, which were abruptly terminated by the militia drum.

As I am now entering on a more ample field of society and study, I can only hope to avoid a vain and prolix garrulity, by overlooking the vulgar crowd of my acquaintance, and confining myself to such intimate friends among books and men, as are best entitled to my notice by their own merit and reputation, or by the deep impression which they have left on my mind. Yet I will embrace this occasion of recommending to the young student a practice, which about this time I myself adopted. After glancing my eye over the design and order of a new book, I suspended the perusal till I had finished the task of self-examination, till I had revolved, in a solitary walk, all that I knew or believed, or had thought on the subject of the whole work, or of some particular chapter: I was then qualified to discern how much the author added to my original stock; and I was sometimes satisfied by the agreement, I was sometimes armed by the opposition of our ideas. The favourite companions of my leisure were our English writers since the Revolution: they breathe the spirit of reason and liberty; and the most seasonable contributed to restore the purity of my own language, which had been corrupted by the long use of a foreign idiom. By the judicious advice of Mr Mallet, I was directed to the writings of Swift and Addison; wit and simplicity are their common attributes; but the style of Swift is supported by manly original vigour; that of Addison is adorned by the female graces of elegance and mildness. The old reproach, that no British altars had been raised to the muse of history, was recently disproved by the first performances of Robertson and Hume, the histories of Scotland and of the Stuarts. I will assume the presumption of saying, that I was not unworthy to read them: nor will I disguise my different feelings in the repeated perusals. The perfect composition, the nervous language, the well-tuned periods of Dr. Robertson, inflamed me to the ambitious hope that I might one day tread in his footsteps: the calm philosophy, the careless inimitable beauties of his friend and rival, often forced me to close the volume with a mixed sensation of delight and despair.

CHAP. XIII.

MR. GIBBON PUBLISHES HIS FIRST WORK.

THE design of my first work, the Essay on the Study of Literature, was suggested by a refinement of vanity, the desire of justifying and praising the object of a favourite pursuit. In France, to which my ideas were confined, the learning and language of Greece and Rome were neglected by a philosophic age. The guardian of those studies, the Academy of Inscriptions, was degraded to the lowest rank among the three royal societies of Paris: the new appellation of Erudits was contemptuously applied to the successors of Lipsius and Casaubon; and I was provoked to hear (see M. d'Alembert, Discours préliminaire à l'Encyclopédie) that the exercise of the memory, their sole merit, had been superseded by the nobler faculties of the imagination and the judgment. I was ambitious of proving by my own example, as well as by my precepts, that all the faculties of the mind may be exercised and displayed by the study of ancient literature: I began to select and adorn the various proofs and illustrations which had offered themselves in reading the classics; and the first pages or chapters of my essay were composed before my departure from Lausanne. The hurry of the journey, and of the first weeks of my English life, suspended all thoughts of serious applica-

tion: but my object was ever before my eyes; and no
more than ten days, from the first to the eleventh of July,
were suffered to elapse after my summer establishment
at Buriton. My essay was finished in about six weeks;
and as soon as a fair copy had been transcribed by one
of the French prisoners at Petersfield, I looked round for a
critic and judge of my first performance. A writer can
seldom be content with the doubtful recompense of solitary approbation; but a youth, ignorant of the world and
of himself, must desire to weigh his talents in some scales
less partial than his own: my conduct was natural, my
motive laudible, my choice of Dr. Maty judicious and
fortunate. By descent and education Dr. Maty, though
born in Holland, might be considered as a Frenchman; but
he was fixed in London by the practice of physic, and an
office in the British Museum. His reputation was justly
founded on the eighteen volumes of the Journal Britannique, which he had supported, almost alone, with perseverance and success. This humble though useful labour,
which had once been dignified by the genius of Bayle
and the learning of Le Clerc, was not disgraced by the
taste, the knowledge, and the judgment of Maty: he
exhibits a candid and pleasing view of the state of literature in England during a period of six years (January,
1750—December, 1755); and, far different from his
angry son, he handles the rod of criticism with the tenderness and reluctance of a parent. The author of the
Journal Britannique sometimes aspires to the character
of a poet and philosopher: his style is pure and elegant;
and in his virtues, or even in his defects, he may be
ranked as one of the last disciples of the school of Fon-

tenelle. His answer to my first letter was prompt and polite: after a careful examination he returned my manuscript, with some animadversion and much applause; and when I visited London in the ensuing winter, we discussed the design and execution in several free and familiar conversations. In a short excursion to Buriton I reviewed my essay, according to his friendly advice; and after suppressing a third, adding a third, and altering a third, I consummated my first labour by a short preface, which is dated February 3rd, 1759. Yet I still shrunk from the press with the terrors of virgin modesty: the manuscript was safely deposited in my desk; and as my attention was engaged by new objects, the delay might have been prolonged till I had fulfilled the precept of Horace, "nonumque prematur in annum." Father Sirmund, a learned jesuit, was still more rigid, since he advised a young friend to expect the mature age of fifty, before he gave himself or his writings to the public. (Olivet, Histoire de l'Académie Française tom. ii. p. 143.) The counsel was singular; but it is still more singular that it should have been approved by the example of the author. Sirmond was himself fifty-five years of age when he published (in 1614) his first work, an edition of Sidonius Apollinaris, with many valuable annotations. (See his life, before the great edition of his works in five volumes folio, Paris, 1696, e Typographiâ Regiâ).

Two years elapsed in silence: but in the spring of 1761 I yielded to the authority of a parent, and complied, like a pious son, with the wish of my own heart.* My

JOURNAL, March 8th, 1758.]—I began my Essay on the Study of Literature, and wrote the first twenty-three chapters (excepting the following ones, 11, 12. 13, 18, 19, 20, 21, 22) before I left Switzerland.

private resolves were influenced by the state of Europe. About this time the belligerent powers had made and accepted overtures of peace; our English plenipotentiaries were named to assist at the Congress of Augsburg, which never met; I wished to attend them as a gentleman or a secretary; and my father fondly believed that the proof of some literary talents might introduce me to public notice, and second the recommendations of my friends. After a last revisal, I consulted with Mr Mallet and Dr. Maty, who approved the design, and promoted the execution. Mr. Mallet, after hearing me read my manuscript, received it from my hands, and delivered it into those of Becket, with whom he made an agreement in my name; an easy agreement: I required only a certain number of copies; and, without transferring my property, I devolved on the bookseller the charges and

July 11th.]—I again took in hand my Essay; and in about six weeks finished it, from C. 23—55 (excepting 27, 28, 39, 30, 31, 32, 33, and note to C. 88) besides a number of chapters from C. 55 to the end, which are now struck out.

Feb. 11, 1759.]—I wrote the chapters of my Essay, 27, 28, 29, 30, 31, the note to C. 33, and the first part of the preface.

April 23, 1761.]—Being at length, by my father's advice, determined to publish my essay, I revised it with great care, made many alterations, struck out a considerable part, and wrote the chapters from 57—58, which I was obliged myself to copy out fair,

June 10th, 1761.]—Finding the printing of my book proceeded but slowly, I went up to town, where I found the whole was finished. I gave Becket orders for the presents; twenty for Lausanne; copies for the Duke of Richmond, Marquis of Carnarvon, Lords Waldegrave, Litchfield, Bath, Granville, Bute, Shelburne, Chesterfield, Hardwicke, Lady Hervey, Sir Joseph Yorke, Sir Matthew Featherstone, Messieurs Mallet, Maty, Scott, Wray, Lord Egremont, M. de Bussy, Mademoiselle la Duchesse d'Aiguillon, and M. le Compte de Caylus;—great part of these were only my father's or Mallet's acquaintance.

profits of the edition. Dr. Maty undertook, in my absence, to correct the sheets: he inserted, without my
knowledge, an elegant and flattering epistle to the author;
which is composed, however, with so much art, that, in
case of a defeat, his favourite report might have been
ascribed to the indulgence of a friend for the rash attempt
of a *young English* gentleman. The work was printed
and published, under the title of Essai sur l'Etude de la
Littérature, à Londres, chez T. Becket et P. A. de Hondt,
1761, in a small volume in duodecimo: my dedication to
my father, a proper and pious address, was composed the
twenty-eighth of May: Dr. Maty's letter is dated the 16th
of June; and I received the first copy (June 23) at Alresford, two days before I marched with the Hampshire
militia. Some weeks afterwards, on the same ground, I
presented my book to the late Duke of York, who break-
fasted in Colonel Pitt's tent. By my father's direction,
and Mallet's advice, many literary gifts were distributed
to several eminent characters in England and France;
two books were sent to the Compte de Caylus, and the
Duchesse d'Auiguillon, at Paris; I had reserved twenty
copies for my friends at Lausanne, as the first fruits of
my education, and a grateful token of my remembrance:
and on all these persons I levied an unavoidable tax of
civility and compliment. It is not surprising that a work,
of which the style and sentiments were so totally foreign,
should have been more successful abroad than at home.
I was delighted by the copious extracts, the warm com-
mendations, and the flattering predictions of the journals
of France and Holland; and the next year (1762) a new
edition (I believe at Geneva) extended the fame, or at

least the circulation of the work. In England it was received with cold indifference, little read, and speedily forgotten: a small impression was slowly dispersed; the bookseller murmured, and the author, had his feelings been more exquisite, might have wept over the blunders and boldness of the English translation. The publication of my history fifteen years afterwards revived the memory of my first performance, and the essay was eagerly sought in the shops. But I refused the permission which Becket solicited of reprinting it: the public curiosity was imperfectly satisfied by a pirated copy of the booksellers of Dublin; and when a copy of the origininal edition has been discovered in a sale, the primitive value of half a crown has risen to the fanciful price of a guinea or thirty shillings.

I have expatiated on the petty circumstances and period of my first publication, a memorable æra in the life of a student, when he ventures to reveal the measure of his mind: his hopes and fears are multiplied by the idea of self-importance, and he believes for a while that the eyes of mankind are fixed on his person and performance. Whatever may be my present reputation, it no longer rests on the merit of this first essay; and at the end of twenty-eight years I may appreciate my juvenile work with the impartiality, and almost with the indifference, of a stranger. In his answer to Lady Hervey, the Comte de Caylus admires, or affects to admire, " les livres sans nombre que Mr. Gibbon a lus et très bien lus*." But, alas! my stock of erudition at that time was scanty and superficial; and, if I allow myself

* See Letter, No. X.

the liberty of naming the Greek masters, my genuine and
personal acquaintance was confined to the Latin classics.
The most serious defect of my Essay is a kind of obscurity and abruptness which always fatigues, and may
often elude, the attention of the reader. Instead of a
precise and proper definition of the title itself, the sense
of the word *Littérature* is loosely and variously applied:
a number of remarks and examples, historical, critical,
philosophical, are heaped on each other without method
or connection: and if we except some introductory
pages, all the remaining chapters might indifferently be
reversed or transposed. The obscurity of many passages is often affected, " brevis esse laboro, obscurus fio;"
the desire of expressing perhaps a common idea with
sententious and oracular brevity: alas! how fatal has
been the imitation of Montesquieu! But this obscurity
sometimes proceeds from a mixture of light and darkness
in the author's mind; from a partial ray which strikes
upon an angle, instead of spreading itself over the surface
of an object. After this fair confession I shall presume
to say, that the Essay does credit to a young writer of
·two and twenty years of age, who had read with taste,
who thinks with freedom, and who writes in a foreign
language with spirit and elegance. The defence of the
early History of Rome and the New Chronology of Sir
Isaac Newton form a specious argument. The patriotic
and political design of the Georgics is happily conceived ;
and any probable conjecture, which tends to raise the
dignity of the poet and the poem, deserves to be adopted,
without a rigid scrutiny. Some dawnings of a philosophic spirit enlighten the general remarks on the study
of history and of man. I am not displeased with the inquiry into the origin and nature of the gods of polytheism.

which might deserve the illustration of a riper judgment.
Upon the whole, I may apply to the first labour of my
pen the speech of a far superior artist, when he surveyed
the first productions of his pencil. After viewing some
portraits which he had painted in his youth, my friend
Sir Joshua Reynolds acknowledged to me, that he was
rather humbled than flattered by the comparison with his
present works; and that after so much time and study,
he had conceived his improvement to be much greater
than he found it to have been.

At Lausanne I composed the first chapters of my
Essay in French, the Familiar language of my conversation and studies, in which it was easier for me to write
than in my mother-tongue. After my return to England
I continued the same practice, without any affectation, or
design of repudiating (as Dr. Bentley would say) my ver-
nacular idiom. But I should have escaped some anti-
gallican clamour, had I been content with the more natural character of an English author. I should have
been more consistent had I rejected Mallet's advice, of
prefixing an English dedication to a French book; a
confusion of tongues that seemed to accuse the ignorance
of my patron. The use of a foreign dialect might be excused by the hope of being employed as a negotiator, by
the desire of being generally understood on the Continent;
but my true motive was doubtless the ambition of new
and singular fame, an Englishman claiming a place among
the writers of France. The Latin tongue had been consecrated by the service of the church, it was refined by
the imitation of the ancients; and in the fifteenth and
sixteenth centuries the scholars of Europe enjoyed the
advantage, which they gradually resigned, of conversing and writing in a common and learned idiom. As that

idiom was no longer in any country the vulgar speech, they all stood on a level with each other; yet a citizen of old Rome might have smiled at the best Latinity of the Germans and Britons : and we may learn from the Ciceronianus of Erasmus, how difficult it was found to steer a middle course between pedantry and barbarism. The Romans themselves had sometimes attempted a more perilous task, of writing in a living language, and appealing to the taste and judgment of the natives. The vanity of Tully was doubly interested in the Greek memoirs of his own consulship; and if he modestly supposes that some Latinisms might be detected in his style, he is confident of his own skill in the art of Isocrates and Aristotle; and he requests his friend Atticus to disperse the copies of his work at Athens, and in the other cities of Greece. (Ad Atticum, i. 19, ii. 1.) But it must not be forgotten, that from infancy to manhood Cicero and his contemporaries had read, and declaimed, and composed with equal diligence in both languages; and that he was not allowed to frequent a Latin school till he had imbibed the lessons of the Greek grammarians and rhetoricians. In modern times, the language of France has been diffused by the merit of her writers, the social manners of the natives, the influence of the monarchy, and the exile of the Protestants. Several foreigners have seized the opportunity of speaking to Europe in this common dialect, and Germany may plead the authority of Leibnitz and Frederick, of the first of her philosophers, and the greatest of her kings. The just pride and laudable prejudice of England has restrained this communication of idioms; and of all the nations on this side of the Alps, my countrymen are the least practiced and least perfect in the exercise of the French tongue. By

Sir William Temple and Lord Chesterfield it was only used on occasions of civility and business, and their printed letters will not be quoted as models of composition. Lord Bolingbroke may have published in French a sketch of his Reflections on Earle: but his reputation now reposes on the address of Voltaire, " Docte sermones utriusque linguæ ;" and by his English dedication to Queen Caroline, and his Essay on Epic Poetry, it should seem that Voltaire himself wished to deserve a return of the same compliment. The exception of Count Hamilton cannot fairly be urged; though an Irishman by birth, he was educated in France from his childhood. Yet I am surprised that a long residence in England, and the habits of domestic conversation, did not affect the ease and purity of his inimitable style; and I regret the omission of his English verses, which might have afforded an amusing object of comparison. I might therefore assume the *primus ego in patriam, &c.;* but with what success I have explored this untrodden path must be left to the decision of my French readers. Dr. Maty, who might himself be questioned as a foreigner, has secured his retreat at my expense. " Je ne crois pas que vous vous piquiez d'être moins facile à reconnaitre pour un Anglais que Lucullus pour un Romain." My friends at Paris have been more indulgent, they received me as a countryman, or at least as a provincial; but they were friends and Parisians. The defects which Maty insinuates, " Ces traits saillans, ces figures hardies, ce sacrifice de la règle au sentiment, et de la cadence à la force," are the faults of the youth, rather than of the stranger: and after the long and laborious exercise of my own language, I am conscious that my French style has been ripened and improved.

CHAP. XIV.

THE AUTHOR IN THE HAMPSHIRE MILITIA.

I have already hinted, that the publication of my Essay was delayed till I had embraced the military profession. I shall now amuse myself with the recollection of an active scene, which bears no affinity to any other period of my studious and social life.

In the outset of a glorious war, the English people had been defended by the aid of German mercenaries. A national militia has been the cry of every patriot since the Revolution; and this measure, both in parliament and in the field, was supported by the country gentlemen or Tories, who insensibly transferred their loyalty to the house of Hanover: in the language of Mr. Burke, they have changed the idol, but they have preserved the idolatry. In the act of offering our names and receiving our commissions, as major and captain in the Hampshire regiment, (June 12th, 1759,) we had not supposed that we should be dragged away, my father from his farm, myself from my books, and condemned during two years and a half, (May 10, 1760—December 23, 1762,) to a wandering life of military servitude. But a weekly or monthly exercise of thirty-thousand provincials would have left them useless and ridiculous; and after the pretence of an invasion had vanished, the popularity of Mr.

Pitt gave a sanction to the illegal step of keeping them till the end of the war under arms, in constant pay and duty, and at a distance from their respective homes. When the King's order for our embodying came down, it was too late to retreat, and too soon to repent. The South battalion of the Hampshire militia was a small independent corps of four hundred and seventy-six, officers and men, commanded by lieutenant-colonel Sir Thomas Worsley, who, after a prolix and passionate contest, delivered us from the tyranny of the lord lieutenant, the Duke of Bolton. My proper station, as first captain, was at the head of my own, and afterwards of the grenadier company; but in the absence, or even in the presence, of the two field officers, I was entrusted by my friend and my father with the effective labour of dictating the orders, and exercising the battalion. With the help of an original journal, I could write the history of my bloodless and inglorious campaigns; but as these events have lost much of their importance in my own eyes, they shall be dispatched in a few words.

From Winchester, the first place of assembly, (June 4, 1760,) we were removed, at our own request, for the benefit of a foreign education. By the arbitrary, and often capricious, orders of the War-office, the battalion successively marched to the pleasant and hospitable Blandford (June 17); to Hilsea barracks, a seat of disease and discord (September 1); to Cranbrook in the Weald of Kent (December 11); to the sea-coast of Dover (December 27); to Winchester camp (June 25, 1761); to the populous and disorderly town of Devizes (October 23); to Salisbury (February 28, 1762); to our beloved

Blandford a second time (March 9); and finally, to the fashionable resort of Southampton (June 2); where the colours were fixed till our final dissolution (December 23). On the beach at Dover we had exercised in sight of the Gallic shores. But the most splendid and useful scene of our life was a four months encampment on Winchester Down, under the command of the Earl of Effingham. Our army consisted of the thirty-fourth regiment of foot and six militia corps. The consciousness of our defects was stimulated by friendly emulation. We improved our time and opportunities in morning and evening field days: and in the general reviews the South Hampshire were rather a credit than a disgrace to the line. In our subsequent quarters of the Devizes and Blandford, we advanced with a quick step in our military studies; the ballot of the ensuing summer renewed our vigour and youth; and had the militia subsisted another year, we might have contested the prize with the most perfect of our brethren.

The loss of so many busy and idle hours was not compensated by any elegant pleasure; and my temper was insensibly soured by the society of our rustic officers. In every state there exists, however, a balance of good and evil. The habits of a sedentary life were usefully broken by the duties of an active profession: in the healthful exercise of the field I hunted with a batallion, instead of a pack; and at that time I was ready at any hour of the day or night, to fly from quarters to London, from London to quarters, on the slightest call of private or regimental business. But my principal obligation to the militia, was the making me an Englishman and a soldier.

After my foreign education, with my reserved temper, I should long have continued a stranger in my native country, had I not been shaken in this various scene of new faces and new friends: had not experience forced me to feel the characters of our leading men, the state of parties, the forms of office, and the operation of our civil and military system. In this peaceful service, I imbibed the rudiments of the language and science of tactics, which opened a new field of study and observation. I diligently read, and meditated, the Mémoires Militaires of Quintus Icilius, (Mr. Guichardt), the only writer who has united the merits of a professor and a veteran. The discipline and evolutions of a modern battalion gave me a clearer notion of the phalanx and the legion; and the captain of the Hampshire grenadiers (the reader may smile) has not been useless to the historian of the Roman empire.

A youth of any spirit is fired even by the play of arms, and in the first sallies of my enthusiasm I had seriously attempted to embrace the regular profession of a soldier. But this military fever was cooled by the enjoyment of our mimic Bellona, who soon unveiled to my eyes her naked deformity. How often did I sigh for my proper station in society and letters. How often (a proud comparison) did I repeat the complaint of Cicero in the command of a provincial army : "Clitellæ bovi sunt impositæ. Est incredibile quam me negotii tædeat. Non habet satis magnum campum ille tibi non ignotus cursus animi; et industriæ meæ præclara opera cessat. Lucem, *libros,* urbem, domum, vos desidero. Sed feram, ut potero; sit modo annum. Si prorogatur, actum est·"* From a ser-

* Epist. ad Atticum, lib. v. 15.

vice without danger, I might indeed have retired without disgrace; but as often as I hinted a wish of resigning, my fetters were riveted by the friendly entreaties of the colonel, the parental authority of the major, and my own regard for the honour and welfare of the battalion. When I felt that my personal escape was impracticable, I bowed my neck to the yoke: my servitude was protracted far beyond the annual patience of Cicero; and it was not till after the preliminaries of peace that I received my discharge from the act of government which disembodied the militia.*

*Journal, January 11, 1761.]—In these seven or eight months of a most disagreeably active life, I have had no studies to set down: indeed, I hardly took a book in my hand the whole time. The first two months at Blandford, I might have done something; but the novelty of the thing, of which for some time I was so fond as to think of going into .the army, our field days, our dinners abroad, and the drinking and late hours we got into, prevented any serious reflections. From the day we marched from Blandford I had hardly a moment I could call my own, almost continually in motion; if I was fixed for a day, it was in the guard room, a barrack, or an inn. Our disputes consumed the little time I had left. Every letter, every memorial relative to them fell to my share; and our evening conferences were used to hear all the morning hours strike. At last I got to Dover and Sir Thomas left us for two months. The charm was over, I was sick of so hateful a service; I was settled in a comparatively quiet situation. Once more I began to taste the pleasure of thinking.

Recollecting some thoughts I had formerly had in relation to the system of Paganism, which I intended to make use of in my Essay, I resolved to read Tully de Naturâ Deorum, and finished it in about a month. I lost some time before I could recover my habit of application.

October 23rd.]—Our first design was to march to Marlborough; but finding on inquiry that it was a bad road and a great way about, we resolved to push for the Devizes in one day, though nearly thirty miles. We accordingly arrived there about three o'clock in the afternoon.

Nov. 2nd.]—I have very little to say for this and the following month.

When I complain of the loss of time, justice to myself
and to the militia must throw the greatest part of that

Nothing could be more uniform than the life I led there.   The little civility
of the neighboring gentlemen gave us no opportunity of dining out; the
time of year did not tempt us to any excursions round the country; and at
first my indolence, and afterwards a violent cold, prevented my going over
to Bath.   I believe in the two months I never dined or lay from quarters.
I can therefore only set down what I did in the literary way.   Designing to
recover my Greek, which I had somewhat neglected, I set myself to read
Homer, and finished the four first books of the Iliad, with Pope's translation
and notes; at the same time, to understand the geography of the Iliad, and
particularly the catalogue, I read the 8th, 9th, 10th, 11th, 12th, 13th, and
14th books of Strabo, in Casaubon's Latin translation; I likewise read
Hume's History of England to the reign of Henry the Seventh, just published, *ingenious but superficial;* and the Journals des Savans, for August,
September, and October, 1761, with the Bibliothèque des Sciences, &c.
from July to October; both these Journals speak very handsomely of my
book.   .

December 25th, 1761.]—When, upon finishing the year, I take a review
of what I have done, I am not dissatisfied with what I did in it, upon
making proper allowances.   On the one hand, I could begin nothing before
the middle of January.   The Deal duty lost me part of February; although
I was at home part of March, and all April, yet electioneering is no friend to
the Muses.   May, indeed, though dissipated by our sea parties, was pretty
quiet, but June was absolutely lost, upon the march, at Alton, and settling
ourselves in camp.   The four succeeding months in camp allowed me little
leisure and little quiet.   November and December were indeed as much my
own as any time can be whilst I remain in the militia; but still it is, at
best, not a life for a man of letters.   However, in this tumultuous year,
(besides smaller things which I have set down), I read four books of
Homer in Greek, six of Strabo in Latin, Cicero de Naturâ Deorum, and the
great philosophical and theological work of M. de Beausobre; I wrote in
the same time a long dissertation on the succession of Naples; reviewed,
fitted for the press, and augmented above a fourth, my Essai sur l'Etude de
la Littérature.

In the six weeks I passed at Beriton, as I never stirred from it, every day
was like the former.   I had neither visits, hunting, nor walking.   My only

reproach on the first seven or eight months, while I was obliged to learn as well as to teach. The dissipation of

resources were myself, my books, and family conversations.—But to me these were great resources.

April 24th, 1762.]—I waited upon Colonel Hervey in the morning, to get him to apply for me to be brigade-major to Lord Effingham, as a post I should be very fond of, and for which I am not unfit. Hervey received me with great good-nature and candour, told me he was both willing and able to serve me; that indeed he had already applied to Lord Effingham for * * * *, one of his own officers, and though there would be more than one brigade-major, he did not think he could properly recommend two; but that if I could get some other person to break the ice, he would second it, and believed he should succeed; should that fail, as * * * * * was in bad circumstances, he believed he could make a compromise with him (this was my desire) to let me do the duty without pay. I went from him to the Malleis, who promised to get Sir Charles Howard to speak to Lord Effingham.

August 22nd.]—I went with Ballard to the French church where I heard a most indifferent sermon preached by M******. A very bad style, a worse pronunciation and action, and a very great vacuity of ideas, composed this excellent performance. Upon the whole, which is preferable, the philosophic method of the English, or the rhetoric of the French preachers? The first, (though less glorious) is certainly safer for the preacher. It is difficult for a man to make himself ridiculous, who proposes only to deliver plain sense on a subject he has thoroughly studied. But the instant he discovers the least pretensions towards the sublime, or the pathetic, there is no medium; we must either admire or laugh; and there are so many various talents requisite to form the character of an orator, that it is more than probable we shall laugh. As to the advantage of the hearer, which ought to be the great consideration, the dilemma is much greater. Excepting in some particular cases, where we are blinded by popular prejudices, we are in general so well acquainted with our duty, that it is almost superfluous to convince us of it. It is the heart, and not the head, that holds out: and it is certainly possible, by a moving eloquence, to rouse the sleeping sentiments of that heart, and incite it to acts of virtue. Unluckily it is not so much acts, as habits of virtue, we should have in view; and the preacher, who is inculcating, with the eloquence of a Bourdaloue,

Blandford, and the disputes of Portsmouth, consumed

the necessity of a virtuous life, will dismiss his assembly full of emotions, which a variety of other objects, the coldness of our northern constitutions, and no immediate opportunity of exerting their good resolutions, will dissipate in a few moments.

August 24th.]—The same reason that carried so many people to the assembly to-night, was what kept me away ; I mean the dancing.

28th.]—To-day Sir Thomas came to us to dinner.   The Spa has done him a great deal of good, for he looks another man.   Pleased to see him, we kept bumperizing till after roll-calling : Sir Thomas assuring us, every fresh bottle, how infinitely sober he was grown.

29th.]—I felt the usual consequences of Sir Thomas's company, and lost a morning because I had lost the day before. However, having finished Voltaire, I returned to Le Clerc, (I mean for the amusement of my leisure hours) ; and laid aside for some time his Bibliothèque Universelle, to look into the Bibliothèque Choisie, which is by far the better work.

September the 23rd.]—Colonel Wilkes, of the Buckinghamshire Militia, dined with us, and renewed the acquaintance Sir Thomas and myself had begun with him at Reading. I scarcely ever met with a better companion; he has inexhaustible spirits, infinite wit and humour, and a great deal of knowledge. He told us himself, that in this time of public dissension, he was resolved to make his fortune. Upon this principle, he has connected himself closely with Lord Temple and Mr. Pitt, commenced a public adversary to Lord Bute, whom he abuses weekly in the North Briton, and other political papers in which he is concerned. This proved a very debauched day: we drank a good deal both after dinner and supper ; and when at last Wilkes had retired, Sir Thomas and some others (of whom I was not one) broke into his room, and made him drink a bottle of claret in bed.

October 5th.]—The review, which lasted about three hours, concluded, as usual, with marching by Lord Effingham, by grand divisions. Upon the whole, considering the camp had done both the Winchester and the Gosport duties all the summer, they behaved very well, and made a fine appearance. As they marched by, I had my usual curiosity to count their files. The following is my field return, I think it a curiosity; I am sure it is more exact than is commonly made to a reviewing general.

.the hours which were not employed in the field; .and

		Numbes of files.	Number of men.	Establishment.
Berkhire,	{ Grenadiers, 19 } { Battalion, 72 }	91 . . .	273 . . .	560
W. Essex,	{ Grenadiers, 15 } { Battalion, 80 }	95 . . .	285 . . .	480
S. Glo'ster,	{ Grenadiers, 20 } { Battalion, 84 }	94	312	600
N. Glo'ster,	{ Grenadiers, 13 } { Battalion, 52 }	65 . . .	195 . . .	360
Lancashire,	{ Grenadiers, 20 } { Battalion, 88 }	108 . . .	324 . . .	800
Wiltshire,	{ Grenadiers, 24 } { Battalion, 120 }	144 . . .	432 . . .	800
	Total, 607		1821	3600

N. B. The Gosport detachment from tne Lancashire consisted of two hundred and fifty men. The Buckinghamshire took the Winchester duty that day.

So that this camp in England, supposed complete, with only one detachment, had under arms, on the day of the grand review, but little more than half their establishment. This amazing deficiency, (though exemplified in every regiment I have seen) is an extraordinary military phenomenon; what must it be upon foreign service? I doubt whether a nominal army of a hundred thousand men often brings fifty into the field.

Upon our return to Southampton in the evening, we found Sir Thomas Worsley.

October 21st.]—One of those impulses, which it is neither very easy nor very necessary to withstand, drew me from Longinus to a very different subject, the Greek Calendar. Last night, when in bed, I was thinking of a dissertation of M. de la Nauze upon the Roman Calendar, which I read last year. This led me to consider what was the Greek, and finding myself very ignorant of it, I determined to read a short, but very excellent extract of Mr. Dodwell's book De Cyclis, by the famous Dr. Halley. It is only twenty-five pages; but as I meditated it thoroughly, and verified all the calculations, it was a very good morning's work.

October 28th.]—I looked over a new Greek Lexicon, which I have just received from London. It is that of Robert Constantine, Lugdun, 1637. It is a very large volume in folio, in two parts, comprising in the whole 1785 pages. After the great Thesaurus, this is esteemed the best Greek Lexicon. It seems to be so. Of a variety of words for which I looked, I always found

amid the perpetual hurry of an inn, a barrack, or a guard.

an exact definition; the various senses well distinguished and properly supported, by the best authorities. However, I still prefer the radical method of Scapula to this alphabetical one.

December 11th]—I have already given an idea of the Gosport duty; I shall only add a trait which characterises admirably our unthinking sailors. At a time when they knew that they should infallibly be discharged in a few weeks, numbers, who had considerable wages due to them, were continually jumping over the walls, and risking the losing of it for a few hours' amusement at Portsmouth.

17th.]—We found old Captain Meard at Alresford, with the second division of the fourteenth. He and all his officers supped with us, and made the evening rather a drunken one.

18th.]—About the same hour our two corps paraded to march off: they, an old corps of regulars, who had been two years quiet in Dover castle; we, part of a young body of militia, two-thirds of our men recruits of four months standing, two of which they had passed upon very disagreeable duty. Every advantage was on their side, and yet our superiority, both as to appearance and discipline, was so striking, that the most prejudiced regular could not have hesitated a moment. At the end of the town our two companies separated: my father's struck off for Petersfield, whilst I continued my rout to Alton; into which place I marched my company about noon; two years six months and fifteen days after my first leaving it. I gave the men some beer at roll-calling, which they received with great cheerfulness and decency. I dined and lay at Harrison's, where I was received with that old-fashioned breeding which is at once so honourable and so troublesome.

23rd.]—Our two companies were disembodied: mine at Alton, and my father's at Buriton. Smith marched them over from Petersfield: they fired three volleys, lodged the major's colours, delivered up their arms, received their money, partook of a dinner at the major's expense, and then separated with great cheerfulness and regularity. Thus ended the militia; I may say ended, since our annual assemblies in May are so very precarious, and can be of so little use. However, our sergeants and drums are still kept up, and quartered at the rendezvous of their company, and the adjutant remains at Southampton in full pay.

As this was an extraordinary scene of life, in which I was engaged above three years and a half from the date of my commission, and above two

room, all literary ideas were banished from my mind.

years and a half, from the time of our embodying, I cannot take my leave of it without some few reflections. When I engaged in it, I was totally ignorant of its nature and consequences. I offered, because my father did, without ever imagining that we should be called out, till it was too late to retreat with honour. Indeed, I believe it happens throughout, that our most important actions have been often determined by chance, caprice, or some very inadequate motive. After our embodying, many things contributed to make me support it with impatience. Our continual disputes with the Duke of Bolton; our unsettled way of life, which hardly allowed me books or leisure for study; and, more than all, the disagreeable society in which I was forced to live.

After mentioning my sufferings, I must say something of what I found agreeable. Now it is over, I can make the separation much better than I could at the time. 1. The unsettled way of life itself had its advantages. The exercise and change of air and of objects amused me, at the same time that it fortified my health. 2. A new field of knowledge and amusement opened itself to me; that of military affairs, which both in my studies and travels, will give me eyes for a new world of things, which before would have passed unheeded. Indeed, in that respect I can hardly help wishing our battalion had continued another year. We had got a fine set of new men, all our difficulties were over; we were perfectly well clothed and appointed; and, from the progress our recruits had already made, we could promise ourselves that we should be one of the best militia corps by next summer: a circumstance that would have been the more agreeable to me, as I am now established the real acting major of the battalion. But what I value most, is the knowledge it has given me of mankind in general, and of my own country in particular. The general system of our government, the methods of our several offices, the departments and powers of their respective officers, our provincial and municipal administration, the views of our several parties, the characters, connexions, and influence of our principal people, have been impressed on my mind, not by vain theory, but by the indellible lessons of action and experience. I have made a number of valuable acquaintances, and am myself much better known, than (with my reserved character) I should have been in ten years, passing regularly my summers at Beriton, and my winters in London. So that the sum of all is, I am glad the militia has been, and glad that it is no more.

CHAP. XV.

THE AUTHOR RESUMES HIS STUDIES.

AFTER this long fast, the longest which I have ever known, I once more tasted at Dover the pleasures of reading and thinking; and the hungry appetite with which I opened a volume of Tully's philosophical works is still present to my memory. The last review of my essay before its publication, had prompted me to investigate the *nature of the gods :* my inquiries led me to the Histoire Critique du Manichéisme of Beausobre, who discusses many deep questions of pagan and christian theology; and from this rich treasury of facts and opinions, I deduced my own consequences, beyond the holy circle of the author. After this recovery I never relapsed into indolence; and my example might prove, that in the life most averse to study, some hours may be stolen, some minutes may be snatched. Amidst the tumult of Winchester camp I sometimes thought and read in my tent; in the more settled quarters of the Devizes, Blandford, and Southampton, I always secured a separate lodging, and the necessary books; and in the summer of 1762, while the new militia was raising, I enjoyed at Beriton two or three months of literary repose.* In forming a

* JOURNAL, May 8th, 1762.]—This was my birth-day, on which I entered into the twenty-sixth year of my age. This gave me occasion to look

new plan of study, I hesitated between the mathematics
and the Greek language; both of which I had neglected
since my return from Lausanne.   I consulted a learned
and friendly mathematician, Mr. George Scott, a pupil of
De Moivre ; and his map of a country which I have never
explored may perhaps be more serviceable to others.*
As soon as I had given the preference to Greek, the example of Scaliger and my own reason determined me on the
choice of Homer, the father of poetry, and the Bible of
the ancients : but Scaliger ran through the Iliad in one
and twenty days ; and I was not dissatisfied with my
own diligence for performing the same labour in an equal
number of weeks.   After the first difficulties were sur-
mounted, the language of nature and harmony soon became easy and familiar ; and each day I sailed upon the
ocean with a brisker gale and a more steady course.

a little into myself, and consider impartially my good and bad qualities.   It
appeared to me, upon this inquiry, that my character was virtuous, incapable of a base action, and formed for generous ones; but that it was proud,
violent, and disagreeable in society.   These qualities I must endeavour to
cultivate, extirpate, or restrain, according to their different tendency.   Wit
I have none.   My imagination is rather strong than pleasing.   My memory
both capacious and retentive.   The shining qualities of my understanding
are extensiveness and penetration; but I want both quickness and exact-
ness.   As to my situation in life, though I may sometimes repine at it, it
perhaps is the best adapted to my character.   I can command all the con-
veniences of life, and I can command too that independence, (that first
earthly blessing) which is hardly to be met with in a higher or lower fortune.
When I talk of my situation, I must exclude that temporary one, of being
in the militia.   Though I go through with spirit and application, it is unfit
for and unworthy of me.

* See Letter, No. XIV. *excellent*, from Mr. Scott to Mr. Gibbon.

'E δ' άνεμος ςρησεν μεσον ίστιον, άμφι δε κυμα
Στειρη ςορφυρεον μεγαλ' ίαχε, νηος ίουσης·
'Η δ'ίθεεν κατα κυμα διαςρησσουσα κελευθα.*—*Ilias*, A. 481.

In the study of a poet who has since become the most
intimate of my friends, I successively applied many passages and fragments of Greek writers; and among these
I shall notice a life of Homer, in the Opuscula Mytholo-
gica of Gale, several books of the geography of Strabo,
and the entire treatise of Longinus, which, from the title
and the style, is equally worthy of the epithet of *sublime*.
My grammatical skill was improved, my vocabulary was
enlarged; and in the militia I acquired a just and indelible knowledge of the first of languages. On every
march, in every journey, Horace was always in my
pocket, and often in my hand; but I should not mention
his two critical epistles, the amusement of a morning,
had they not been accompanied by the elaborate commentary of Dr. Hurd, now Bishop of Worcester. On
the interesting subjects of composition and imitation of
epic and dramatic poetry, I presumed to think for myself;
and thirty close written pages in folio could scarcely
comprise my full and free discussion of the sense of the
master and the pedantry of the servant.

After his oracle Dr. Johnson, my friend Sir Joshua
Reynolds denies all original genuis, any natural propen-

* ——Fair wind, and blowing fresh,
Apollo sent them; quick they rear'd the mast,
Then spread th' unsullied canvas to the gale,
And the wind fill'd it. Roar'd the sable flood
Around the bark, that ever as she went
Dash'd wide the brine, and scudded swift away.—*Cowper's Homer*.

sity of the mind to one art or science rather than
another. Without engaging in a metaphysical or rather
verbal dispute, I *know*, by experience, that from my
early youth I aspired to the character of an historian.
While I served in the militia, before and after the publication of my essay, this idea ripened in my mind; nor
can I paint in more lively colours the feelings of the
moment, than by transcribing some passages, under their
respective dates, from a journal which I kept at that
time.

"Beriton, April 14, 1761.—(In a short excursion from
Dover.)—Having thought of several subjects for an historical composition, I chose the expedition of Charles
VIII. of France into Italy. I read two memoirs of Mr.
De Foncemagne in the Academy of Inscriptions (tom.
xvii. p. 539—607), and abstracted them. I likewise
finished this day a dissertation, in which I examine the
right of Charles VIII. to the crown of Naples, and the
rival claims of the House of Anjou and Arragon: it consists of ten folio pages, besides large notes."

"Beriton, August 4, 1761.—(In a week's excursion
from Winchester Camp.)—After having long revolved
subjects for my intended historical essay, I renounced
my first thought of the expedition of Charles VIII. as
too remote from us, and rather an introduction to great
events, than great and important in itself. I successively chose and rejected the Crusade of Richard the
First, the barons' wars against John and Henry the
Third, the history of Edward the Black Prince, the lives
and comparisons of Henry V. and the Emperor Titus,
the life of Sir Philip Sydney, and that of the Marquis of

Montrose. At length I have fixed on Sir Walter
Raleigh for my hero. His eventful story is varied by
the characters of the soldier and sailor, the courtier and
historian; and it may afford such a fund of materials as
I desire, which have not yet been properly manufactured.
At present I cannot attempt the execution of this work.
Free leisure, and the opportunity of consulting many books,
both printed and manuscript, are as necessary as they
are impossible to be attained in my present way of life.
However, to acquire a general insight into my subject
and resources, I read the life of Sir Walter Raleigh by
Dr. Birch, his copious article in the General Dictionary
by the same hand, and the reigns of Queen Elizabeth
and James the First, in Hume's History of England."

"Beriton, January, 1762.—(In a month's absence from
the Devizes.)—During this interval of repose, I again
turned my thoughts to Sir Walter Raleigh, and looked
more closely into my materials. I read the two volumes
in quarto of the Bacon papers, published by Dr. Birch:
the Fragmenta Regalia of Sir Robert Naunton, Mallet's
Life of Lord Bacon, and the political treatises of that
great man in the first volume of his works, with many
of his letters in the second; Sir William Monson's Naval
Tracts, and the elaborate life of Sir Walter Raleigh,
which Mr. Oldys has prefixed to the best edition of his
History of the World. My subject opens upon me, and
in general improves upon a nearer prospect."

"Beriton, July 26, 1762.—(During my summer residence.)—I am afraid of being reduced to drop my hero;
but my time has not, however, been lost in the research
of his story, and of a memorable æra of our English

annals. The Life of Sir Walter Raleigh, by Oldys, is a
very poor performance; a servile panegyric, or flat
apology, tediously minute, and composed in a dull and
affected style. Yet the author was a man of diligence
and learning, who had read every thing relative to his
subject and whose ample collections are arranged with
perspicuity and method. Excepting some anecdotes
lately revealed in the Sydney and Bacon papers, I know
not what I should be able to add. My ambition (exclusive of the uncertain merit of style and sentiment)
must be confined to the hope of giving a good abridgment of Oldys. I have even the disappointment of finding some parts of this copious work dry and barren;
and these parts are unluckily some of the most charac-
teristic: Raleigh's colony of Virginia, his quarrels with
Essex, the true secret of his conspiracy, and above all,
the detail of his private life, the most essential and important to a biographer. My best resource would be
in the circumjacent history of the times, and perhaps in
some digressions artfully introduced, like the fortunes of the
peripatetic philosophy in the portrait of Lord Bacon. But
the reigns of Elizabeth and James the First are the periods
of English history, which have been the most variously
illustrated: and what new lights could I reflect on a
subject, which has exercised the accurate industry of
Birch, the lively and curious acuteness of Walpole, the
critical spirit of Hurd, the vigorous sense of Mallet and
Robertson, and the impartial philosophy of Hume?
Could I even surmount these obstacles, I should shrink
with terror from the modern history of England, where
every character is a problem, and every reader a friend

or an enemy; where a writer is supposed to hoist a flag of party, and is devoted to damnation by the adverse faction. Such would be *my* reception at home: and abroad the historian of Raleigh must encounter an indifference far more bitter than censure or reproach. The events of his life are interesting; but his character is ambiguous, his actions are obscure, his writings are English, and his fame is confined to the narrow limits of our language and our island. I must embrace a safer and more extensive theme.

"There is one which I should prefer to all others, the History of the Liberty of the Swiss, of that independence which a brave people rescued from the house of Austria, defended against a Dauphin of France, and finally sealed with the blood of Charles of Bergundy. From such a theme, so full of public spirit, of military glory, of examples of virtue, of lessons of government, the dullest stranger would catch fire: what might not *I* hope, whose talents, whatsoever they may be, would be inflamed with the zeal of patriotism. But the materials of this history are inaccessable to me, fast locked in the obscurity of an old barbarous German dialect, of which I am totally ignorant, and which I cannot resolve to learn for this sole and peculiar purpose.

"I have another subject in view, which is the contrast of the former history: the one a poor, warlike, virtuous republic, which emerges into glory and freedom; the other a commonwealth, soft, opulent, and corrupt; which, by just degrees, is precipitated from the abuse to the loss of her liberty: both lessons are, perhaps, equally instructive. This second subject is, the History of the

Republic of Florence under the house of Medicis : a period of one hundred and fifty years, which rises or descends from the dregs of the Florentine democracy, to the title and dominion of Cosmo de Medicis in the grand duchy of Tuscany.   I might deduce a chain of revolutions not unworthy the pen of Vertot; singular men, and singular events; the Medicis four times expelled, and as often recalled; and the Genius of Freedom, reluctantly yielding to the arms of Charles V. and the policy of Cosmo.   The character and fate of Savanerola, and the revival of arts and letters in Italy, will be essentially connected with the elevation of the family and the fall of the republic.   The Medicis (stirps quasi fataliter nota ad instauranda vel fovenda studia. Lipsius ad Germanos et Gallos, Epist. viii.) were illustrated by the patronage of Learning; and enthusiasm was the most formidable weapon of their adversaries.   On this splendid subject I shall most probably fix; but *when*, or *where*, or *how* will it be executed?   I behold in a dark and doubtful perspective."

Res altâ terrâ, et caligine mersas.*

* JOURNAL, July 27, 1762.]—The reflections which I was making yesterday, I continued and digested to-day. I don't absolutely look on that time as lost, but that it might have been better employed than in revolving schemes, the execution of which is so far distant. I must learn to check these wanderings of my imagination.

Nov 24.]—I dined at the Cocoa Tree with ****'; who, under a great appearance of oddity, conceals more real honour, good sense, and even knowledge, than half those who laugh at him. We went thence to the play (the Spanish Friar); and when it was over, returned to the Cocoa Tree. That respectable body, of which I have the honour of being a member afford every evening a sight truly English. Twenty or thirty, per-

haps, of the first men in the kingdom, in point of fashion and fortune, sup-
ping at little tables covered with a napkin, in the middle of a coffee-room,
upon a bit of cold meat, or a sandwich, and drinking a glass of punch. At
present, we are full of king's counsellors and lords of the bedchamber;
who, having jumped into the ministry, make a very singular medley of
their old principles and language with their modern ones.

Nov. 26.]—I went with Mallet to breakfast with Garrick ; and thence
to Drury-lane House, where I assisted at a very private rehearsal, in the
Green-room, of a new tragedy of Mallet's, called Elvira. As I have not
since seen it acted, I shall defer my opinion till then ; but I cannot help
mentioning the surprising versatility of Mrs. Pritchard's talents, who re-
hearsed, almost at the same time, the part of a furious queen in the Green-
room, and that of a coquette on the stage and passed several times from
one to the other with the utmost ease and happiness.

Dec. 30.]—Before I close the year I must balance my accounts—not of
money, but of time. I may divide my studies into four branches : 1. Books
that I have read for themselves, classic writers or capital treatises upon any
science ; such books as ought to be perused with attention, and meditated
with care. Of these I read the twenty last books of the Iliad twice, the
three first books of the Odyssey, the life of Homer, and Longinus περι
Υψους. 2. Books which I have read, or consulted, to illustrate the former.
Such as this year, Blackwall's Inquiry into the Life and writings of Homer,
Burke's Sublime and Beautiful, Hurd's Horace, Guichard's Mémoires Militaires, a great variety of passages of the ancients, occasionally useful ; large
extracts from Mezeriac, Bayle, and Potter ; and many memoires and abstracts from the Academy of Belles Lettres : among these I shall only mention
here two long and curious suits of dissertations—the one upon the Temple
of Delphi, the Amphictyonic Council, and the Holy Wars, by MM. Hardion
and de Valois ; the other upon the Games of the Grecians, by MM. Burette,
Gedoyne, and de la Barre. 3. Books of amusement and instruction, perused at my leisure hours, without any reference to a regular plan of study.
Of these, perhaps, I read too many, since I went through the Life of Erasmus, by Le Clerc and Burigny, many extracts from Le Clerc's Biblio-
thèques, the Ciceronianus, and Colloquies of Erasmus, Barclay's Argenis,
Terrasson's Sethos, Voltaire's Siècle de Louis XIV., Madame de Motteville's
Memoirs, and Fontenelle's Works. 4. Compositions of my own. I find
hardly any, except this Journal, and the Extract of Hurd's Horace, which
(like a chapter of Montaigne) contains many things very different from its

title. To these four heads I must this year add a fifth. 5. Those treatises
of English history which I read in January, with a view to my now abortive scheme of the Life of Sir Walter Raleigh. I ought indeed to have
known my own mind better before I undertook them. Upon the whole,
after making proper allowances, I am not dissatisfied with the year.

The three weeks which I passed at Beriton, at the end of this and the
beginning of the ensuing year, are almost a blank. I seldom went out;
and as the scheme of my travelling was at last entirely settled, the hurry of
impatience, the cares of preparations, and the tenderness of friends I was
going to quit, allowed me hardly any moments for study.

CHAP. XVI.

MR. GIBBON AT PARIS.

THE youthful habits of the language and manners of France had left in my mind an ardent desire of revisiting the Continent on a larger and more liberal plan. According to the law of custom, and perhaps of reason, foreign travel completes the education of an English gentleman; my father had consented to my wish, but I was detained above four years by my rash engagement in the militia. I eagerly grasped the first moments of freedom: three or four weeks in Hampshire and London were employed in the preparations of my journey, and the farewell visits of friendship and civility: my last act in town was to applaud Mallet's new tragedy of Elvira;* a post-

---

* JOURNAL, January 11th, 1763.]—I called upon Dr. Maty in the morning. He told me that the Duke de Nivernois desired to be acquainted with me. It was indeed with that view that I had written to Maty from Beriton to present, in my name, a copy of my book to him. Thence I went to Becket, paid him his bill, (fifty-four pounds,) and gave him back his translation. It must be printed, though very indifferent. My comfort is, that my misfortune is not an uncommon one. We dined and supped at the Mallets.

12th. I went with Maty to visit the Duke in Albemarle-street. He is a little emaciated figure, but appears to possess a good understanding, taste, and knowledge. He offered me very politely letters for Paris. We dined at our lodgings. I went to Covent Garden to see Woodward in Bobadil, and supped with the Mallets at George Scott's.

JOURNAL, Jan. 19th, 1763.]—I waited upon Lady Hervey and the Duke

chaise conveyed me to Dover, the packet to Boulogne, and
such was my diligence, that I reached Paris on the 28th
of January, 1763, only thirty-six days after the disband-

de Nivernois, and received my credentials. Lady Hervey's are for M. le
Comte de Caylus, and Madame Geoffrin. The Duke received me civilly,
but (perhaps through Maty's fault) treated me more as a man of letters
than as a man of fashion. His letters are entirely in that style; for the
Comte de Caylus and MM. de la Bleterie, de Ste. Palaye, Caperonnier, du
Clos, de Foncemagne, and d'Alembert. I then undressed for the play
My father and I went to the Rose, in the passage of the play-house, where
we found Mallet, with about thirty friends. We dined together, and went
thence into the pit, where we took our places in a body, ready to silence
all opposition. However, we had no occasion to exert ourselves. Notwith
standing the malice of party, Mallet's nation, connexions, and, indeed, im-
prudence, we heard nothing but applause. I think it was deserved. The
plan was borrowed from De la Motte, but the details and language have
great merit. A fine vein of dramatic poetry runs through the piece. The
scenes between the father and son awaken almost every sensation of the
human breast ; and the counsel would have equally moved, but for the
inconvenience unavoidable upon all theatres, that of intrusting fine speeches
to indifferent actors. The perplexity of the catastrophe is much, and I
believe justly criticised. But another defect made a stronger impression
upon me. When the poet ventures upon the dreadful situation of a father
who condemns his son to death, there is no medium, the father must either
be a monster or a hero. The obligations of justice, of the public good,
must be as binding, as apparent, as perhaps those of the first Brutus. The
cruel necessity consecrates his actions. and leaves no room for repentance.
The thought is shocking if not carried into action. In the execution of
Brutus's sons I am sensible of that fatal necessity. Without such an example, the unsettled liberty of Rome would have perished the instant after its
birth. But Alonzo might have pardoned his son for a rash attempt, the
cause of which was a private injury, and whose consequences could never
have disturbed an established government. He might have pardoned
such a crime in any other subject; and as the laws could exact only an
equal rigour for a son, a vain appetite for glory, and a mad affectation of
heroism, could alone have influenced him to exert an unequal and superior
severity.

ing of the militia. Two or three years were loosely
defined for the term of my absence; and I was left at
liberty to spend that time in such places and in such a
manner as was most agreeable to my taste and judgment.

In this first visit I passed three months and a half,
(January 28—May 9,) and a much longer space might
have been agreeably filled, without any intercourse with
the natives. At home we are content to move in the
daily round of pleasure and business; and a scene which
is always present is supposed to be within our knowledge, or at least within our power. But in a foreign
country, curiosity is our business and our pleasure; and
the traveller, conscious of his ignorance, and covetous of
his time, is diligent in the search and the view of every
object that can deserve his attention. I devoted many
hours in the morning to the circuit of Paris and the
neighbourhood, to the visit of churches and palaces conspicuous by their architecture, to the royal manufactures,
collections of books and pictures, and all the various
treasures of art, of learning, and of luxury. An Englishman may hear without reluctance, that in these curious
and costly articles Paris is superior to London; since the
opulence of the French capital arises from the defects of
its government and religion. In the absence of Louis
XIV. and his successors, the Louvre has been left
unfinished: but the millions which have been lavished on
the sands of Versailles, and the morass of Marli, could
not be supplied by the legal allowance of a British king.
The splendour of the French nobles is confined to their
town residence; that of the English is more usefully distributed in their country seats; and we should be

astonished at our own riches, if the labours of architecture, the spoils of Italy and Greece, which are now scattered from Inverary to Wilton, were accumulated in a few streets between Marylebone and Westminster. All superfluous ornament is rejected by the cold frugality of the Protestants; but the catholic superstition, which is always the enemy of reason, is often the parent of the arts. The wealthy communities of priests and monks expend their revenues in stately edifices; and the parish church of St. Sulpice, one of the noblest structures in Paris, was built and adorned by the private industry of a late curé. In this outset, and still more in the sequel of my tour, my eye was amused; but the pleasing vision cannot be fixed by the pen: the particular images are darkly seen through the medium of five-and-twenty years, and the narrative of my life must not degenerate into a book of travels.*

* JOURNAL, February 21, 1763.]—To-day I commenced my tour around the city, to see such places as were worthy of notice. D'Augny accompanied me. We went first to the library of the Abbey of St. Germain des Prés, where every body was busy, arranging a cabinet of curiosities; then to the Hôpital des Invalides, where the cupola was shut up on account of repairs going forward. I must therefore defer the visit and description of these two places. From thence we went to see the Ecole Militaire. As this edifice stands beside the Invalides, many persons would there perceive a very easy method of appreciating the different minds of their respective founders. In one, every thing is grand and magnificent; in the other, every thing is little and mean. Small white apartments, tolerably clean, (which, instead of the 500 gentlemen talked about, contain 258) compose the whole establishment; for the riding school and stables are nothing. It is true that these buildings are but a scaffolding, which should be taken away, to erect the real work on their ruins. Indeed, they could not have been built for eternity, since in twenty years' time the greater part of the beams are rotten. We afterwards glanced at the church of St. Sulpicius, whose façade (the pretext and product of so many lotteries) is not yet finished.

But the principal end of my journey was to enjoy the society of a polished and amiable people, in whose favour I was strongly prejudiced, and to converse with some authors, whose conversation, as I fondly imagined, must be far more pleasing and instructive than their writings. The moment was happily chosen. At the close of a successful war, the British name was respected on the Continent.

> Clarum et venerabile nomen
> Gentibus.

Our opinions, our fashions, even our games, were adopted in France, a ray of national glory illuminated each individual, and every Englishman was supposed to be born a patriot and a philosopher. For myself, I carried a personal recommendation; my name and my Essay were already known; the compliment of having written in the French language entitled me to some returns of civility and gratitude. I was considered as a man of letters who wrote for amusement. Before my departure I had obtained from the Duke de Nivernois, Lady Hervey, the Mallets, Mr. Walpole, &c., many letters of recommendation to their private or literary friends. Of these epistles the reception and success were determined by the character and situation of the persons by whom and to whom they were addressed; the seed was sometimes cast on a barren rock, and it sometimes multiplied an hundred fold in the production of new shoots, spreading branches, and exquisite fruit. But upon the whole, I had reason to praise the national urbanity, which from the court has diffused its gentle influence to the shop, the cottages, and

the schools. Of the men of genius of the age, Montesquieu and Fontenelle were no more; Voltaire resided on
his own estate near Geneva; Rousseau in the preceding
year had been driven from his hermitage in Montmorency;
and I blush at my having neglected to seek, in this journey, the acquaintance of Buffon. Among the men of letters
whom I saw, D'Alembert and Diderot held the foremost
rank in merit, or at least in fame. I shall content myself
with enumerating the well-known names of the Comte
de Caylus, of the Abbé de la Bleterie, Barthelemy, Reynal,
Arnaud, of Messieurs de la Condamine, du Clos, de Sainte
Palaye, de Bougainville, Caperonnier, de Guignes, Suard,
&c., without attempting to discriminate the shades of
their charcters, or the degrees of our connexion. Alone,
in a morning visit, I commonly found the artists and
authors of Paris less vain, and more reasonable, than in
the circles of their equals, with whom they mingle in the
houses of the rich. Four days in a week I had a place,
without invitation, at the hospitable tables of Mesdames
Geoffrin and du Bocage, of the celebrated Helvetius, and
of the Baron d'Olbach. In these symposia the pleasures
of the table were improved by lively and liberal conversation; the company was select, though various and
voluntary.*

* JOURNAL, February 23, 1763.]—I paid a visit to the Abbé de la Bleterie, who wished to take me to the Duchess of Aiguillon's: I wrote to M.
de Bougainville, whom I much wished to become acquainted with, and I
afterwards went to Baron d'Olbach's the friend of M. Helvetius. This
was my first visit, and the first step made into a very good house. The
Baron possesses genius and learning, and, above all, he very often gives
capital dinners.

February 24.]—The Abbé Barthelemy is a very amiable man, and has

The society of Madame du Bocage was more soft and
moderate than that of her rivals, and the evening conversations of M. de Foncemagne were supported by the
good sense and learning of the principal members of the
Academy of Inscriptions.   The opera and the Italians I
occasionally visited; but the French theatre, both in
tragedy and comedy, was my daily and favourite amuse-

nothing of the antiquary about him but a great depth of erudition. I
finished the evening by a very agreeable supper at Madame Bontem's with
the Marquis de Mirabeau. He is a singular man; he has imagination
enough for ten more, and not enough sound sense for himself alone. I
asked him several questions about the titles of the French nobility; but all
I could understand was, that nobody has very clear ideas about them.

   May, 1763.]—Fortified with a double letter of recommendation for the
Comte de Caylus, I imagined that I should find, united in him, the man of
letters and the man of quality. I saw him three or four times, and found
him a simple, ingenuous, good man, who showed me the utmost kindness. If I have not profited more by him I attribute it less to his character than to his mode of life. He rises early, runs through the artists,
painting-rooms all day long, comes home again at six o'clock in the evening,
puts on his dressing-gown, and shuts himself up in his closet. Is this the
way to see one's friends.

   If these recommendations were fruitless, there were others which were
as productive in their effects as they were agreeable in themselves. In a
capital like Paris, it is just and necessary that you should be distinguished
from the crowd by letters of recommendation, but when the ice is once
broken, your acquaintance multiply themselves, and your new friends feel
pleasure in introducing you to others newer still. A most happy effect of
the light and amiable character of the French, which has established
in Paris a suavity and liberty in society, unknown to antiquity and still
unknown to other nations. At London one must make one's way into each
house, which opens to us with the utmost difficulty. There they think
they afford you pleasure in receiving you; here they feel pleasure in it
themselves. So that I am acquainted with more houses in Paris than in
London; the fact is not probable, but it is true.

ment. Two famous actresses then divided the public
applause. For my own part, I preferred the consummate art of the Clairon, to the intemperate sallies of the
Dumesnil, which were extolled by her admirers, as the
genuine voice of nature and passion. Fourteen weeks
insensibly stole away; but had I been rich and independent, I should have prolonged, and perhaps have fixed,
my residence at Paris.

Between the expensive style of Paris and of Italy it was
prudent to interpose some months of tranquil simplicity;
and at the thoughts of Lausanne I again lived in the
pleasures and studies of my early youth. Shaping my
course through Dijon and Besançon, in the last of which
places I was kindly entertained by my cousin Acton, I
arrived in the month of May, 1763, on the banks of the
Leman Lake. It had been my intention to pass the Alps
in the autumn, but such are the simple attractions of the
place, that the year had almost expired before my departure from Lausanne in the ensuing spring. An absence
of five years had not made much alteration in manners, or
even in persons. My old friends, of both sexes, hailed
my voluntary return; the most genuine proof of my
attachment. They had been flattered by the present of
my book, the produce of their soil; and the good Pavilliard shed tears of joy as he embraced a pupil, whose
literary merit he might fairly impute to his own labours.
To my old list, I added some new acquaintance, and
among the strangers I shall distinguish Prince Lewis of
Wirtemberg, the brother of the reigning Duke, at whose
country-house, near Lausanne, I frequently dined: a wandering meteor, and at length a falling star, his light and

ambitious spirit had successively dropped from the firma-
ment of Prussia, of France, and of Austria; and his faults,
which he styled his misfortunes, had driven him into philosophic exile in the Pays de Vaud. He could now
moralize on the vanity of the world, the equality of mankind, and the happiness of a private station. His address
was affable and polite, and as he had shone in courts
and armies, his memory could supply, and his eloquence
could adorn, a copious fund of interesting anecdotes.
His first enthusiasm was that of charity and agriculture;
but the sage gradually lapsed into the saint, and Prince
Lewis of Wirtemberg is now buried in a hermitage near
Mayence, in the last stage of mystic devotion. By some
ecclesiastical quarrel, Voltaire had been provoked to
withdraw himself from Lausanne, and retired to his
castle at Ferney, where I again visited the poet and the
actor without seeking his more intimate acquaintance, to
which I might now have pleaded a better title. But the
theatre which he had founded, the actors whom he had
formed, survived the loss of their master; and recent
from Paris, I attended with pleasure at the representation
of several tragedies and comedies. I shall not descend
to specify particular names and characters; but I cannot
forget a private institution, which will display the innocent freedom of Swiss manners. My favourite society
had assumed, from the age of its members, the proud
denomination of the Spring (la Société du Printemps).
It consisted of fifteen or twenty young unmarried ladies,
of genteel, though not of the very first families; the
eldest perhaps about twenty, all agreeable, several handsome, and two or three of exquisite beauty. At each

other's houses they assembled almost every day, without
the control, or even the presence, of a mother or an aunt;
they were trusted to their own prudence, among a crowd
of young men of every nation in Europe. They laughed,
they sung, they danced, they played at cards, they acted
comedies; but in the midst of this careless gaiety, they
respected themselves, and were respected by the men;
the invisible line between liberty and licentiousness was
never transgressed by a gesture, a word, or a look, and
their virgin chastity was never sullied by the breath of
scandal or suspicion. A singular institution, expressive
of the innocent simplicity of Swiss manners. After having
tasted the luxury of England and Paris, I could not have
returned with satisfaction to the coarse and homely
table of Madame Pavilliard; nor was her husband offended
that I now entered myself as a *pensionnaire*, or boarder,
in the elegant house of Mr. De Mesery, which may be
entitled to a short remembrance, as it has stood above
twenty years, perhaps, without a parallel in Europe. The
house in which we lodged was spacious and convenient,
in the best street, and commanding, from behind, a noble
prospect over the country and the Lake. Our table was
served with neatness and plenty; the boarders were
select; we had the liberty of inviting any guests at a
stated price: and in the summer the scene was occasionally transferred to a pleasant villa, about a league
from Lausanne. The characters of master and mistress
were happily suited to each other, and to their situation.
At the age of seventy-five, Madame de Mesery, who
has survived her husband, is still a graceful, and I had
almost said, a handsome woman. She was alike quali-

fied to preside in her kitchen and her drawing-room,
and such was the equal propriety of her conduct, that of
two or three hundred foreigners, none ever failed in respect, none could complain of her neglect, and none could
ever boast of her favour.   Mesery himself, of the noble
family of De Crousaz, was a man of the world, a jovial
companion, whose easy manners and natural sallies
maintained the cheerfulness of his house.   His wit
could laugh at his own ignorance; he disguised, by
an air of profusion, a strict attention to his interest; and
in this situation, he appeared like a nobleman who spent
his fortune and entertained his friends.   In this agreeable
society I resided nearly eleven months (May, 1763—April
1764); and in this second visit to Lausanne, among a
crowd of my English companions, I knew and esteemed
Mr. Holroyd (now Lord Sheffield); and our mutual attachment was renewed and fortified in the subsequent stages
of our Italian journey.   Our lives are in the power of
chance, and a slight variation on either side, in time or
place, might have deprived me of a friend, whose activity
in the ardour of youth was always prompted by a benevolent heart, and directed by a strong understanding.*

* JOURNAL, September 16, 1763.]—**** and **** have left us.   The
former is a vile beast, gross, ignorant, and unmannerly.   His violence has
got him into twenty scrapes here.   However, they would have had him
make the journey to Italy, but **** refusing to accompany him, they have
resolved to send for him back again to England via Paris.   **** is a philosopher, and very well read, but cold and not at all a man of talent.   He is
weary of running over the world with young blockheads.   After having
returned this one back to his family, he expects to come and seek repose
and seclusion in this country.   How right he is !

September 21.]—I have sustained a slight mortification at the society.

Frey's departure had occasioned the office of strangers' director to be vacant. It was intimated that it was intended for me, and my natural frankness had not permitted me to conceal that I should be glad to accept it, and that I was in expectation of it. Nevertheless, the majority of votes gave it to M. Roel Hollandois. I saw that they had taken advantage of the very first moment the laws allowed for balloting, and that, if I had wished to assemble my friends, I might have gained it; but I know, at the same time, that I should have had it three months ago without a moment's care about it. My reputation is, with some reason, declining here, and I have enemies.

September 25.]—I have passed the afternoon at Madame de ****'s. I had not seen her since the 14th of this month. She has not spoken a single word about me, or appeared to have noticed my absence. This silence has hurt me. I had a very good reputation here for morality, but I see they now begin to confound me with my fellow-countrymen, and to look upon me as a man who loves wine and dissipation.

October 15.]—I have passed the afternoon at Madame de Mesery's. She wished to introduce me to a young French lady, whom she had invited to supper. This young lady, who calls herself Le Franc, is six feet high. Her stature, countenance, voice, and conversation, all announce the most determined grenadier, but a grenadier who has talent, intelligence, and knowledge of the world. So that her sex, name, and condition are all a mystery. She says she is a Parisian lady of quality, who has retired into this country on account of her religion   May it not rather be on account of an affair of honour?

Lausanne, December 1763.]—I got up late, and a very friendly visit from M. de Chandieu Villars* took away what was left of the morning. M. de. Chandieu has served with distinction in France, and retired with the rank of field-marshal. He is a man of great politeness, of a free and lively spirit; and now, at sixty, he would form the agreeable attraction in a company of young ladies. He is almost the only foreigner who has succeeded in acquiring the ease of French manners, without at the same time falling into bullying and blustering airs.

Lausanne, December, 18, 1763.]—This was Communion Sunday. Religious ceremonies are well observed in this country. They are rare, and

---

* The father of Madame de Severy, whose family were Mr. Gibbon's most intimate friends, after he had settled at Lausanne in the year 1783.—S.

on that very account more respected. Old folks complain, indeed, of the cooling of devotion; but a day like this still affords an edifying spectacle. There is neither business nor parties; and they interdict even whist, so necessary to the very existence of a Lausannese.

December 31.]—Let us glance back at this year 1763, and see how I have employed this portion of my existence, which is passed away, and will never return. The month of January was spent in the bosom of my family, to whom I was forced to sacrifice all my time, for it was the last part of my stay, and mingled with the cares of departure and the bustle of a journey. In that journey, however, I found means of reading the letters of Busequius, imperial minister at the Port. They are equally interesting and instructive. I remained at Paris from the 28th of January to the 9th of May. During all this time, I did not study at all. Amusements took up a great deal of my time, and the habit of dissipation, which is so easily acquired in large cities, did not allow me to profit by what remained. Indeed, if I turned over but few books, the observation of all the curious objects which are presented to view in a large metropolis, and conversation with the greatest men of the age, taught me many things that are not to be found in books. The last seven or eight months of the year have been more tranquil. When I found myself settled at Lausanne, I undertook a consecutive course of study on the ancient geography of Italy. My enthusiasm kept up very well for six weeks, till the end of the month of June. Then, a journey to Geneva a little interrupted my diligence. Mesery's dwelling presented a thousand attractions, and Saussure's society put the finishing stroke to the loss of my time. I resumed my work at this Journal about the middle of August, and from that time to the beginning of November, I put every instant to profit. I must confess, that during the last two . months my ardour is a little slackened. I. In this course of study I read, 1. Nearly two books of Strabo's Geography upon Italy, twice over. 2. Part of the second book of Pliny's Natural History. 3. The fourth chapter of the second book of Pomponious Mela. 4. The Itineraries of Antoninus and Jerusalem, as far as regards Italy. I read them with the Commentaries of Wesselling, &c. I have extracted tables of all the great roads in Italy, every where reducing the Roman into English miles, according to the calculations of M. d'Anville. 5. The History of the Great Roman Empire, by M. Bergier, 2 vols. 4to. 6. Some select extracts from Cicero, Livy, Velleius Paterculus, Tacitus, and the two Plinies. The Roma Vetus of Nardini, and several other little treatises on the same subject, which compose almost all the fourth volume of Grævius' Trésor des Antiquités Romaines. 7. The Italia Antiqua of Cluverius, 2 vols. folio. 8. The Iter (or Journey) of Claudius Rutilius Numatianus among the Gauls. 9. Virgil's Catalogues. 10. That of Silius Italicus. 11. Horace's Journey to Brundusium. N. B. These last three I read twice over. 12. D'Anville's Treatise on the Itinerary Measures, and some Memoires of the Académie des Belles Lettres. II. I had to wait for Nardini from the library of Geneva; I wished to fill up this spare moment in reading Juvenal, a poet whom I as yet knew only by reputation. I read him twice over carefully, and with pleasure. III. During the year, I have read some periodicals; among others, the Journal Etranger, from its commencement, a volume of Bayle's Nouvelles, and the first 35 volumes of the Bibliothèque raisonnée. IV. I have written a great deal of my Recueil Géogarphique d'Italie, which is already very ample, and tolerably curious. V. I ought not to forget this very Journal, which has grown into a book; 214 well filled pages, in four months and a half, are a considerable object. For, without reckoning a great number of detached observations, there are in it several learned and orderly dissertations. That upon Hannibal's expedition includes ten pages, and that on the civil war twelve. But these pieces are too long, and the Journal itself stands in need of a reform, which should retrench from it a number of pieces that are foreign to its real plan. After having reflected some time upon the subject, here are some rules that I have made on the objects that are proper for it. I. All my domestic and private life, my amusements, connexions, and even my rambles; as well as all the reflections that strike me on subjects that are merely personal. I allow that all this is interesting only to myself, but then it is only for myself that I write this Journal. II. All that I learn by observation and conversation. With respect to this, I shall only put down what I have from persons, who are at once both perfectly well informed and honest, when it regards facts, or from that small number who merit the title of great men, when it regards sentiments and opinions. III. I shall carefully put in it all that may be termed the material part of my studies; how many hours I have worked, how many pages I have written or read, with a short notice of their contents. IV. I should be sorry to read without reflecting on my readings, giving correct judgments upon my authors, and carefully culling their ideas and expressions. But all reading does not alike furnish them. There are books to be skimmed over, and books to be read. My observations on those of the first class can only

be short and detached. These will be proper for the Journal. Those
on the second class will only enter it so far as they may come under the
same character. V. My reflections on those few classic authors that are to
be carefully meditated upon, will naturally be deeper, and more consecutive. For them, and for more lengthy and original dissertations, which
reading or reflection may give rise to, I shall make a separate collection.
I shall, nevertheless, preserve its connexion with the Journal by constant
references which will mark the number of each treatise, together with
the time and occasion of its composition. Making use of these precautions, my Journal cannot but be useful to me. This exact account of my
time will make me more justly appreciate its value it will, by its minuteness, dissipate the illusion that we fall into of looking only at months
and years, and neglecting hours and days. I say nothing of the
pleasure of it. It is, however, a very great one to be able to review each
epoch of one's life, and, whenever we please, to place ourselves in the
midst of all the little scenes that we have formerly acted, or seen
acted.

April 6, 1764.]—I was awakened by Pavilliard and H****, in order
to put a stop to an unfortunate affair, which took place at the ball after
we left. G****, who has for a long time paid his addresses to Miss ****,
was grieved to see that **** threatened to supplant him. He replied to
his rival's politeness only by rudeness; and, at last, on a dispute for Miss
****'s hand, he treated him in the worst possible manner, and called him,
before every body, "a fool," &c. I understood from Pavilliard, that
**** had sent him a challenge, and, that G****'s answer not having
satisfied him, they were to have a meeting at five o'clock this evening.
Being exceedingly vexed to see my friend engaged in an affair which
could not but do him wrong, I hastened to the house of M. de Crousaz,
where **** lived. I soon saw that it merely needed a very slight ex-
planation, added to some sort of apology from G****, to appease him, and
I went to the house of the latter with H****, to request him to give it.
We convinced him that the acknowldgment of a real fault was never
injurious to honour, and that his insult to the ladies, as well as to ****, was
inexcusable. I dictated to him an appropriate note, but without the least
meanness, which I carried to the Dutchman. He laid down his arms
immediately, returned him the most polite answer, and thanked me a
thousand times for the part I had acted. Indeed, he is by no means an
untractable man. After dinner, I saw the ladies, to whom I took an

apologizing note. The mother was willing to accept G****'s excuses ; but Miss **** is afflicted at the injury this affair may do her with the world. This business has occupied me the whole day; but could it have been better employed than in saving the life, perhaps, of two persons, and in preserving a friend's reputation ?   Besides, I have seen deeply into more than one character.   G**** is brave, true, and sensible, but has an impetuosity that is only the more dangerous for being ordinarily suppressed. C**** is as rude as a school-boy.   De S**** has an indifference, which is much more attributable to a defect of sensibility than to an excess of reason.   I have conceived a real friendship for H****.   He has a high degree of rationality and honourable sentiments, with one of the best regulated hearts,

CHAP. XVII.

MR. GIBBON PREPARES FOR HIS ITALIAN JOURNEY.

If my studies at Paris had been confined to the study of the world, three or four months would not have been unprofitably spent. My visits, however superficial, to the Academy of Medals and the public libraries, opened a new field of inquiry; and the view of so many manuscripts of different ages and characters induced me to consult the two great Benedictine works, the Diplomatica of Mabillon, and the Palæographia of Montfaucon. I studied the theory without attaining the practice of the art; nor should I complain of the intricacy of Greek abbreviations and Gothic alphabets, since every day, in a familiar language, I am at a loss to decypher the hieroglyphics of a female note. In a tranquil scene, which revived the memory of my first studies, idleness would have been less pardonable: the public libraries of Lausanne and Geneva liberally supplied me with books; and if many hours were lost in dissipation, many more were employed in literary labour. In the country, Horace and Virgil, Juvenal and Ovid, were my assiduous companions: but, in town, I formed and executed a plan of study for the use of my transalpine expedition: the topography of old Rome. the ancient geography of Italy, and the science of medals. 1. I diligently read, almost always

with my pen in my hand, the elaborate treatises of
Nardini, Donatus, &c., which fill the fourth volume of
the Roman Antiquities of Grævius. 2. I next undertook
and finished the Italia Antiqua of Cluverius, a learned
native of Prussia, who had measured, on foot, every spot,
and has compiled and digested every passage of the
ancient writers. These passages in Greek or Latin
authors I perused in the text of Cluverius, in two folio
volumes: but I separately read the descriptions of Italy
by Strabo, Pliny, and Pomponius Mela, the Catalogues of
the Epic poets, the Itineraries of Wesselling's Antonius,
and the coasting Voyage of Rutilius Mumatianus; and I
studied two kindred subjects in the Mesures Itinéraires of
D'Anville, and the copious work of Bergier, Histoire des
grands Chemins de l'Empire Romain. From these materials I formed a table of roads and distances reduced to
our English measure; filled a folio common-place book
with my collections and remarks on the geography of
Italy, and inserted in my journal many long and learned
notes on the insulæ and populousness of Rome, the social
war, the passage of the Alps by Hannibal, &c. 3. After
glancing my eye over Addison's agreeable dialogues, I
more seriously read the great work of Ezechiel Span-
heim de Præstantiâ et Usû Numismatum, and applied
with him the medals of the kings and emperors, the families and colonies, to the illustration of ancient history.
And thus was I armed for my Italian journey.*

JOURNAL, Lausanne, April 17, 1764.]—Guise and myself gave an excellent dinner and plenty of wine to Dupleix and several others. After
dinner, we made our escape to pay some visits to the ****, the ****, and
the ****. I leave with some regret: but a little wine, and a cheerfulness

that I could not account for, gave me an unparralleled impudence with these little lasses. I said a hundred nonsensical things to them, and we embraced each other with a laugh. Mesery gave us a very prime supper, with some of the morning's company, increased by the addition of Bourgeois and Pavilliard. This supper, the adieux to Pavilliard especially, (whom I sincerely love,) and the preparations for departure, occupied me till two in the morning. I leave Lausanne with less regret than at the first time. I now only leave acquaintances there. Then, it was the loss of the mistress and the friend that I deplored. Formerly, I saw Lausanne with the inexperienced eyes of a youth, who owed to it the rational part of his existence, and who judged without comparison of objects. Now I see in it an ill-built town, in the midst of a delightful country, which enjoys peace and repose, and takes them to be liberty; a numerous and well-educated population, who are fond of society, and judicious in the conduct of it, and who admit strangers into their circles, which would be much more agreeable if conversation had not given place to play. The women are pretty, and notwithstanding their extensive liberty, are very prudent At the farthest, they can only be a little complaisant in the innocent but uncertain hope of entangling a stranger in their nets. Affectation is the original sin of the Lausannese; affectation of magnificence, nobility, and talent; the two first are very common, while the latter is extremely rare. As this vice is constantly clashing with the same quality in others, Lausanne is divided into a great number of states, whose principles and language are infinitely varied, and which have nothing in common but their reciprocal hatred for each other. Their taste for expense accords but badly with that for nobility. They would perish sooner than renounce their grandeur, or embrace the only profession that would support them. M. Mesery's is a delightful house; the open and generous character of the husband, the engaging qualities of the wife, a charming situation, excellent cheer, the company of his fellow-countrymen, and an unrestrained freedom, make every English love the dwelling. Oh, that I could find a similar one in London! I regret leaving Holroyd, who is, however, following us close.

CHAP. XVIII.

MR. GIBBON'S TOUR IN ITALY.

I shall advance with rapid brevity in the narrative of this tour, in which somewhat more than a year (April, 1764—May, 1765) was agreeably employed. Content with tracing my line of march, and slightly touching on my personal feelings, I shall waive the minute investigation of the scenes which have been viewed by thousands, and described by hundreds, of our modern travellers. Rome is the great object of our pilgrimage: 1st, the journey; 2d, the residence; and 3d, the return, will form the most proper and conspicuous division. 1. I climbed Mount Cenis, and descended into the plain of Piedmont, not on the back of an elephant, but on a light osier seat, in the hands of the dexterous and intrepid chairman of the Alps. The architecture and government of Turin presented the same aspect of tame and tiresome uniformity; but the court was regulated with decent and splendid economy; and I was introduced to his Sardinian Majesty,* Charles Emanuel, who, after the incomparable Frederic, held the second rank (proximus longo tamen intervallo) among the kings of Europe. The size and populousness of Milan could not surprise an inhabitant of

* See Letter, No. XVIII.

London : but the fancy is amused by a visit to the Borro-
mean islands, an enchanted palace, a work of the fairies
in the midst of a lake encompassed with mountains, and
far removed from the haunts of men.   I was less amused
by the marble palaces of Genoa than by the recent
memorials of her deliverance (in December, 1746) from
the Austrian tyranny; and I took a military survey of
every scene of action within the enclosure of her double
walls.   My steps were detained at Parma and Modena,
by the precious relics of the Farnese and Este collections: but, alas! the far greater part had been already
transported, by inheritance or purchase, to Naples and
Dresden.   By the road of Bologna and the Appenines, I
at last reached Florence, where I reposed from June to
September, during the heat of the summer months.   In
the Gallery, and especially in the Tribune, I first acknowledged, at the feet of the Venus of Medicis, that the
chisel may dispute the pre-eminence with the pencil, a
truth in the fine arts which cannot on this side of the
Alps be felt or understood.   At home I had taken some
lessons of Italian: on the spot I read, with a learned
native, the classics of the Tuscan idiom: but the short-
ness of my time, and the use of the French language,
prevented my acquiring any facility of speaking; and I
was a silent spectator in the conversations of our envoy,
Sir Horace Mann, whose most serious bus'ness was that
of entertaining the English at his hospitable table.*

* JOURNAL, Florence, August 9, 1764.]—Cocchi dined with us. We
chatted a good deal, but I did not find in him the genius that is attributed to
him ; perhaps because our minds are not analogous. I can perceive extravagance in his ideas, and affectation in his manners. He is every moment

After leaving Florence, I compared the solitude of Pisa with the industry of Lucca and Leghorn, and continued my journey through Sienna to Rome, where I arrived in the beginning of October. 2. My temper is not very susceptible of enthusiasm; and the enthusiasm which I do not feel, I have ever scorned to affect. But, at the distance of twenty-five years, I can neither forget nor express the strong emotions which agitated my mind as I first approached and entered the *eternal city*. After a sleepless night, I trod, with a lofty step, the ruins of the Forum; each memorable spot where Romulus *stood*, or Tully spoke, or Cæsar fell, was at once present to my eye; and several days of intoxication were lost or enjoyed before I could descend to a cool and minute investigation. My guide was Mr. Byers, a Scotch antiquary of experience and taste; but, in the daily labour of eighteen weeks, the powers of attention were sometimes fatigued, till I was myself qualified, in a last review, to select and study the capital works of ancient and modern art. Six weeks were borrowed for my tour of Naples, the most populous of cities, relative to its size; whose luxurious inhabitants seem to dwell on the confines of paradise and hell-fire. I was presented to the boy-king by our new envoy, Sir William Hamilton; who, wisely diverting his correspondence from the Secretary of State to the Royal Society and British Museum, has elucidated a country of

complaining of his poverty. He knows but little of the true dignity of a man of letters. If his knowledge is extensive, it is inclined towards physics. He asked me if Lord Spenser could not make bishops, and told me a story about Lord Lyttleton (whose son he cannot bear) while we were talking about country parliaments.

such inestimable value to the naturalist and antiquarian. On my return, I fondly embraced, for the last time, the miracles of Rome; but I departed without kissing the feet of Rezzonico (Clement XIII.), who neither possessed the wit of his predecessor Lambertini, nor the virtues of his successor Ganganelli. 3. In my pilgrimage from Rome to Loretto, I again crossed the Appenine; from the coast of the Adriatic I traversed a fruitful and populous country, which could alone disprove the paradox of Montesquieu, that modern Italy is a desert. Without adopting the exclusive prejudice of the natives, I sincerely admire the paintings of the Bologna school. I hastened to escape from the sad solitude of Ferrera, which in the age of Cæsar was still more desolate. The spectacle of Venice afforded some hours of astonishment; the university of Padua is a dying taper: but Verona still boasts her amphitheatre, and his native Vicenza is adorned by the classic architecture of Balladia; the road of Lombardy and Piedmont (did Montesquieu find them without inhabitants?) led me back to Milan, Turin, and the passage of Mount Cenis, where I again crossed the Alps in my way to Lyons.

The use of foreign travel has been often debated as a general question; but the conclusion must be finally applied to the character and circumstances of each individual. With the education of boys, *where* or *how* they may pass over some juvenile years with the least mischief to themselves or others, I have no concern. But after supposing the previous and indispensable requisites of age, judgment, a competent knowledge of men and books, and a freedom from domestic prejudices, I will briefly describe the qualification which I deem most essential to a traveller. He should be endowed with an active, indefatigable vigour of mind and body, which can seize every mode of conveyance, and support, with a careless smile, every hardship of the road, the weather, or the inn. The benefits of foreign travel will correspond with the degrees of these qualifications : but, in this sketch, those to whom I am known will not accuse me of framing my own panegyric. It was at Rome, on the 15th of October, 1764, as I sat musing amidst the ruins of the Capitol, while the bare-footed friars were singing vespers in the temple of Jupiter,* that the idea of writing the decline and fall of the city first started to my mind. But my original plan was circumscribed to the decay of the city rather than of the empire : and, though my reading and reflections began to point towards that object, some years elapsed, and several avocations intervened, before I was seriously engaged in the execution of that laborious work.

I had not totally renounced the southern provinces of France, but the letters which I found at Lyons were expressive of some impatience. Rome and Italy had satiated my curious appetite, and I was now ready to return to the peaceful retreat of my family and books. After a happy fortnight I reluctantly left Paris, embarked at Calais, again landed at Dover, after an interval of two years and five months, and hastily drove through the summer dust and solitude of London. On the 25th of June, 1765, I arrived at my father's house : and the five

* Now the church of the Zoccolants, or Franciscan Friars.

years and a half between my travels and my father's
death (1770) are the portion of my life which I passed
with the least enjoyment, and which I remember with
the least satisfaction.   Every spring I attended the
monthly meeting and exercise of the militia at Southampton; and by the resignation of my father, and the
death of Sir Thomas Worsley, I was successively promoted to the rank of major and lieutenant-colonel com-
mandant: but I was each year more disgusted with the
inn, the wine, the company, and the tiresome repetition
of annual attendance and daily exercise.   At home, the
economy of the family and farm still maintained the same
creditable appearance.   My connexion with Mrs. Gibbon
was mellowed into a warm and solid attachment: my
growing years abolished the distance that might yet
remain between a parent and a son, and my behaviour
satisfied my father, who was proud of the success, however imperfect in his own life-time, of my literary talents.
Our solitude was soon and often enlivened by the visit of
the friend of my youth, Dr. Deyverdun, whose absence
from Lausanne I had sincerely lamented.   About three
years after my first departure, he had emigrated from
his native lake to the banks of the Oder in Germany.
The *res angusta domi*, the waste of a decent patrimony,
by an improvident father, obliged him, like many of his
countrymen, to confide in his own industry; and he was
entrusted with the education of a young prince, the
grandson of the Margrave of Schavedt, of the roya.
family of Prussia.   Our friendship was never cooled, our
correspondence was sometimes interrupted; but I rather
wished than hoped to obtain Mr Deyverdun for the com

panion of my Italian tour.   An unhappy, though honourable passion, drove him from his German court; and the
attractions of hope and curiosity were fortified by the
expectation of my speedy return to England.   During
four successive summers he passed several weeks or
months at Beriton, and our free conversation, on every
topic that could interest the heart or understanding,
would have reconciled me to a desert or a prison.   In
the winter months of London my sphere of knowledge
and action were somewhat enlarged, by the many new
acquaintances which I had contracted in the militia and
abroad; and I must regret, as more than an acquaintance, Mr. Godfrey Clarke of Derbyshire, an amiable and
worthy young man, who was snatched away by an
untimely death.   A weekly convivial meeting was established by myself and travellers, under the name of the
Roman Club.*

The renewal, or perhaps the improvement of my
English life embittered by the alteration of my own feelings.   At the age of twenty-one I was, in my proper
station of a youth, delivered from the yoke of education,
and delighted with the comparative state of liberty and
affluence.   My filial obedience was natural and easy;
and in the gay prospect of futurity, my ambition did not
extend beyond the enjoyment of my books, my leisure,
and my patrimonial estate, undisturbed by the cares of a

* The members were Lord Mountstuart (now Earl of Bute), Colonel Ed-
monstone, Weddal, Palgrave, Lord Berkley, Godfrey Clark, Holroyd
(Lord Sheffield), Major Ridley, Sir William Guise, Sir John Aubrey, Lord
Abingdon, Hon. Peregrine Bertie, Cleaver, Hon. John Damer, Hon. George
Damer (Lord Milton), Sir Thomas Gascoyne, Sir John Hort, E. Gibbon, Esq.

family and the duties of a profession. But in the militia
I was armed with power; in my travels, I was exempt
from control; and as I approached, as I gradually passed
my thirtieth year, I began to feel the desire of being
master in my own house. The most gentle authority
will sometimes frown without reason, the most cheerful
submission will sometimes murmur without cause; and
such is the law of our imperfect nature, that we must
either command or obey; that our professional liberty is
supported by the obsequiousness of our own dependants.
While so many of my acquaintance were married or in
parliament, or advancing with a rapid step in the various
roads of hononr and fortune, I stood alone, immoveable
and insignificant; for after the monthly meeting of 1770,
I had even withdrawn myself from the militia, by the
resignation of an empty and barren commission. My
temper is not susceptible of envy, and the view of successful merit has always excited my warmest applause.
The miseries of a vacant life were never known to a man
whose hours were insufficient for the inexhaustible
pleasures of study. But I lamented that at the proper
age I had not embraced the lucrative pursuits of the law
or of trade, the chances of civil office or India adventure,
or even the fat slumbers of the church; and my repentance
became more lively as the loss of time was more irretrievable. Experience showed me the use of grafting my
private consequence on the importance of a great professional body; the benefits of those firm connexions which
are cemented by hope and interest, by gratitude and
emulation, by the mutual exchange of services and
favours. From the emoluments of a profession I might

have derived an ample fortune, or a competent income, instead of being stinted to the same narrow allowance, to be increased only by an event which I sincerely deprecated. The progress and the knowledge of our domestic disorders aggravated my anxiety, and 1 began to apprehend that I might be left in my old age without the fruits either of industry or inheritance.

In the first summer after my return, whilst I enjoyed at Beriton the society of my friend Deyverdun, our daily conversations expatiated over the field of ancient and modern literature; and we freely discussed my studies, my first essay, and my future projects. The Decline and Fall of Rome I still contemplated at an awful distance: but the two historical designs which had balanced my choice were submitted to his taste; and in the parallel between the Revolutions of Florence and Switzerland, our common partiality for a country which was *his* by birth, and *mine* by adoption, inclined the scale in favour of the latter. According to the plan, which was soon conceived and digested, I embraced a period of two hundred years, from the association of three peasants of the Alps to the plenitude and prosperity of the Helvetic body in the sixteenth century. I should have described the deliverance and victory of the Swiss, who have never shed the blood of their tyrants but in the field of battles the laws and manners of the confederate states; the splendid trophies of the Austrian, Burgundian, and Italian wars; and the wisdom of a nation, who, after some sallies of martial adventure, has been content to guard the blessings of peace with the sword of freedom.

———Manus hæc inimica tyrannis
Ense petit placidam sub libertate quietem.

My judgment, as well as my enthusiasm, was satisfied
with the glorious theme : and the assistance of Deyverdun
seemed to remove an insuperable obstacle.   The French
or Latin memorials, of which I was not ignorant, are
inconsiderable in number and weight: but in the perfect
acquaintance of my friend with the German language, I
found the key of a more valuable collection.   The most
necessary books were procured ; he translated, for my
use, the folio volume of Schilling, a copious and contem-
porary relation of the war of Burgundy ; we read and
marked the most interesting parts of the great chronicle
of Tschudi : and by his labour, or that of an inferior
assistant, large extracts were made from the History
of Lauffer, and the Dictionary of Lew ; yet such was the
distance and delay, that two years elapsed in these preparatory steps ; and it was late in the third summer
(1767) before I entered, with these slender materials, on
the more agreeable task of composition.   A specimen of
my history, the first book, was read the following winter
in a literary society of foreigners in London ; and as the
author was unknown, I listened, without observation, to
the free strictures and unfavourable sentence of my
judges.*   The momentary sensation was painful ; but their

* Mr. Hume seems to have had a different opinion of this work.

From Mr. Hume to Mr. Gibbon.

"Sir,—It is but a few days ago since Mr. Deyverdun put your manuscript
into my hands, and I have perused it with great pleasure and satisfaction.
I have only one objection, derived from the language in which it is written.
Why do you compose in French, and carry faggots into the wood, as
Horace says with regard to Romans who wrote in Greek ?   I grant that
you have a like motive to those Romans, and adopt a language much more
generally diffused than your native tongue ; but have you not remarked
the fate of those two ancient languages in following ages ?   The Latin,

condemnation was ratified by my cooler thoughts. I delivered my imperfect sheets to the flames,* and for ever renounced a design in which some expense, much labour, and more time, had been so vainly consumed. I cannot regret the loss of a slight and superficial essay; for such the work must have been in the hands of a stranger, uninformed by the scholars and statesmen, and remote from the libraries and archieves of the Swiss republica. My ancient habits, and the presence of Deyverdun, encouraged me to write in French for the Continent of Europe; but I was conscious myself that my style, above

though then less celebrated, and confined to more narrow limits, has in some measure outlived the Greek, and is now more generally understood by men of letters. Let the French, therefore, triumph in the present diffusion of their tongue. Our solid and increasing establishments in America, where we need less dread the inundation of barbarians, promise a superior stability and duration to the English language.

"Your use of the French tongue has also led you into a style more poetical and figurative, and more highly coloured, than our language seems to admit of in historical productions; for such is the practice of French writers, particularly the more recent ones, who illuminate their pictures more than custom will permit us. On the whole, your history, in my opinion, is written with spirit and judgment; and I exhort you earnestly to continue it. The objections that occurred to me on reading it, were so frivolous, that I shall not trouble you with them, and should, I believe, have a difficulty to recollect them. I am, with great esteem, sir, your most obedient and most humble servant,

(Signed)   DAVID HUME."

"London, 24th of Oct. 1767.

* He neglected to burn them. He left at Sheffield-place the introduction, or first book, in forty-three pages folio, written in a very small hand, besides a considerable number of notes. If Mr. Gibbon had not declared his judgment, perhaps Mr. Hume's opinion, expressed in the letter in the last note, might have justified the publication of it.—S.

prose and below poetry, degenerated into a verbose and
turgid declamation.   Perhaps I may impute the failure to
an injudicious choice of a foreign language.   Perhaps I
may suspect that the language itself is ill adapted to sustain the vigour and dignity of an important narrative.
But if France, so rich in literary merit, had produced a
great original historian, his genius would have formed
and fixed the idiom to the proper tone, the peculiar mode
of historical eloquence.

CHAP. XIX.

MR. GIBBON COMMENCES A PERIODICAL.

It was in search of some liberal and lucrative employment that my friend Deyverdun had visited England. His remittances from home were scanty and precarious. My purse was always open, but it was often empty; and I bitterly felt the want of riches and power, which might have enabled me to correct the errors of his fortune. His wishes and qualifications solicited the station of the travelling governor of some wealthy pupil; but every vacancy provoked so many eager candidates, that for a long time I struggled without success; nor was it till after much application that I could even place him as a clerk in the office of the secretary of state. In a residence of several years he never acquired the just pronunciation and familiar use of the English tongue, but he read our most difficult authors with ease and taste: his critical knowledge of our language and poetry was such as few foreigners have possessed; and few of our countrymen could enjoy the theatre of Shakspeare and Garrick with more exquisite feeling and discernment. The consciousness of his own strength, and the assurance of my aid, emboldened him to imitate the example of Dr. Maty, whose Journal Britannique was esteemed and

regretted; and to improve his model, by uniting with the
transactions of literature a philosophic view of the arts
and manners of the British nation.   Our journal for the
year 1767, under the title of Mémoires Littéraires de la
Grande Bretagne, was soon finished and sent to the
press.   For the first article, Lord Lyttleton's History of
Henry II., I must own myself responsible; but the public
has ratified my judgment of that voluminous work, in
which sense and learning are not illuminated by a ray of
genius.   The next specimen was the choice of my friend,
the Bath Guide, a light and whimsical performance, of
local, and even verbal, pleasantry.   I started at the
attempt: he smiled at my fears: his courage was justified by success; and a master of both languages will
applaud the curious felicity with which he has transfused
into French prose the spirit, and even the humour, of the
English verse.   It is not my wish to deny how deeply I
was interested in these Memoirs, of which I need not
surely be ashamed; but at the distance of more than
twenty years, it would be impossible for me to ascertain
the respective shares of the two associates.   A long and
intimate communication of ideas had cast our sentiments
and style in the same mould.   In our social labours we
composed and corrected by turns; and the praise which
I might honestly bestow would fall perhaps upon some
article or passage most properly my own.   A second
volume (for the year 1768) was published of these
Memoirs.   I will presume to say, that their merit was
superior to their reputation; but it is not less true, that
they were productive of more reputation than emolument.
They introduced my friend to the protection, and myself

to the acquaintance of the Earl of Chesterfield, whose age and infirmities secluded him from the world; of Mr. David Hume, who was under secretary to the office in which Deyverdun was more humbly employed. The former accepted a dedication (April 12th, 1769,) and reserved the author for the future education of his successor; the latter enriched the journal with a reply to Mr. Walpole's Historical Doubts, which he afterwards shaped into the form of a note. The materials of the third volume were almost completed, when I recommended Deyverdun as governor to Sir Richard Worsley, a youth, the son of my old lieutenant-colonel, who was lately deceased. They set forwards on their travels; nor did they return to England till some time after my father's death.

My next publication was an accidental sally of love and resentment; of my reverence for modest genius, and my aversion for insolent pedantry. The sixth book of Æneid is the most pleasing and perfect composition of Latin poetry. The descent of Æneas and the Sybil to the infernal regions, to the world of spirits, expands an awful and boundless prospect, from the nocturnal gloom of the Cumæan grot,

> Ibant obscuri solâ sub nocte per umbram,

to the meridian brightness of the Elysian fields;

> Largior hic campos æther et lumine vestit
> Purpureo ——————

from the dreams of simple nature, to the dreams, alas! of Egyptian theology, and the philosophy of the Greeks.

But the final dismission of the hero through the ivory gate, whence

Falsa ad cœlum mittunt insomnia manes,

seems to dissolve the whole enchantment, and leaves the reader in a state of cold and anxious scepticism. This most lame and impotent conclusion has been variously imputed to the taste or irreligion of Virgil; but, according to the more elaborate interpretation of Bishop Warburton, the descent to hell is not a false but a mimic scene; which represents the initiation of Æneas in the character of a lawgiver, to the Eleusinian mysteries. This hypothesis, a singular chapter in the Divine Legation of Moses, had been admitted by many as true; it was praised by all as ingenius; nor had it been exposed, in a space of thirty years, to a fair and critical discussion. The learning and the abilities of the author had raised him to a just eminence; but he reigned the dictator and tyrant of the world of literature. The real merit of Warburton was degraded by the pride and presumption with which he pronounced his infallible decrees; in his polemic writings he lashed his antagonists without mercy or moderation; and his servile flatterers, (see the base and malignant Essay on the Delicacy of Friendship,) exalting the master critic far above Aristotle and Longinus, assaulted every modest dissenter who refused to consult the oracle, and adore the idol. In a land of liberty, such despotism must provoke a general opposition, and the zeal of opposition is seldom candid or impartial. A late professor of Oxford (Dr. Lowth), in a pointed and polished epistle, (August 31st, 1765,) defended himself, and attacked the bishop; and, whatsoever might be the merits of an insignificant controversy, his victory was clearly established by the silent confusion of Warburton and his slaves.   I, too, without any private offence, was ambitious of breaking a lance against the giant's shield; and in the beginning of the year 1770, my Critical Observations on the Sixth Book of the Æneid were sent, without my name, to the press.   In this short essay, my first English publication, I aimed my strokes against the person and the hypothesis of Bishop Warburton. I proved, at least to my own satisfaction, *that* the ancient lawgivers did not invent the mysteries, and *that* Æneas was never invested with the office of lawgiver; *that* there is not any argument, any circumstance, which can melt a fable into allegory, or remove the scene from the Lake Avernus to the Temple of Ceres: *that* such a wild supposition is equally injurious to the poet and the man; *that* if Virgil was not initiated he could not, if he were he would not, reveal the secrets of the initiation: *that* the anathema of Horace ("vetabo qui Cereris sacrum vulgarit," &c.) at once attests his own ignorance and the innocence of his friend. As the Bishop of Gloucester and his party maintained a discreet silence, my critical disquisition was soon lost among the pamphlets of the day; but the public coldness was over-balanced to my feelings by the weighty approbation of the last and best editor of Virgil, Professor Heyne, of Gottingen, who acquiesces in my confutation, and styles the unknown author, "doctus .... et elegantisimus Brittannus."   But I cannot resist the temptation of transcribing the favourable judgment of Mr. Hayley, himself a poet and a scholar : " An intricate hypothesis, twisted into a long and laboured chain of quotation and argument, the Dissertation on the Sixth Book of Virgil remained some time unrefuted. . . . . At length a superior, but anonymous, critic arose, who, in one of the most judicious and spirited essays that our nation has produced, on a point of classical literature, completely overturned this ill-founded edifice, and exposed the arrogance and futility of its assuming architect." He even condescends to justify an acrimony of style, which had been gently blamed by the more unbiassed German ; " Paullo acrius quam velis . . . . perstrinxit."* But I can never forgive myself the contemptuous treatment of a man who with all his faults, was entitled to my esteem ;† and I can less forgive, in a personal attack, the cowardly concealment of my name and character.

In the fifteen years between my Essay on the Study of Literature and the first volume of the Decline and Fall, (1761—1776,) this criticism on Warburton, and some articles in the journal, were my sole publications.

* The editor of the Warburtonian Tracts, Dr. Parr (p. 192), considers the allegorical interpretation " as completely refuted in a most clear, elegant, and decisive work of criticism ; which could not, indeed, derive authority from the greatest name ; but to which the greatest name might with propriety have been affixed."

† The Divine Legation of Moses is a monument already crumbling in the dust, of the vigour and weakness of the human mind. If Warburton's new argument proved anything, it would be a demonstration against the legislator who left his people without the knowledge of a future state. But some episodes of the work, on the Greek philosophy, the hieroglyphics of Egypt, &c. are entitled to the praise of learning, imagination and discernment.

It is more especially encumbent on me to mark the employment, or to confess the waste of time, from my travels to my father's death, an interval in which I was not diverted by any professional duties from the labours and pleasures of a studious life.   1. As soon as I was released from the fruitless task of the Swiss revolutions, (1768,) I began to advance gradually from the wish to the hope, from the hope to the design, from the design to the execution, of my historical work, of whose limits and extent I had yet a very inadequate notion. The classics, as low as Tacitus, the younger Pliny, and Juvenal, were my old and familiar companions.   I insensibly plunged into the ocean of the Augustan history; and in the descending series I investigated, with my pen almost always in my hand, the original records both Greek and Latin, from Dion Cassius to Ammianus Marcellinus, from the reign of Trajan to the last age of the Western Cæsars.   The subsidary rays of medals and inscriptions, of geography and chronology, were thrown on their proper objects; and I applied the collections of Tillemont whose inimitable accuracy almost assumes the character of genius, to fix and arrange within my reach the loose and scattered atoms of historical information. Through the darkness of the middle ages I explored my way in the Annals and Antiquities of Italy of the learned Muratori;   and diligently compared them with the parallel or transverse lines of Sigonius and Maffei, Baronius and Pagi, till I almost grasped the ruins of Rome in the fourteenth century, without suspecting that this final chapter must be attained by the labour of six quartos and twenty years.   Among the books which

I purchased, the Theodosian Code, with the commentary of James Godefroy, must be gratefully remembered. I used (and much I used it) as a work of history, rather than of jurisprudence: but in every light it may be considered as a full and capacious repository of the political state of the empire in the fourth and fifth centuries. As I believed, and as I still believe, that the propagation of the Gospel and the triumph of the church are inseparably connected with the decline of the Roman monarchy, I weighed the causes and effects of the revolution, and contrasted the narratives and apologies of the Christians themselves, with the glances of candour or enmity which the Pagans have cast on the rising sects. The Jewish and Heathen testimonies, as they are collected and illustrated by Dr. Lardner, directed, without superseding, my search of the originals ; and in an ample dissertation on the miraculous darkness of the passion, I privately drew my conclusions from the silence of an unbelieving age. I have assembled the preparatory studies, directly or indirectly, relative to my history ; but in strict equity, they must be spread beyond this period of my life, over the two summers (1771 and 1772) that elapsed between my father's death and my settlement in London. 2. In a free conversation with books and men, it would be endless to enumerate the names and characters of all who are introduced to our acquaintance: but in this general acquaintance we may select the degrees of friendship and esteem. According to the wise maxim, " Multum legere potius quam multa," I reviewed, again and again, the immortal works of the French and English, the Latin and Italian classics. My Greek studies (though less assiduous than I designed) maintained and extended my knowledge of that incomparable idiom. Homer and Xenophon were still my favourite authors; and I had almost prepared for the press an Essay on the Cyropœdia, which, in my own judgment, is not unhappily laboured.   After a certain age, the new publications of merit are the sole food of the many; and the most austere student will be often tempted to break the line, for the sake of indulging his own curiosity, and of providing the topics of fashionable currency.   A more respectable motive may be assigned for the third perusal of Blackstone's Commentaries, and a copious and critical abstract of that English work was my first serious production in my native language.   3. My literary leisure was much less complete and independent than it might appear to the eye of a stranger.   In the hurry of London I was destitute of books; in the solitude of Hampshire I was not master of my time.   My quiet was gradually disturbed by our domestic anxiety, and I should be ashamed of my unfeeling philosophy, had I found much time or taste for study in the last fatal summer (1770) of my father's decay and dissolution.

The disembodying of the militia at the close of the war (in 1763) had restored the Major (a new Cincinnatus) to a life of agriculture.   His labours were useful, his pleasures innocent, his wishes moderate; and my father *seemed* to enjoy the state of happiness which is celebrated by poets and philosophers, as the most agreeable to nature, and the least accessible to fortune.

Beatus ille, qui procul negotiis
(Ut prisca gens mortalium)
Paterna rura bubus exercet suis,
Solutus omni fœnore.*   *Hor. Epod.* ii.

But the last indispensable condition, the freedom from
debt, was wanting to my father's felicity; and the vani-
ties of his youth were severely punished by the solicitude and sorrow of his declining age. The first mortgage, on my return from Lausanne (1758), had afforded
him a partial and transient relief. The annual demand
of interest and allowance was a heavy deduction from
his income; the militia was a source of expense, the
farm in his hands was not a profitable adventure, he was
loaded with the costs and damages of an obsolete lawsuit; and each year multiplied the number and exhausted
the patience of his creditors. Under these painful circumstances I consented to an additional mortgage, to
the sale of Putney, and to every sacrifice that could
alleviate his distress. But he was no longer capable of
a rational effort, and his reluctant delays postponed
not the evils themselves, but the remedies of those
evils ("remedia malorum potius quam mala differebat").
The pangs of shame, tenderness, and self-reproach, incessantly preyed on his vitals; his constitution was
broken; he lost his strength and his sight; the rapid
progress of a dropsy admonished him of his end, and he
sunk into the grave on the 10th of November, 1770, in

* Like the first mortals blest is he,
From debts, and usury, and business free,
     With his own team who ploughs the soil,
Which grateful once confess'd his father's toil. *Francis.*

the sixty-fourth year of his age. A family tradition insinuates that Mr. William Law had drawn his pupil in the light and inconstant character of Flatus, who is ever confident and ever disappointed in the chase of happiness. But these constitutional failings were happily compensated by the virtues of the head and heart, by the warmest sentiments of honour and humanity. His graceful person, polite address, gentle manners, and unaffected cheerfulness, recommended him to the favour of every company; and in the change of times and opinions, his liberal spirit had long since delivered him from the zeal and prejudice of a Tory education. I submitted to the order of Nature; and my grief was soothed by the conscious satisfaction that I had discharged all the duties of filial piety.

CHAP. XX.

MR. GIBBON SETTLES IN LONDON.

As soon as I had paid the last solemn duties to my father, and obtained, from time and reason, a tolerable composure of mind, I began to form the plan of an independent life, most adapted to my circumstances and inclination. Yet so intricate was the net, my efforts were so awkward and feeble, that nearly two years (November, 1770—October, 1772) were suffered to elapse before I could disentangle myself from the management of the farm, and transfer my residence from Beriton to a house in London. During this interval I continued to divide my year between town and the country; but my new situation was brightened by hope; my stay in London was prolonged into the summer; and the uniformity of the summer was occasionally broken by visits and excursions at a distance from home. The gratification of my desires (they were not immoderate) has been seldom disappointed by the want of money or credit; my pride was never insulted by the visit of an importunate tradesman; and my transient anxiety for the past or future has been dispelled by the studious or social occupation of the present hour. My conscience does not accuse me of an act of extravagance or injustice, and the remnant of my estate affords an ample and honourable provision for my declining age. I shall not expatiate on my economical affairs, which cannot be instructive or amusing to the reader. It is a rule of prudence, as well as of politeness, to reserve such confidence for the ear of a private friend, without exposing our situation to the envy or pity of strangers; for envy is productive of hatred, and pity borders too nearly on contempt. Yet I may believe, and even assert, that in circumstances more indigent or more wealthy, I should never have accomplished the task, or acquired the fame, of an historian; that my spirit would have been broken by poverty and contempt, and that my industry might have been relaxed in the labour and luxury of a superfluous fortune.

I had now attained the first of earthly blessings, independence: I was the absolute master of my hours and actions: nor was I deceived in the hope that the establishment of my library in town would allow me to divide the day between study and society. Each year the circle of my acquaintance, the number of my dead and living companions, was enlarged. To a lover of books, the shops and sales of London present irresistible temptations; and the manufacture of my history required a various and growing stock of materials. The militia, my travels, the House of Commons, the fame of an author, contributed to multiply my connexions: I was chosen a member of the fashionable clubs; and, before I left England in 1783, there were few persons of any eminence in the literary or political world to whom I was a stranger.*

* From the mixed, though polite, company of Boodle's, White's, and Brookes's, I must honourably distinguish a weekly society which was instituted in the year 1764, and which still continues to flourish, under the

It would most assuredly be in my power to amuse the
reader with a gallery of portraits and a collection of
anecdotes. But I have always condemned the practice
of transforming a private memorial into a vehicle of satire or praise. By my own choice I passed in town the
greatest part of the year; but whenever I was desirous
of breathing the air of the country, I possessed an hospitable retreat at Sheffield-place in Sussex, in the family of
my valued friend Mr. Holroyd, whose character, under
the name of Lord Sheffield, has since been more conspicuous to the public.

No sooner was I settled in my house and library, than
I undertook the composition of the first volume of my
history. At the outset all was dark and doubtful; even
the title of the work, the true æra of the decline and fall
of the empire, the limits of the introduction, the division
of the chapters, and the order of the narrative: and I
was often tempted to cast away the labour of seven
years. The style of an author should be the image of
his mind, but the choice and command of language is the
fruit of exercise. Many experiments were made before
I could hit the middle tone between a dull chronicle and
a rhetorical declamation: three times did I compose the
first chapter, and twice the second and third, before I
was tolerably satisfied with their effect. In the remain-

title of the Literary Club. (Hawkins's Life of Johnson, p. 415. Bos-
well's Tour to the Hebrides, p. 97.) The names of Dr. Johnson, Mr.
Burke, Mr. Tophan Beauclerc, Mr. Garrick, Dr. Goldsmith, Sir Joshua
Reynolds, Mr. Colman, Sir William Jones, Dr. Percy, Mr. Fox, Mr. Sheri-
dan, Mr. Adam Smith, Mr. Steevens, Mr. Dunning, Sir Joseph Banks, Dr.
Wharton, and his brother, Mr. Thomas Wharton, Dr. Burney, &c., form
a large and luminous constellation of British stars.

der of the way I advanced with a more equal and easy pace; but the fifteenth and sixteenth chapters have been reduced, by three successive revisals, from a large volume to their present size; and they might still be compressed, without any loss of facts or sentiments. An opposite fault may be imputed to the concise and superficial narrative of the first reigns from Commodus to Alexander; a fault of which I have never heard, except from Mr. Hume in his last journey to London. Such an oracle might have been consulted and obeyed with rational devotion; but I was soon disgusted with the modest practice of reading the manuscript to my friends. Of such friends some will praise from politeness, and some will criticise from vanity. The author himself is the best judge of his own performance; no one has so deeply meditated on the subject; no one is so sincerely interested in the event.

By the friendship of Mr. (now Lord) Eliot, who had married my first cousin, I was returned at the general election for the borough of Liskeard. I took my seat at the beginning of the memorable contest between Great Britain and America, and supported with many a sincere and silent vote, the rights, though not, perhaps, the interest, of the mother country. After a fleeting illusive hope, prudence condemned me to acquiesce in the humble station of a mute. I was not armed by nature and education with the intrepid energy of mind and voice.

Vincentem strepitus, et natum rebus agendis.

Timidity was fortified by pride, and even the success of

my pen discouraged the trial of my voice.* But I assisted at the debates of a free assembly; I listened to the attack and defence of eloquence and reason; I had a near prospect of the characters, views, and passions of the first men of the age. The cause of government was ably vindicated by Lord North, a statesman of spotless integrity, a consummate master of debate, who could wield, with equal dexterity, the arms of reason and of ridicule. He was seated on the treasury bench, between his attorney and solicitor general, the two pillars of the law and state, "magis pares quam similes;" and the minister might indulge in a short slumber, whilst he was upholden on either hand by the majestic sense of Thurlow, and the skilful eloquence of Wedderburne. From the adverse side of the house an ardent and powerful opposition was supported, by the lively declamation of Barré, the legal acuteness of Dunning, the profuse and philosophic fancy of Burke, and the argumentative vehemence of Fox, who in the conduct of a party approved himself equal to the conduct of an empire. By such men every operation of peace and war, every principle of

* A French sketch of Mr. Gibbon's Life, written by himself, probably for the use of some foreign journalist or translator, contains no fact not mentioned in his English Life. He there describes himself with his usual candour. For the last eight years he has assisted at the most important deliberations, but he never found in himself either courage or talent sufficient to speak in a public assembly. This sketch was written before the publication of his three last volumes, as in closing it he says of his history—this enterprise still requires from him several years of continued application; but whatever may be its success, he finds in this very application a pleasure ever varied and ever new.

justice or policy, every question of authority and freedom, was attacked and defended ; and the subject of the momentous contest was the union or separation of Great Britain and America. The eight sessions that I sat in parliament were a school of civil prudence, the first and most essential virtue of an historian.

The volume of my history, which had been somewhat delayed by the novelty and tumult of a first session, was now ready for the press. After the perilous adventure had been declined by my friend Mr. Elmsly, I agreed, upon easy terms, with Mr. Thomas Cadell, a respectable bookseller, and Mr. William Strahan an eminent printer ; and they undertook the care and risk of the publication, which derived more credit from the name of the - shop than from that of the author. The last revisal of the proofs was submitted to my vigilance ; and many blemishes of style, which had been invisible in the manuscript, were discovered and corrected in the printed sheet. So moderate were our hopes, that the original impression had been stinted to five hundred, till the number was doubled by the prophetic taste of Mr. Strahan. During this awful interval I was neither elated by the ambition of fame, nor depressed by the apprehension of contempt. My diligence and accuracy were attested by my own conscience. History is the most popular species of writing, since it can adapt itself to the highest or the lowest capacity. I had chosen an illustrious subject. Rome is familiar to the school-boy and the statesman ; and my narrative was deduced from the last period of classical reading. I had likewise flattered myself, that an age of light and liberty would receive, without scandal, an inquiry into the human *causes* of the progress and establishment of Christianity.

I am at a loss how to describe the success of the work without betraying the vanity of the writer. The first impression was exhausted in a few days; a second and third edition were scarcely adequate to the demand; and the bookseller's property was twice invaded by the pirates of Dublin. My book was on every table, and almost on every toilette; the historian was crowned by the taste or fashion of the day; nor was the general voice disturbed by the barking of any *profane* critic. The favour of mankind is most freely bestowed on a new acquaintance of any original merit; and the mutual surprise of the public and their favourite is productive of those warm sensibilities, which at a second meeting can no longer be rekindled. If I listened to the music of praise, I was more seriously satisfied with the approba-tion of my judges. The candour of Dr. Robertson em-braced his disciple. A letter from Mr. Hume overpaid the labour of ten years; but I have never presumed to accept a place in the triumverate of British historians.

That curious and original letter will amuse the reader, and his gratitude should shield my free communication from the reproach of vanity.

"*Edinburgh*, 18*th March* 1776.

"Dear Sir,—As I ran through your volume of history with great avidity and impatience, I cannot forbear dis-covering somewhat of the same impatience in returning you thanks for your agreeable present, and expressing the satisfaction which the performance has given me. Whether I consider the dignity of your style, the depth of your matter, or the extensiveness of your learning, I must regard the work as equally the object of esteem; and I own that if I had not previously had the happiness of your personal acquaintance, such a performance from an Englishman in our age would have given me some surprise. You may smile at this sentiment; but as it seems to me that your countrymen, for almost a whole generation, have given themselves up to barbarous and absurd faction, and have totally neglected all polite letters, I no longer expected any valuable production ever to come from them. I know it will give you pleasure, as it did me, to find that all the men of letters in this place concur in their admiration of your work, and in their anxious desire of your continuing it.

"When I heard of your undertaking, which was some time ago, I own I was a little curious to see how you would extricate yourself from the subject of your two last chapters. I think you have observed a very prudent temperament; but it was impossible to treat the subject so as not to give grounds of suspicion against you, and you may expect that a clamour will arise. This, if any thing, will retard your success with the public; for in every other respect your work is calculated to be popular. But among many other marks of decline, the prevalence of superstition in England prognosticates the fall of philosophy and decay of taste; and though nobody be more capable than you to revive them, you will probably find a struggle in your first advances.

"I see you entertain a great doubt with regard to the

authenticity of the poems of Ossian. You are certainly right in so doing. It is indeed strange that any men of sense could have imagined it possible, that above twenty thousand verses, along with numberless historical facts, could have been preserved by oral tradition during fifty generations, by the rudest, perhaps, of all the European nations, the most necessitous, the most turbulent, and the most unsettled. Where a supposition is so contrary to common sense, any positive evidence of it ought never to be regarded. Men run with great avidity to give their evidence in favour of what flatters their passions and their national prejudices. You are therefore over and above indulgent to us in speaking of the matter with hesitation.

"I must inform you that we are all very anxious to hear that you have fully collected the materials for your second volume, and that you are even considerably advanced in the composition of it. I speak this more in the name of my friends than in my own; as I cannot expect to live so long as to see the publication of it. Your ensuing volume will be more delicate than the preceding, but I trust in your prudence for extricating you from the difficulties; and at all events, you have courage to despise the clamour of bigots. I am, with great regard, dear sir, your most obedient, and most humble servant,

"DAVID HUME."

Some weeks afterwards I had the melancholy pleasure of seeing Mr. Hume in his passage through London; his body feeble, his mind firm. On the 25th of August of the same year, 1776, he died at Edinburgh the death of a philosopher.

My second excursion to Paris was determined by the
pressing invitation of M. and Madame Necker, who had
visited England in the preceding summer.   On my arrival I found M. Necker director-general of the finances, in
the first bloom of power and popularity.   His private
fortune enabled him to support a liberal establishment;
and his wife, whose talents and virtues I had long
admired, was admirably qualified to preside in the conversation of her table and drawing-room.   As their
friend, I was introduced to the best company of both
sexes; to the foreign ministers of all nations, and to the
first names and characters of France; who distinguished
me by such marks of civility and kindness, as gratitude will
not suffer me to forget, and modesty will not allow me
to enumerate.   The fashionable suppers often broke into
the morning hours; yet I occasionally consulted the
royal library, and that of the abbey of St. Germain, and
in the free use of their books at home, I had always
reason to praise the liberality of those institutions.   The
society of men of letters I neither courted nor declined;
but I was happy in the acquaintance of M. de Buffon,
who united with a sublime genius the most amiable simplicity of mind and manners.   At the table of my old
friend, M. de Foncemagne, I was involved in a dispute
with the Abbé de Mably; and his jealous, irascible spirit
revenged itself on a work which he was incapable of
reading in the original.

As I might be partial in my own cause, I shall transcribe the words of an unknown critic, observing only,
that this dispute had been preceded by another on the
English constitution, at the house of the Countess de
Froulay, and old Jansenist lady.

"You were, my dear Theodon, at M. de Foncemagne's
house when the Abbé Mably and Mr. Gibbon dined there
with a number of guests. The conversation ran almost
entirely upon history. The Abbé, being a profound politician, turned it, while at the dessert, upon the administration of affairs; and as by genius, temper, and a habit
of admiring Livy, he values only the republican system,
he began to boast of the excellence of republics; being
well persuaded that the learned Englishman would
approve of all he said, and admire the profundity of
genius that had enabled a Frenchman to discover all
these advantages. But Mr. Gibbon, knowing by experience the inconveniences of a popular government, was
not at all of his opinion, and generously took up the
defence of monarchy. The Abbé wished to convince
him out of Livy, and by some arguments drawn from
Plutarch in favour of the Spartans. Mr. Gibbon, being
endowed with a most excellent memory, and having all
events present to his mind, soon got the command of the
conversation. The Abbé grew angry, they lost possession of themselves, and said hard things of each other;
the Englishman, retaining his native coolness, watched
for his advantages, and pressed the Abbé with increasing
success, in proportion as he was more disturbed by passion. The conversation grew warmer, and was broken
off by M. de Foncemagne's rising from table and passing
into the parlour, where no one was tempted to renew it."
—Supplément de la Manière d'ecrire l'Histoire, page
125, &c.*

* Of the voluminous writings of the Abbé de Mably, (see his Eloge by
the Abbé-Brizard,) the Principes du Droit public de l'Europe, and the
first part of the Observations sur l'Histoire de France, may be deservedly

Nearly two years had elapsed between the publication of my first and the commencement of my second volume: and the causes must be assigned of this long delay. 1. After a short holiday, I indulged my curiosity in some studies of a very different nature, a course of anatomy, which was demonstrated by Dr. Hunter; and some lessons of chymistry, which were delivered by Mr. Higgins. The principles of these sciences, and a taste for books of natural history, contributed to multiply my ideas and images; and the anatomist and chymist may sometimes track me in their own snow. 2. I dived, perhaps too deeply, into the mud of the Arian controversy; and many days of reading, thinking, and writing were consumed in the pursuit of a phantom. 3. It is difficult to arrange, with order and perspecuity, the various transactions of the age of Constantine; and so much was I displeased with the first essay, that I committed to the flames about fifty sheets. 4. The six months of Paris and pleasure must be deducted from the account. But

praised; and even the Manière d'ecrire l'Histoire contains several useful precepts and judicious remarks. Mably was a lover of virtue and freedom; but his virtue was austere, and his freedom was impatient of an equal. Kings, magistrates, nobles, and successful writers, were the objects of his contempt, or hatred, or envy; but his illiberal abuse of Voltaire, Hume Buffon, the Abbé Raynal, Dr Robertson, and *tutti quanti*, can be injurious only to himself.

" Is anything more tedious," says the polite censor, " than a Mr Gibbon, who, in his never ending history of the Roman Emperors, interrupts every instant his slow and insipid narration to explain to you the causes of events that you are going to read." (Manière d'ecrire l'Histoire, p. 184. See another passage, p. 280.) Yet I am indebted to the Abbé de Mably for two such advocates as the anonymous French critic and my friend Mr. Hayley. (Hayley's Works, 8vo. edit. vol. ii. p. 261—263.)

when I resumed my task I felt my improvement; I was now master of my style and subject, and while the measure of my daily performance was enlarged, I discovered less reason to cancel or correct. It has always been my practice to cast a long paragraph in a single mould, to try it by my ear, to deposit it in my memory, but to suspend the action of the pen till I had given the last polish to my work. Shall I add, that I never found my mind more vigorous, nor my composition more happy, than in the winter hurry of society and parliament?

Had I believed that the majority of English readers were so fondly attached even to the name and shadow of Christianity; had I foreseen that the pious, the timid, and the prudent, would feel, or affect to feel, with such exquisite sensibility; I might, perhaps, have softened the two invidious chapters, which would create many enemies, and conciliate few friends. But the shaft was shot, the alarm was sounded, and I could only rejoice, that if the voice of our priests was clamorous and bitter, their hands were disarmed from the power of persecution. I adhered to the wise resolution of trusting myself and my writings to the candour of the public, till Mr. Davis of Oxford presumed to attack, not the faith, but the fidelity of the historian. My Vindication, expressive of less anger than contempt, amused for a moment the busy and idle metropolis; and the most rational part of the laity, and even of the clergy, appear to have been satisfied of my innocence and accuracy. I would not print this Vindication in quarto, lest it should be bound and preserved with the history itself. At the distance of twelve years, I calmly affirm my judgment of Davis, Chelsum, &c. A

victory over such antagonists was a sufficient humilia-
tion. They, however, were rewarded in this world.
Poor Chelsum was indeed neglected; and I dare not
boast the making Dr. Watson a bishop; he is a prelate
of a large mind and liberal spirit:* but I enjoyed the
pleasure of giving a Royal pension to Mr. Davis, and of
collating Dr. Apthorpe to an archi-episcopal living. Their
success encouraged the zeal of Taylor the Arian,† and
Milner the Methodist,‡ with many others, whom it would
be difficult to remember, and tedious to rehearse. The
list of my adversaries, however, was graced with the
more respectable names of Dr. Priestly, Sir David Dalrymple, and Dr. White; and every polemic, of either
university, discharged his sermon or pamphlet against the
impenetrable silence of the Roman historian. In his History of the Corruptions of Christianity, Dr. Priestly threw
down his two gauntlets to Bishop Hurd and Mr. Gibbon.
I declined the challenge in a letter, exhorting my oppo-
nent to enlighten the world by his philosophical discoveries, and to remember that the merit of his predecessor Servetus is now reduced to a single passage, which

* See Letters, No. LXXXIII. LXXXVIII. and CXIV.

† The stupendous title, Thoughts on the Causes of the grand Apostacy,
at first agitated my nerves, till I discovered that it was the apostacy of the
whole church, since the Council of Nice, from Mr. Taylor's private religion.
His book is a thorough mixture of *high* enthusiasm and *low* buffoonery, and
the Millenium is a fundamental article of his creed.

‡ From his grammar-school at Kingston-upon-Hull, Mr. Joseph Milner
pronounces an anathema against all rational religion. *His* faith is a divine
taste, a spiritual inspiration; *his* church is a mystic and invisible body: the
natural Christians, such as Mr. Locke, who believe and interpret the
Scriptures, are, in his judgment, no better than profane infidels.

indicates the smaller circulation of the blood through the lungs, from and to the heart.* Instead of listening to this friendly advice, the dauntless philosopher of Birmingham continued to fire away his double battery against those who believed too little, and those who believed too much. *From my* replies he has nothing to hope or fear: but his Socinian shield has repeatedly been pierced by the spear of Horsley, and his trumpet of sedition may at length awaken the magistrates of a free country.

The profession and rank of Sir David Dalrymple (now a Lord of Session) has given a more decent colour to his style. But he scrutinized each separate passage of the two chapters with the dry minuteness of a special pleader; and as he was always solicitous to make, he may have succeeded sometimes in finding a flaw. In his Annals of Scotland, he has shown himself a diligent collector and an accurate critic.

I have praised, and I still praise, the eloquent sermons which were preached in St. Mary's pulpit at Oxford by Dr. White. If he assaulted me with some degree of illiberal acrimony, in such a place, and before such an audience, he was obliged to speak the language of the country. I smiled at a passage in one of his private letters to Mr. Badcock: "The part where we encounter Gibbon must be brilliant and striking."

In a sermon preached before the University of Cambridge, Dr. Edwards complimented a work, "which can only perish with the language itself;" and esteems the author a formidable enemy. He is, indeed, astonished that more learning and ingenuity has not been shown in

* Astruc, de la Structure du Cœur, tom. i. 77, 79, Letter CXLIV.

the defence of Israel; that the prelates and dignitaries of the church (alas, good man!) did not vie with each other whose stone should sink the deepest in the forehead of this Goliah.

"But the force of truth will oblige us to confess, that in the attacks which have been levelled against our scep- tical historian, we can discover but slender traces of profound and exquisite erudition, of solid criticism and accurate investigation; but we are too frequently dis- gusted by vague and inconclusive reasoning; by unsea- sonable banter and senseless witticisms; by embittered bigotry and enthusiastic jargon; by futile cavils and illiberal invectives. Proud and elated by the weakness of his antagonists, he condescends not to handle the sword of controversy."*

Let me frankly own that I was startled at the first dis- charge of ecclesiastical ordinance; but as soon as I found that this empty noise was mischievous only in the inten- tion, my fear was converted into indignation; and every feeling of indignation or curiosity has long since subsided in pure and placid indifference.

* Monthly Review, Oct. 1790.

CHAP. XXI.

MR. GIBBON ENGAGES IN POLITICS.

THE prosecution of my history was soon afterwards checked by another controversy of a very different kind. At the request of the Lord Chancellor, and of Lord Weymouth, then secretary of state, I vindicated, against the French manifesto, the justice of the British arms. The whole correspondence of Lord Stormont, our late ambassador at Paris, was submitted to my inspection, and the Mémoire Justificatif, which I composed in French, was first approved by the cabinet ministers, and then delivered as a state paper to the courts of Europe. The style and manner are praised by Beumarchais himself, who, in his private quarrel, attempted a reply; but he flatters me, by ascribing the memoir to Lord Stormont; and the grossness of his invective betrays the loss of temper and of wit; he acknowledged,* that "the style would not be ungraceful, nor the reasoning unjust," &c., if the facts were true which he undertakes to disprove. For these facts my credit is not pledged; I spoke as a

* Œuvres de Beaumarchais, tom. iii. p. 299, 355.

lawyer from my brief. But the veracity of Beaumarchais may be estimated from the assertion that France,
by the treaty of Paris (1763), was limited to a certain
number of ships of war. On the application of the
Duke of Choiseul, he was obliged to retract this daring
falsehood.

Among the honourable connexions which I had formed,
I may justly be proud of the friendship of Mr. Wedderburne, at that time attorney-general, who now illustrates
the title of Lord Loughborough, and the office of Chief
Justice of the Common Pleas. By his strong recommendation, and the favourable disposition of Lord North,
I was appointed one of the lords commissioners of trade
and plantations; and my private income was enlarged by
a clear addition of between seven and eight hundred
pounds a year. The fancy of an hostile orator may paint,
in the strong colours of ridicule, "the perpetual virtual
adjournment, and the unbroken sitting vacation of the
board of trade."* But it must be allowed that our duty
was not intolerably severe, and that I enjoyed many
days and weeks of repose, without being called away
from the library to the office. My acceptance of a place
provoked some of the leaders of opposition, with whom I
had lived in habits of intimacy; and I was most unjustly

---

* I can never forget the delight with which that diffusive and ingenious
orator, Mr. Burke, was heard by all sides of the house, and even by those
whose existence he proscribed. (See Mr. Burke's speech on the Bill of
Reform, p. 72—80.) The lords of trade blushed at their insignificancy,
and Mr. Eden's appeal to the 2500 volumes of our Reports, served only to
excite a general laugh. I take this opportunity of certifying the correctness of Mr. Burke's printed speeches, which I have heard and read.

accused of deserting a party, in which I had never en-
listed.*

* *From Edward Gibbon, Esq. to —— Esq.*

" 2nd July, 1779.

" Dear Sir,—Yesterday I received a very interesting communication
from my friend, the attorney-general, whose kind and honourable behaviour
towards me I must always remember with the highest gratitude.　He informed me that, in consequence of an arrangement, a place at the board of
trade was reserved for me, and that as soon as I signified my acceptance
of it, he was satisfied no farther difficulties would arise.　My answer to him
was sincere and explicit.　I told him that I was far from approving all the
past measures of the administration, even some of those in which I myself
had silently concurred: that I saw, with the rest of the world, many
capital defects in the characters of some of the present ministers, and was
sorry that in so alarming a situation of public affairs, the country had not
the assistance of several able and honest men who are now in opposition.
But that I had not formed with any of those persons in opposition any
engagements or connexions which could in the least restrain or affect my
parliamentary conduct; that I could not discover among them such superior advantages, either of measures or of abilities, as could make me consider it as a duty to attach myself to their cause; and that I clearly understood, from the public and private language of ——, one of their
leaders, that in the actual state of the country, he himself was seriously of
opinion that opposition could not tend to any good purpose, and might be
productive of much mischief; that, for those reasons, I saw no objections
which could prevent me from accepting an office under the present
government, and that I was ready to take a step which I found to be consistent both with my interest and my honour.

" It must now be decided, whether I may continue to live in England,
or whether I must soon withdraw myself into a kind of philosophical exile
in Switzerland.　My father left his affairs in a state of embarrassment, and
even of distress.　My attempts to dispose of a part of my landed property
have hitherto been disappointed, and are not likely at present to be more
successful; and my plan of expense, though moderate in itself, deserves
the name of extravagance, since it exceeds my real income.　The addition
of the salary which is now offered will make my situation perfectly easy;
but I hope you will do me the justice to believe that my mind could not
be so, unless I were satisfied of the rectitude of my own conduct."

The aspect of the next session of parliament was stormy and perilous; county meetings, petitions, and committes of correspondence, announced the public discontent; and instead of voting with a triumphant majority, the friends of government were often exposed to a struggle, and sometimes to a defeat. The House of Commons adopted Mr. Dunning's motion, "That the influence of the Crown had increased, was increasing, and ought to be diminished:" and Mr. Burke's bill of reform was framed with skill, introduced with eloquence, and supported by numbers. Our late president, the American secretary of state, very narrowly escaped the sentence of proscription; but the unfortunate board of trade was abolished in the committee by a small majority (207 to 199) of eight votes. The storm, however, blew over for a time; a large defection of country gentlemen eluded the sanguine hopes of the patriots: the lords of trade were revived; adminstration recovered their strength and spirit; and the flames of London, which were kindled by a mischievous madman, admonished all thinking men of the danger of an appeal to the people. In the premature dissolution which followed this session of parliament, I lost my seat. Mr. Eliot was now deeply engaged in the measures of opposition, and the electors of Liskeard* are commonly of the same opinion as Mr. Eliot.

In this interval of my senatorial life, I published the second and third volumes of the Decline and Fall. My ecclesiastical history still breathed the same spirit of free-

* The borough which Mr. Gibbon had represented in Parliament.

dom; but protestant zeal is more indifferent to the characters and controversies of the fourth and fifth centuries. My obstinate silence had damped the ardour of the polemics. Dr. Watson, the most candid of my adversaries, assured me that he had no thoughts of renewing the attack, and my impartial balance of the virtues and vices of Julian was generally praised. This truce was interrupted only by some animadversions of the Catholics of Italy, and by some angry letters of Mr. Travis, who made me personally responsible for condemning, with the best critics, the spurious text of the three heavenly witnesses.

The piety or prudence of my Italian translator has provided an antidote against the poison of his original. The 5th and 7th volumes are armed with five letters from an anonymous divine to his friends, Foothead and Kirk, two English students at Rome; and this meritorious service is commended by Monsignor Stonor, a prelate of the same nation, who discovers much venom in the *fluid* and nervous style of Gibbon. The critical essay at the end of the third volume was furnished by the Abbate Nicola Spedalieri, whose zeal has gradually swelled to a more solid confutation in two quarto volumes.—Shall I be excused for not having read them?

The brutal insolence of Mr. Travis's challenge can only be excused by the absence of learning, judgment, and humanity; and to that excuse he has the fairest or foulest pretension. Compared with Archdeacon Travis, Chelsum and Davis assumes the title of respectable enemies.

The bigoted advocate of popes and monks may be turned over even to the bigots of Oxford; and the

wretched Travis still smarts under the lash of the merciless
Porson. I consider Mr. Porson's answer to Archdeacon
Travis as the most acute and accurate piece of criticism
which has appeared since the days of Bentley. His
strictures are founded in argument, enriched with learning, and enlivened with wit; and his adversary neither
deserves nor finds any quarter at his hands. The evidence of the three heavenly witnesses would now be rejected in any court of justice: but prejudice is blind,
authority is deaf, and our vulgar bibles will ever be polluted by this spurious text, "sedet æternumque sedebit."
The more learned ecclesiastics will indeed have the
secret satisfaction of reprobating in the closet what they
read in the church.

I perceived, and without surprise, the coldness and
even prejudice of the town; nor could a whisper escape
my ear, that, in the judgment of many readers, my continuation was much inferior to the original attempts. An
author who cannot ascend will always appear to sink:
envy was now prepared for my reception, and the zeal of
my religious, was fortified by the motive of my political
enemies. Bishop Newton, in writing his own life, was
at full liberty to declare how much he himself and two
eminent brethren were disgusted by Mr. G.'s prolixity,
tediousness, and affectation. But the old man should not
have indulged his zeal in a false and feeble charge
against the historian,* who had faithfully and even cau-

* *Extract from Mr. Gibbon's Common-place Book.*

Thomas Newton, Bishop of Bristol and Dean of St. Paul's, was born at
Litchfield on the 21st of December, 1703, O. S. (1st January, 1704, N. S.),
and died the 14th of February, 1782, in the 79th year of his age. A few

tiously rendered Dr. Burnet's meaning by the alternative
of sleep or repose.   That philosophic divine supposes,

days before his death he finished the memoirs of his own life, which have
been prefixed to an edition of his posthumous works, first published in
quarto, and since (1787) republished in six volumes octavo.

P. 173, 174. Some books were published in 1781, which employed
some of the Bishop's leisure hours, and during his illness. Mr. Gibbon's
History of the Decline and Fall of the Roman Empire he read throughout,
but it by no means answered his expectation ; for he found it rather a prolix
and tedious performance, his matter uninteresting, and his style affected; his
testimonials not to be depended upon, and his frequent scoffs at religion
offensive to every sober mind. He had before been convicted of making
false quotations, which should have taught him more prudence and cau-
tion. But, without examining his authorities, there is one which must
necessarily strike every man who has read Dr. Burnet's Treatise de Statû
Mortuorum. In vol. iii. p. 99, Mr. G. has the following note,—"Burnet
(de S. M. p. 56—84) collects the opinions of the Fathers, as far as they
assert the sleep or repose of human souls till the day of judgment. He
afterwards exposes (p. 91) the inconveniences which must arise if they
possessed a more active and sensible existence. Who would not from
hence infer that Dr. B. was an advocate for the sleep or insensible existence of
the soul after death ! whereas his doctrine is directly the contrary. He
has employed some chapters in treating of the state of human souls in the
interval between death and the resurrection; and after various proofs from
reason, from Scripture, and the Fathers, his conclusions are, that human
souls exist after their separation from the body, that they are in a good or
evil state according to their good or evil behaviour, but that neither their
happiness nor their misery will be complete or perfect before the day of
judgment. His argumentation is thus summed up at the end of the 4th
chapter—"Ex quibus constat primo, animas superesse extincto corpore ;
secundo, bonas bene, malas male se habituras ; tertio, nec illis summam
felicitatem, nec his summam miseriam, accessuram esseante diem judicii.' "
(The Bishop's reading the whole was a greater compliment to the work
than was paid to it by two of the most eminent of his brethren for their
learning and station. The one entered upon it, but was soon wearied and
laid it aside in disgust : the other returned it upon the bookseller's hands

that, in the period between death and the resurrection, human souls exist without a body, endowed with internal consciousness, but destitute of all active or passive con-nexion with the external world. " Secundum communem dictionem sacræ scripturæ, mors dicitur somnus, et mori-entes dicuntur *abdormire,* quod innuere mihi vidętur statum mortis esse statum quietis, silentii, et αϵργαϭϵας." (De Statû Mortuorum, ch. v. p. 98.)

and it is said that Mr. G. himself happened unluckily to be in the shop at the same time.)

Does the Bishop comply with his own precept in the next page ! (p. 175.) " Old age should lenify, should soften men's manners, and make them more mild and gentle; but often has the contrary effect, hardens their hearts, and makes them more sour and crabbed."—He is speaking of Dr. Johnson.

Have I ever insinuated that preferment-hunting is the great occupation of an ecclesiastical life! (Memoirs passim) that a minister's influence and a bishop's patronage are sometimes pledged eleven deep! (p. 151) that a prebendary considers the audit-week as the better part of the year! (p. 127) or that the most eminent of priests, the pope himself, would change their religion if anything better could be offered them! (p. 56). Such things are more than insinuated in the Bishop's Life, which afforded some scandal to the church, and some diversion to the profane laity.

CHAP. XXII.

THE AUTHOR PROCEEDS WITH HIS HISTORY.

I was however encouraged by some domestic and foreign testimonies of applause; and the second and third volumes insensibly rose in sale and reputation to a level with the first. But the public is seldom wrong; and I am inclined to believe that, especially in the beginning, they are more prolix, and less entertaining than the first: my efforts had not been relaxed by success, and I had rather deviated into the opposite fault of minute and superfluous diligence. On the Continent, my name and writings were slowly diffused: a French translation of the first volume had disappointed the booksellers of Paris; and a passage in the third was construed as a personal reflection on the reigning monarch.*

Before I could apply for a seat at the general election the list was already full; but Lord North's promise was sincere, his recommendation was effectual, and I was

---

* It may not be generally known that Louis the Sixteenth is a great reader, and a reader of English books. On perusing a passage of my History which seems to compare him to Arcadius or Honorius, he expressed his resentment to the Prince of B***** from whom the intelligence was conveyed to me. I shall neither disclaim the allusion, nor examine the likeness: but the situation of the late King of France excludes all suspicion of flattery ; and I am ready to declare that the concluding observations of my third volume were written before his accession to the throne.

soon chosen on a vacancy for the borough of Lymington,
in Hampshire. In the first session of the new parliament,
administration stood their ground; their final overthrow
was reserved for the second. The American war had
once been the favourite of the country: the pride of
England was irritated by the resistance of her colonies,
and the executive power was driven by national clamour
into the most vigorous and coercive measures. But the
length of a fruitless contest, the loss of armies, the accumulation of debt and taxes, and the hostile confederacy
of France, Spain, and Holland, indisposed the public to
the American war, and the persons by whom it was conducted; the representatives of the people, followed at a
slow distance, the changes of their opinion; and the
ministers who refused to bend, were broken by the tempest. As soon as Lord North had lost or was about to
lose, a majority in the House of Commons, he surren-
dered his office, and retired to a private station, with the
tranquil assurance of a clear conscience and a cheerful
temper: the old fabric was dissolved, and the posts of
government were occupied by the victorious and veteran
troops of opposition. The lords of trade were not immediately dismissed, but the board itself was abolished
by Mr. Burke's bill, which decency had compelled the
patriots to revive; and I was stripped of a convenient
salary, after having enjoyed it about three years.

So flexible is the title of my history, that the final æra
might be fixed at my own choice; and I long hesitated
whether I should be content with the three volumes, the
Fall of the Western Empire, which fulfilled my first engagement with the public. In this interval of suspense,

nearly a twelvemonth, I returned, by a natural impulse, to the Greek authors of antiquity: I read with new pleasure the Iliad and the Odyssey, the histories of Herodotus, Thucydides, and Xenophon, a large portion of the tragic and comic theatre of Athens, and many interesting dialogues of the Socratic school. Yet in the luxury of freedom I began to wish for the daily task, the active pursuit, which gave a value to every book, and an object to every inquiry: the preface of a new edition announced my design, and I dropped without reluctance from the age of Plato to that of Justinian. The original texts of Procopius and Agathias supplied the events and even the characters of his reign: but a laborious winter was devoted to the Codes, the Pandects, and the modern interpreters, before I presumed to form an abstract of the civil law. My skill was improved by practice, my diligence, perhaps, was quickened by the loss of office; and. excepting the last chapter, I had finished the fourth volume before I sought a retreat on the banks of the Leman Lake.

It is not the purpose of this narrative to expatiate on the public or secret history of the times: the schism which followed the death of the Marquis of Rockingham, the appointment of the Earl of Shelburne, the resignation of Mr. Fox, and his famous coalition with Lord North. But I may assert, with some degree of assurance, that in their political conflict those great antagonists had never felt any personal animosity to each other, that their reconciliation was easy and sincere, and that their friendship has never been clouded by the shadow of suspicion or jealousy. The most violent or venal of their respective followers embraced this fair occasion of revolt, but their alliance still commanded a majority in the House of Commons; the peace was censured, Lord Shelburne resigned, and the two friends knelt on the same cushion to take the oath of secretary of state. From a principle of gratitude I adhered to the coalition: my vote was counted in the day of battle, but I was overlooked in the division of the spoil. There were many claimants more deserving and importunate than myself; the board of trade could not be restored; and while the list of places was curtailed, the number of candidates was doubled. An easy dismission to a secure seat at the board of customs or excise was promised on the first vacancy; but the chance was distant and doubtful; nor could I solicit with much ardour an ignoble servitude, which would have robbed me of the most valuable of my studious hours: at the same time the tumult of London, and the attendance on Parliament, were grown more irksome; and, without some additional income, I could not long or prudently maintain the style of expense to which I was accustomed.

From my early acquaintance with Lausanne I had always cherished a secret wish, that the school of my youth might become the retreat of my declining age. A moderate fortune would secure the blessings of ease, leisure, and independence: the country, the people, the manners, tne language, were congenial to my taste; and I might indulge the hope of passing a few years in the domestic society of a friend. After travelling with several English,* Mr. Deyverdun was now settled at

* Sir Richard Worsley, Lord Chesterfield, Broderick Lord Middleton, and Mr. Hume, brother to Sir Abraham.

home, in a pleasant habitation, the gift of his deceased
aunt: we had long been separated, we had long been
silent; yet in my first letter I exposed, with the
most perfect confidence, my situation, my sentiments, and
my designs. His immediate answer was a warm and
joyful acceptance: the picture of our future life provoked
my impatience; and the terms of arrangement were
short and simple, as he possessed the property, and I
undertook the expense of our common house.* Before
I could break my English chain, it was incumbent on me
to struggle with the feelings of my heart, the indolence of
my temper, and the opinion of the world, which unanimously condemned this voluntary banishment. In the
disposal of my effects, the library, a secret deposit, was
alone excepted: as my postchaise moved over West-
minister-bridge I bid a long farewell to the "fumum et
opes strepitumque Romœ." My journey by the direct
road through France was not attended with any accident, and I arrived at Lausanne nearly twenty years
after my second departure. Within less than three
months the coalition struck on some hidden rocks; had I
remained on board, I should have perished in the general
shipwreck.†

Since my establishment at Lausanne, more than seven
years have elapsed: and if every day has not been
equally soft and serene, not a day, not a moment, has
occurred in which I have repented of my choice. During
my absence, a long portion of human life, many changes
had happened: my elder acquaintance had left the stage;
virgins were ripened into matrons, and children were

* See Letters, No. CL, CLI, CLII, CLIII, CLIV, CLVI, CLIX.
† See Letter No. CLXXVI.

grown to the age of manhood. But the same manners were transmitted from one generation to another: my friend alone was an inestimable treasure; my name was not totally forgotten, and all were ambitious to welcome the arrival of a stranger and the return of a fellow-citizen. The first winter was given to a general embrace, without any nice discrimination of persons and characters. After a more regular settlement, a more accurate survey, I discovered three solid and permanent benefits of my new situation. 1. My personal freedom had been somewhat impaired by the House of Commons and the board of trade; but I was now delivered from the chain of duty and dependence, from the hopes and fears of political adventure: my sober mind was no longer intoxicated by the fumes of party, and I rejoiced in my escape, as often as I read of the midnight debates which preceded the dissolution of parliament. 2. My English economy had been that of a solitary bachelor, who might afford some occasional dinners. In Switzerland I enjoyed at every meal, at every hour, the free and pleasant conversation of the friend of my youth; and my daily table was always provided for the reception of one or two extraordinary guests. Our importance in society is less a positive than a relative weight: in London I was lost in the crowd; I ranked with the first families of Lausanne, and my style of prudent expense enabled me to maintain a fair balance of reciprocal civilities. 3. Instead of a small house between a street and a stable-yard, I began to occupy a spacious and convenient mansion, connected on the north side with the city, and open on the south to a beautiful and boundless horizon. A garden of four acres had been laid out by the taste of Mr. Deyverdun: from the garden a rich scenery of meadows and vineyards descends to the Leman Lake, and the prospect far beyond the lake is crowned by the stupenduous mountains of Savoy.   My books and my acquaintance had been first united in London; but this happy position of my library in town and country was finally reserved for Lausanne. Possessed of every comfort in this triple alliance, I could not be tempted to change my habitation with the changes of the seasons.

My friends had been kindly apprehensive that I should not be able to exist in a Swiss town at the foot of the Alps, after having so long conversed with the first men of the first cities of the world.   Such lofty connexions may attract the curious, and gratify the vain; but I am too modest, or too proud, to rate my own value by that of my associates; and whatsoever may be the fame of learning or genius, experience has shown me that the cheaper qualifications of politeness and good sense are of more useful currency in the commerce of life.   By many, conversation is esteemed as a theatre or a school: but, after the morning has been occupied by the labours of the library, I wish to unbend rather than to exercise my mind; and in the interval between tea and supper I am far from disdaining the innocent amusement of a game at cards.   Lausanne is peopled by a numerous gentry, whose companionable idleness is seldom disturbed by the pursuits of avarice or ambition: the women, though confined to a domestic education, are endowed for the most part with more taste and knowledge than their husbands and brothers: but the decent freedom of both sexes is equally remote from the extremes of simplicity and refinement. I shall add as a misfortune rather than a merit, that the situation and beauty of the Pays de Vaud, the long habits of the English, the medical reputation of Dr. Tissot, and the fashion of viewing the mountains and glaciers, have opened us on all sides to the incursions of foreigners. The visits of Mr. and Madame Necker, of Prince Henry of Prussia, and of Mr. Fox, may form some pleasing exceptions; but, in general, Lausanne has appeared most agreeable in my eyes, when we have been abandoned to our own society. I had frequently seen Mr. Necker, in the summer of 1784, at a country house near Lausanne, where he composed his Treatise on the Administration of the Finances. I have since, in October, 1790, visited him in his present residence, the castle and barony of Copet, near Geneva. Of the merits and measures of that statesman various opinions may be entertained; but all impartial men must agree in their esteem of his integrity and patriotism.

In the month of August, 1784, Prince Henry of Prussia, in his way to Paris, passed three days at Lausanne. His military conduct has been praised by professional men; his character has been vilified by the wit and malice of a dæmon;* but I was flattered by his affability, and entertained by his conversation.

In his tour of Switzerland (September, 1788) Mr. Fox gave me two days of free and private society.† He seemed to feel, and even to envy, the happiness of my situation, while I admired the powers of a superior man

* Mémoire Secret de la Cour de Berlin.
† See Letter in the Continuation, October 1, 1788

as they are blended in his attractive character with the softness and simplicity of a child. Perhaps no human being was ever more perfectly exempt from the taint of malevolence, vanity, or falsehood.

My transmigration from London to Lausanne could not be effected without interrupting the course of my historical labours. The hurry of my departure, the joy of my arrival, the delay of my tools, suspended their progress; and a full twelvemonth was lost before I could resume the thread of regular and daily industry. A number of books most requisite and least common had been previously selected; the academical library of Lausanne, which 1 could use as my own, contained at least the fathers and councils; and I have derived some occasional succour from the public collections of Berne and Geneva. The fourth volume was soon terminated, by an abstract of the controversies of the incarnation, which the learned Dr. Prideaux was apprehensive of exposing to profane eyes. It had been the original design of the learned Dean Prideaux to write the history of the ruin of the Eastern Church. In this work it would have been necessary, not only to unravel all those controversies which the Christians made about the hypostatical union, but also to unfold all the niceties and subtle notions which each sect entertained concerning it. The pious historian was apprehensive of exposing that incomprehensible mystery to the cavils and objections of unbelievers; and he durst not, " seeing the nature of this book, venture it abroad in so wanton and lewd an age."*

In the fifth and sixth volumes the revolutions of the

* See preface to the Life of Mahomet, p. 10, 11.

empire and the world are most rapid, various, and instructive; and the Greek or Roman historians are
checked by the hostile narratives of the barbarians of
the East and the West.*

It was not till after many designs, and many trials, that I
preferred, as I still prefer, the method of grouping my picture by nations; and the seeming neglect of chronological
order is surely compensated by the superior merits of
interest and perspicuity.   The style of the first volume
is, in my opinion, somewhat crude and elaborate; in the
second and third it is ripened into ease, correctness and
numbers; but in the three last I may have been seduced
by the facility of my pen, and the constant habit of
speaking one language and writing another may have
infused some mixture of Gallic idioms.   Happily for my
eyes, I have always closed my studies with the day, and
commonly with the morning; and a long, but temperate, labour has been accomplished, without fatiguing
either the mind or body; but when I computed the remainder of my time and my task, it was apparent
that, according to the season of publication, the delay of
a month would be productive of that of a year.   I was
now straining for the goal, and in the last winter, many
evenings were borrowed from the social pleasures of
Lausanne.   I could now wish that a pause, an interval,
had been allowed for a serious revisal.

I have presumed to mark the moment of conception:

* I have followed the judicious precept of the Abbé de Maybly, (Manière d'ecrire l'Histoire, p. 110) who advises the historian not to dwell too
minutely on the decay of the eastern empire; but to consider the bar-
barian conquerors as a more worthy subject of his narrative.   "Fas est et
ab hoste doceri."

I shall now commemorate the hour of my final deliverance. It was on the day, or rather, night of the 27th of June, 1787, between the hours of eleven and twelve, that I wrote the last lines of the last page, in a summer-house in my garden. After laying down my pen, I took several turns in a berceau, or covered walk of acacias, which commands a prospect of the country, the Lake, and the mountains. The air was temperate, the sky was serene, the silver orb of the moon was reflected from the waters, and all nature was silent. I will not dissemble the first emotions of joy on the recovery of my freedom, and, perhaps, the establishment of my fame. But my pride was soon humbled, and a sober melancholy was spread over my mind, by the idea that I had taken an everlasting leave of an old and agreeable companion, and that whatsoever might be the future date of my history, the life of the historian must be short and precarious. I will add two facts which have seldom occurred in the composition of six, or even five quartos. 1. My first rough manuscript, without any intermediate copy, has been sent to the press. 2. Not a sheet has been seen by any human eyes, excepting those of the author and the printer: the faults and the merits are exclusively my own.*

Extract from Mr. Gibbon's Common-place Book.

The fourth volume of the History of the Decline and Fall of the Roman Empire	begun March 1st, 1782—ended June, 1784.
The fifth volume . . .	begun July, 1784—ended May 1st, 1786.
The sixth volume , . .	begun May 18th, 1786—ended June 27th, 1787.

These three volumes were sent to press August 15th, 1787, and the whole impression was concluded April following.

I cannot help recollecting a much more extraordinary fact, which is affirmed of himself by Retif de la Bretorme, a voluminous and original writer of French novels. He laboured, and may still labour, in the humble office of corrector to a printing-house; but this office enabled him to transport an entire volume from his mind to the press; and his work was given to the public without ever having been written with a pen.

CHAP. XXIII.

THE AUTHOR VISITS SHEFFIELD.

AFTER a quiet residence of four years, during which I had never moved ten miles from Lausanne, it was not without some reluctance and terror that I undertook, in a journey of two hundred leagues, to cross the mountains and the sea. Yet this formidable adventure was achieved without danger or fatigue; and at the end of a fortnight I found myself in Lord Sheffield's house and library safe, happy, and at home. The character of my friend, Mr. Holroyd, had recommended him to a seat in parliament for Coventry, the command of a regiment of light dragoons, and an Irish peerage. The sense and spirit of his political writings have decided the public opinion on the great questions of our commercial interest with America and Ireland.*

The sale of his Observations on the American States was diffusive, their effect beneficial; the Navigation Act, the palladium of Britain, was defended, and perhaps saved, by his pen; and he proves, by the weight of fact and argument, that the mother country may survive and flourish after the loss of America. My friend has never

* Observations on the Commerce of the American States, by John Lord Sheffield. 6th edition, London, 1784, in octavo.

cultivated the arts of composition; but his materials are copious and correct, and he leaves on his paper the clear impression of an active and vigorous mind. His Observations on the Trade, Manufactures, and present State of Ireland, were intended to guide the industry, to correct the prejudices, and to assuage the passions of a country which seemed to forget that she could be free and prosperous only by a friendly connexion with Great Britain. The concluding observations are written with so much ease and spirit, that they may be read by those who are the least interested in the subject.

He fell, in 1784, with the unpopular coalition; but his merit has been acknowledged at the last general election, 1790, by the honourable invitation and free choice of the city of Bristol. During the whole time of my residence in England I was entertained at Sheffield-place and in Downing-street by his hospitable kindness; and the most pleasant period was that which I passed in the domestic society of the family. In the larger circle of the metropolis I observed the country and the inhabitants, with the knowledge, and without the prejudices, of an Englishman; but I rejoiced in the apparent increase of wealth and prosperity, which might be fairly divided between the spirit of the nation and the wisdom of the minister. All party resentment was now lost in oblivion: since I was no man's rival, no man was my enemy. I felt the dignity of independence, and as I asked no more, I was satisfied with the general civilities of the world. The house in London which I frequented with most pleasure and assiduity was that of Lord North. After the loss of power and of sight, he was still happy in

himself and his friends; and my public tribute of gratitude and esteem could no longer be suspected of any
interested motive.   Before my departure from England,
I was present at the august spectacle of Mr. Hastings's
trial in Westminster Hall.   It is not my province to ab-
solve or condemn the governor of India; but Mr. Sheri-
dan's eloquence demanded my applause; nor could I
hear without emotion the personal compliment which he
paid me in the presence of the British nation.*

From this display of genius, which blazed four successive days, I shall stoop to a very mechanical circumstance.   As I was waiting in the manager's box, I had
the curiosity to inquire of the short-hand writer, how
many words a ready and rapid orator might pronounce
in an hour?   From 7000 to 7500 was his answer.   The
medium of 7200 will afford 120 words in a minute, and
two words in each second.   But this computation will
only apply to the English language.

* He said the facts that made up the volume of narrative were unparal-
leled in atrociousness, and that nothing equal in criminality was to be traced,
either in ancient or modern history, in the correct periods of Tacitus or the
luminous page of Gibbon.—Morning Chronicle, June 14, 1788.

CHAP. XXIV.

MR. GIBBON PUBLISHES THE REMAINDER OF HIS HISTORY.

As the publication of my three last volumes was the principal object, so it was the first care of my English journey. The previous arrangements with the bookseller and the printer were settled in my passage through London, and the proofs, which I returned more correct, were transmitted every post from the press to Sheffield-place. The length of the operation, and the leisure of the country, allowed some time to review my manuscript. Several rare and useful books, the Assises de Jerusalem, Ramusius de Bello C. P^ro, the Greek acts of the synod of Florence, the Statuta Urbis Romæ, &c. were procured, and introduced in their proper places the supplements which they afforded. The impression of the fourth volume had consumed three months. Our common interest required that we should move with a quicker pace; and Mr. Strahan fulfilled his engagement, which few printers could sustain, of delivering every week three thousand copies of nine sheets. The day of publication was, however, delayed, that it might coincide with the fifty-first anniversary of my own birthday; the double festival was celebrated by a cheerful literary dinner at Mr. Cadell's house; and I seemed to blush while they read an elegant compliment from Mr. Hayley,* whose poetical talents had more than once been

* *Occasional Stanzas, by Mr. Hayley, read after the Dinner at Mr. Cadell's, May 8, 1788; being the day of the publication of the three last volumes of Mr. Gibbon's History, and his Birthday.*

Genii of England and of Rome,
In mutual triumph here assume
  The honours each may claim!
This social scene with smiles survey,
And consecrate the festive day
  To Friendship and to Fame!

Enough, by Desolation's tide,
With anguish and indignant pride,
  Has Rome bewail'd her fate;
And mourn'd that time in Havoc's hour,
Defaced each monument of power
  To speak her truly great;

O'er maim'd Polibius, just and sage,
O'er Livy's mutilated page,
  How deep was her regret!
Touch'd by this queen, in ruin grand,
See! Glory, by an English hand,
  Now pays a mighty debt.

Lo! sacred to the Roman name,
And raised like Rome's immortal fame,
  By genius and by toil,
The splendid work is crown'd to-day,
On which Oblivion ne'er shall prey,
  Nor Envy make her spoil!

England, exult! and view not now
With jealous glance each nation's brow,
  Where History's palm has spread!
In every path of liberal art,
Thy sons to prime distinction start,
  And no superior dread.

employed in the praise of his friend.   Before Mr. Hayley inscribed with my name his epistles on history, 1 was not acquainted with that amiable man and elegant poet. He afterwards thanked me in verse for my second and third volumes ;* and in the summer of 1781, the Roman

Science for thee a Newton raised;
For thy renown a Shakspeare blazed,
   Lord of the drama's sphere !
In different fields to equal praise
See History now thy GIBBON raise
   To shine without a peer !

Eager to honour living worth,
And bless to-day the double birth
   That proudest joy may claim,
Let artless Truth this homage pay,
And consecrate the festive day
   To Friendship and to Fame !

* *Sonnet to Edward Gibbon, Esq. on the publication of his second and third Volumes*, 1781.

With proud delight the imperial founder gazed
   On the new beauty of the second Rome,
When on his eager eye rich temples blazed,
   And his fair city rose in youthful bloom :
A pride more noble may thy heart assume,
   O GIBBON ! gazing on thy growing work,
In which, constructed for a happier doom,
   No hasty marks of vain ambition lurk :
Thou may'st deride both Time's destructive sway,
   And baser Envy's beauty-mangling dirk ;
Thy georgeous fabric, plann'd with wise delay,
   Shall baffle foes more savage than the Turk ;
As ages multiply, its fame shall rise,
And earth must perish ere its splendour dies.

Eagle* (a proud title) accepted the invitation of the
English Sparrow, who chirped in the groves of Eartham,

* *A Card of Invitation to Mr. Gibbon at Brighthelmstone, 1781.*

An English sparrow, pert and free,
Who chirps beneath his native tree,
Hearing the Roman eagle 's near,
And feeling more respect than fear,
Thus, with united love and awe,
Invites him to his shed of straw.

Though he is but a twittering sparrow,
The field he hops in rather narrow,
When nobler plumes attract his view
He ever pays them homage due.
He looks with reverential wonder
On him, whose talons bear the thunder;
Nor could the jackdaws e'er inveigle
His voice to vilify the eagle,
Though issuing from the holy towers,
In which they build their warmest bowers,
Their sovereign's haunt they slyly search,
In hopes to catch him on his perch,
(For Pindar says, beside his god
The thunder-bearing bird will nod,)
Then, peeping round his still retreat,
They pick from underneath his feet
Some molted feather he lets fall,
And swear he cannot fly at all.——

Lord of the sky! whose pounce can tear
These croakers that infest the air,
Trust him—the sparrow loves to sing
The praise of thy imperial wing!
He thinks thou 'lt deem him, on his word,
An honest, though familiar bird;
And hopes thou soon wilt condescend
To look upon thy little friend;
That he may boast around his grove
A visit from the bird of Jove.

near Chichester. As most of the former purchasers
were naturally desirous of completing their sets, the sale
of the quarto edition was quick and easy; and an octavo
size was printed, to satisfy at a cheaper rate the public
demand. The conclusion of my work was generally
read, and variously judged. The style has been exposed
to much academical criticism; a religious clamour was
revived, and the reproach of indecency has been loudly
echoed by the rigid censors of morals. I never could
understand the clamour that has been raised against the
indecency of my three last volumes. 1. An equal degree
of freedom in the former part, especially in the first
volume, had passed without reproach. 2. I am justified
in painting the manners of the times; the vices of Theo-
dora form an essential feature in the reign and character
of Justinian. 3. My English text is chaste, and all licentious passages are left in the obscurity of a learned language. "Le Latin dans ses mots brave l'honnêteté,"
says the correct Boileau, in a country and idiom more
scrupulous than our own. Yet, upon the whole, the
History of the Decline and Fall seems to have struck root,
both at home and abroad, and may, perhaps, a hundred
years hence still continue to be abused. I am less
flattered by Mr. Porson's high encomium on the style and
spirit of my history, than I am satisfied with his honourable testimony to my attention, diligence, and accuracy;
those humble virtues, which religious zeal had most audaciously denied. The sweetness of his praise is tempered
by a reasonable mixture of acid.* As the book may not
be common in England, I shall transcribe my own cha-

* See his preface, page 28, 32.

racter from the Bibliotheca Historica of Meuselius,* a learned and laborious German. "Summis ævi nostri historicis Gibbonus sine dubio adnumerandus est. Inter capitolii ruinas stans primum hujus operis scribendi consilium cepit. Florentissimos vitæ annos colligendo et laborando eidem impendit. Enatum inde monumentum ære perennius, licet passim appareant sinistrè dicta, minus perfecta, veritati non satis consentanea. Videmus quidem ubique fere studium scrutandi veritatemque scribendi maximum: tamen sine Tillemontio duce ubi scilicet hujus historia finitur sæpius noster titubat atque hallucinatur. Quod vel maxime fit, ubi de rebus ecclesiasticis vel de juris prudentiâ Romanâ (tom. iv.) tradit, et in aliis locis. Attamen nævi hujus generis haud impediunt quo minus operis summam et οἰκονομίαν præclare dispositam, delectum rerum sapientissimum, argutum quoque interdum, dictionemque seu stylum historico æque ac philosopho dignissimum, et vix a quoque alio Anglo, Humio ac Robertsono haud exceptis (præreptum?) vehementur laudemus, atque sæculo nostro de hujusmodi historiâ gratulemur. . . . . Gibbonus adversarios cum in tum extra patriam nactus est, quia propagationem religionis Christianæ, non, ut vulgo, fieri solet, aut more theologorum, sed ut historicum et philosophum decet, exposuerat."

The French, Italian, and German translations have been executed with various success; but, instead of patronizing, I should willingly suppress such imperfect copies, which injure the character, while they propagate the name of the author. The first volume had been feebly, though faithfully, translated into French by M. Le

* Vol. iv. part 1, page 342, 844.

Clerc de Septchenes, a young gentleman of a studious character and liberal fortune. After his decease the work was continued by two manufacturers of Paris, MM. Desmuniers and Cantwell: but the former is now an active member in the national assembly, and the undertaking languishes in the hands of his associate. The superior merit of the interpreter, or his language, inclines me to prefer the Italian version: but I wish that it were in my power to read the German, which is praised by the best judges. The Irish pirates are at once my friends and my enemies. But I cannot be displeased with the two numerous and correct impressions which have been published, for the use of the Continent, at Basle in Switzerland.* The conquests of our language and literature are not confined to Europe alone, and a writer who succeeds in London, is speedily read on the banks of the Delaware and the Ganges.

In the preface of the fourth volume, while I gloried in the name of an Englishman, I announced my approaching return to the neighbourhood of the Lake of Lausanne. This last trial confirmed my assurance that I had wisely chosen for my own happiness; nor did I once, in a year's visit, entertain a wish of settling in my native country. Britain is the free and fortunate island; but where is the spot in which I could unite the comforts and beauties of my establishment at Lausanne? The tumult of London astonished my eyes and ears; the amusements of public

---

* Of their fourteen octavo volumes, the two last include the whole body of the notes. The public importunity had forced *me* to remove them from the end of the volume to the bottom of the page; but I have often repented of my compliance.

places were no longer adequate to the trouble; the clubs and assemblies were filled with new faces and young men: and our best society, our long and late dinners, would soon have been prejudicial to my health. Without any share in the political wheel, I must be idle and insignificant: yet the most splendid temptations would not have enticed me to engage a second time in the servitude of parliament or office. At Tunbridge, some weeks after the publication of my History, I reluctantly quitted Lord and Lady Sheffield; and, with a young Swiss friend,* whom I had introduced to the English world, I pursued the road of Dover and Lausanne. My habitation was embellished in my absence, and the last division of books, which followed my steps, increased my chosen library to the number of between six and seven thousand volumes. My seraglio was ample, my choice was free, my appetite was keen. After a full repast on Homer and Aristophanes, I involved myself in the philosophic maze of the writings of Plato, of which the dramatic is, perhaps, more interesting than the argumentative part: but I stepped aside into every path of inquiry which reading or reflection accidentally opened.

* Mr. Wilhelm de Severy.

CHAP. XXV.

DEATH OF MR. DEYVERDUN.

ALAS! the joy of my return, and my studious ardour, were soon damped by the melancholy state of my friend Mr. Deyverdun. His health and spirits had long suffered a gradual decline, a succession of apoplectic fits announced his dissolution: and before he expired, those who loved him could not wish for the continuance of his life. The voice of reason might congratulate his deliverance, but the feelings of nature and friendship could be subdued only by time: his amiable character was still alive in my remembrance: each room, each walk, was imprinted with our common footsteps; and I should blush at my own philosophy, if a long interval of study had not preceded and followed the death of my friend. By his last will he left to me the option of purchasing his house and garden, or of possessing them during my life, on the payment of a stipulated price, or of an easy retribution to his kinsman and heir. I should probably have been tempted by the demon of property, if some legal difficulties had not been started against my title: a contest would have been vexatious, doubtful, and invidious; and the heir most gratefully subscribed an agreement, which rendered my life possession more perfect, and his future condition more advantageous. Yet I had often revolved the judicious lines in which Pope answers the objections of his long-sighted friend:

> Pity to build without or child or wife;
> Why, you'll enjoy it only all your life
> Well, if the use be mine, does it concern one,
> Whether the name belong to Pope or Vernon?

The certainty of my tenure has allowed me to lay out a considerable sum in improvements and alterations· they have been executed with skill and taste; and few men of letters, perhaps, in Europe, are so desirably lodged as myself. But I feel, and with the decline of years I shall more painfully feel that I am alone in paradise. Among the circle of my acquaintance at Lausanne, I have gradually acquired the solid and tender friendship of a respectable family :* the four persons of whom it is composed are all endowed with the virtues best adapted to their age and situation; and I am encouraged to love the parents as a brother, and the children as a father. Every day we seek and find the opportunities of meeting: yet even this valuable connexion cannot supply the loss of domestic society.

* The family of De Severy.

CHAP. XXVI.

OBSERVATIONS ON THE FRENCH REVOLUTION.

WITHIN the last two or three years our tranquillity has been clouded by the disorders of France: many families at Lausanne were alarmed and affected by the terrors of an impending bankruptcy; but the revolution, or rather the dissolution, of the kingdom has been heard and felt in the adjacent lands.

I beg leave to subscribe my assent to Mr. Burke's creed on the revolution of France. I admire his eloquence, I approve his politics, I adore his chivalry, and I can almost excuse his reverence for church establishments. I have sometimes thought of writing a dialogue of the dead, in which Lucian, Erasmus, and Voltaire should mutually acknowledge the danger of exposing an old superstition to the contempt of the blind and fanatic multitude.

A swarm of emigrants of both sexes, who escaped from the public ruin, has been attracted by the vicinity, the manners, and the language of Lausanne; and our narrow habitations in town and country are now occupied by the first names and titles of the departed monarchy. These noble fugitives are entitled to our pity; they may claim our esteem, but they cannot, in their present state of mind and fortune, much contribute to our amusement.

Instead of looking down as calm and idle spectators on the theatre of Europe, our domestic harmony is somewhat embittered by the infusion of party spirit: our ladies and gentleman assume the character of self-taught politicians; and the sober dictates of wisdom and experience are silenced by the clamour of the triumphant democrats. The fanatic missionaries of sedition have scattered the seeds of discontent in our cities and villages, which had flourished above two hundred and fifty years without fearing the approach of war, or feeling the weight of government. Many individuals and some communities appear to be infested with the Gallic frenzy, the wild theories of equal and boundless freedom; but I trust that the body of the people will be faithful to their sovereign and to themselves: and I am satisfied that the failure or success of a revolt would equally terminate in the ruin of the country. While the aristocracy of Berne protects the happiness, it is superfluous to inquire whether it be founded in the rights, of man: the economy of the state is liberally supplied without the aid of taxes; and the magistrates *must* reign with prudence and equity, since they are unarmed in the midst of an armed nation.

The revenue of Berne, excepting some small duties, is derived from church lands, tithes, feudal rights, and interest of money. The republic has nearly £500,000 sterling in the English funds, and the amount of their treasure is unknown to the citizens themselves. For myself (may the omen be averted) I can only declare, that the first stroke of a rebel drum would be the signal of my immediate departure.

When I contemplate the common lot of mortality, I

must acknowledge that I have drawn a high prize in the lottery of life. The far greater part of the globe is overspread with barbarism or slavery: in the civilized world, the most numerous class is condemned to ignorance and poverty; and the double fortune of my birth in a free and enlightened country, in an honourable and wealthy family, is the lucky chance of an unit against millions. The general probability is about three to one, that a new-born infant will not live to complete his fiftieth year.* I have now passed that age, and may fairly estimate the present value of my existence in the three-fold division of mind, body, and estate.

1. The first and indispensable requisite of happiness is a clear conscience, unsullied by the reproach or remembrance of an unworthy action.

> ——Hic murus aheneus esto,
> Nil conscire sibi, nullâ pallescere culpâ

I am endowed with a cheerful temper, a moderate sensibility, and a natural disposition to repose rather than to activity: some mischievous appetites and habits have perhaps been corrected by philosophy or time. The love of study, a passion which derives fresh vigour from enjoyment, supplies each day, each hour, with a perpetual source of independent and rational pleasure; and I am not sensible of any decay of the mental faculties. The original soil has been highly improved by cultivation;

---

* See Buffon, Supplement à l'Histoire naturelle, tom. vii. page 158—164. Of a given number of new-born infants, one half, by the fault of nature or man, is extinguished before the age of puberty and reason.—A melancholy calculation!

but it may be questioned, whether some flowers of fancy, some grateful errors, have not been eradicated with the weeds of prejudice. 2. Since I have escaped from the long perils of my childhood, the serious advice of a physician has seldom been requisite. "The madness of superfluous health" I have never known; but my tender constitution has been fortified by time, and the inestimable gift of the sound and peaceful slumbers of infancy may be imputed both to the mind and body. 3. I have already described the merits of my society and situation; but these enjoyments would be tasteless or bitter if their possession were not assured by an annual and adequate supply. According to the scale of Switzerland, I am a rich man; and I am indeed rich, since my income is superior to my expense, and my expense is equal to my wishes. My friend Lord Sheffield has kindly relieved me from the cares to which my taste and temper are most adverse; shall I add, that since the failure of my first wishes, I have never entertained any serious thoughts of a matrimonial connexion?

I am disgusted with the affectation of men of letters, who complain that they have renounced a substance for a shadow; and that their fame (which sometimes is no insupportable weight) affords a poor compensation for envy, censure, and persecution.* My own experience at least, has taught me a very different lesson: twenty

* M. d'Alembert relates, that as he was walking in the gardens of Sans Souci with the King of Prussia, Frederick said to him, " Do you see that old woman, a poor weeder, asleep on that sunny bank ? she is probably a more happy being than either of us." The king and the philosopher may speak for themselves; for my part, I do not envy the old woman.

happy years have been animated by the labour of my History; and its success has given me a name, a rank, a character, in the world, to which I should not otherwise have been entitled. The freedom of my writings has indeed provoked an implacable tribe; but as I was safe from the stings, I was soon accustomed to the buzzing of the hornets: my nerves were not tremblingly alive, and my literary temper is so happily framed, that I am less sensible of pain than of pleasure. The rational pride of an author may be offended, rather than flattered, by vague indiscriminate praise; but he cannot, he should not, be indifferent to the fair testimonies of private and public esteem. Even his moral sympathy may be gratified by the idea, that now, in the present hour, he is imparting some degree of amusement or knowledge to his friends in a distant land; that one day his mind will be familiar to the grandchildren of those who are yet unborn.* I cannot boast of the friendship or favour of princes; the patronage of English literature has long since been devolved on our booksellers, and the measure of their liberality is the least ambiguous test of our com-

* In the first of ancient or modern romances (Tom Jones), this proud sentiment, this feast of fancy, is enjoyed by the genius of Fielding.—" Come, bright love of fame, &c. fill my ravished fancy with the hopes of charming ages yet to come. Foretel me that some tender maid, whose grandmother is yet unborn, hereafter, when, under the fictitious name of Sophia, she reads the real worth which once existed in my Charlotte, shall from her sympathetic breast send forth the heaving sigh. Do thou teach me not only to foresee but to enjoy, nay even to feed on future praise. Comfort me by the solemn assurance, that, when the little parlour in which I sit at this moment shall be reduced to a worse furnished box, I shall be read with honour by those who never knew nor saw me, and whom I shall neither know nor see." Book xiii. ch. 1.

mon success. Perhaps the golden mediocrity of my fortune has contributed to fortify my application.

The present is a fleeting moment; the past is no more; and our prospect of futurity is dark and doubtful. This day may *possibly* be my last: but the laws of probability, so true in general, so fallacious in particular, still allow about fifteen years.* I shall soon enter into the period which, as the most agreeable of his long life, was selected by the judgment and experience of the sage Fontenelle. His choice is approved by the eloquent historian of nature, who fixes our moral happiness to the mature season in which our passions are supposed to be calmed, our duties fulfilled, our ambition satisfied, our fame and fortune established on a solid basis.† In private conversation, that great and amiable man added the weight of his own experience; and this autumnal felicity might be exemplified in the lives of Voltaire, Hume, and many other men of letters. I am far more inclined to embrace than to dispute this comfortable doctrine. I will not suppose any premature decay of the mind or body; but I must reluctantly observe that two causes, the abbreviation of time, and the failure of hope, will always tinge with a browner shade the evening of life.

* Mr. Buffon, from our disregard of the possibility of death within the four-and-twenty hours, concludes that a chance, which falls below or rises above ten thousand to one, will never affect the hopes or fears of a reasonable man. The fact is true, but our courage is the effect of thoughtlessness, rather than of reflection. If a public lottery were drawn for the choice of an immediate victim, and if our name were inscribed on one of the ten thousand tickets, should we be perfectly easy?

† See Buffon.

LETTERS

FROM

EDWARD GIBBON, ESQ.

TO

LORD SHEFFIELD.

NARRATIVE CONTINUED BY LORD SHEFFIELD.

WHEN I first undertook to prepare Mr. Gibbon's Memoirs for the press, I supposed that it would be necessary to introduce some continuation of them, from the time when they cease, namely, soon after his return to Switzerland in the year 1788; but the examination of his correspondence with me suggested, that the best continuation would be the publication of his letters from that time to his death. I shall thus give more satisfaction, by employing the language of Mr. Gibbon, instead of my own; and the public will see him in a new and admirable light, as a writer of letters. By the insertion of a few occasional sentences, I shall obviate the disadvantages that are apt to arise from an interrupted narration. A prejudiced or a fastidious critic may condemn, perhaps, some parts of the letters as trivial; but many readers, I flatter myself, will be gratified by discovering, even in these, my friend's affectionate feelings, and his character in familiar life. His letters in general bear a strong resemblance to the style and turn of his conversation: the characteristics of which were vivacity, elegance, and precision, with knowledge astonishingly extensive and correct. He never ceased to be instructive and entertaining; and in general there was a vein of pleasantry in his conversation which prevented its becoming languid, even during a residence of many months with a family in the country.

It has been supposed that he always arranged what he intended to say, before he spoke; his quickness in conversation contradicts this notion : but it is very true, that before he sat down to write a note or letter, he completely arranged in his mind what he meant to express. He pursued the same method in respect to other composition; and he occasionally would walk several times about his apartment before he had rounded a period to his taste. He has pleasantly remarked to me, that it sometimes cost him many a turn before he could throw a sentiment into a form that gratified his own criticism. His systematic habit of arrangement in point of style, assisted in his instance, by an excellent memory and correct judgment, is much to be recommended to those who aspire to any perfection in writing.

Although the Memoirs extend beyond the time of Mr. Gibbon's return to Lausanne, I shall insert a few letters written immediately after his arrival there, and combine them so far as to include even the last note which he wrote a few days previously to his death. Some of them contain few incidents; but they connect and carry on the account either of his opinions or of his employment.

Lausanne, July 30, 1788.—Wednesday, 3 o'clock.

I have but a moment so say, before the departure of the post, that after a very pleasant journey, I arrived here about half an hour ago; that I am as well arranged as if I had never stirred from this place; and that dinner on the table is just announced. Severy I dropped at his country-house about two leagues off. I just saluted the family, who dine with me the day after to-morrow, and return to town for some days, I hope weeks, on my account. The son is an amiable and grateful youth; and even this journey has taught me to know and to love him still better. My satisfaction would be complete, had I not found a sad and serious alteration in poor Deyverdun; but thus our joys are chequered! I embrace all; and at this moment feel the last pang of our parting at Tunbridge. Convey this letter or information, without delay, from Sheffield-place to Bath. In a few days I shall write more amply to both places.

October 1, 1788.

After such an act of vigour as my first letter, composed, finished, and despatched within half an hour after my landing, while the dinner was smoking on the table, your knowledge of the animal must have taught you to expect a proportionable degree of relaxation; and you will be satisfied to hear, that, for many Wednesdays and Saturdays, I have consumed more time than would have sufficed for the epistle, in devising reasons for procrastinating it to the next post. At this very moment I begin so very late, as I am just going to dress, and dine in the country, that I can take only the benefit of the date, October the 1st, and I must be content to seal and send my letter next Saturday.

October the 4th.

Saturday is now arrived, and I much doubt whether I shall have time to finish. I arose, as usual, about seven;

but as I knew I should have so much time, you know it
would have been ridiculous to begin any thing before
breakfast. When I returned from my breakfast-room to
the library, unluckily I found on the table some new and
interesting books, which instantly caught my attention;
and without injuring my correspondent, I could safely
bestow a single hour to gratify my curiosity. Some
things which I found in them insensibly led me to other
books, and other inquiries; the morning has stolen away
and I shall be soon summoned to dress and dine with the
two Severys, father and son, who are returned from the
country on a disagreeable errand, an illness of Madame,
from which she is, however, recovering. Such is the
faithful picture of my mind and manners, and from a
single day *disce omnes*. After having been so long
chained to the oar, in a splendid galley indeed, I freely
and fairly enjoyed my liberty as I promised in my preface; range without control over the wide expanse of
my library; converse, as my fancy prompts me, with
poets and historians, philosophers and orators, of every
age and language; and often indulge my meditations in
the invention and arrangement of mighty works, which I
shall probably never find time or application to execute.
My garden, berceau, and pavilion often varied the scene
of my studies; the beautiful weather which we have enjoyed exhilarated my spirits, and I again tasted the wisdom and happiness of my retirement, till that happiness
was interrupted by a very serious calamity, which took
from me, for a fortnight, all thoughts of study, of amusement, and even of correspondence. I mentioned in my
first letter the uneasiness I felt at poor Deyverdun's

declining state of health, how much the pleasure of my
life was embittered by the sight of a suffering and languid friend.   The joy of our meeting appeared at first to
revive him; and, though not satisfied, I began to think,
at least to hope, that he was every day gaining ground;
when, alas! one morning I was suddenly recalled from
my berceau to the house, with the dreadful intelligence of
an apoplectic stroke; I found him senseless: the best
assistance was instantly collected; and he had the aid of
the genius and experience of Mr. Tissot, and of the
assiduous care of another physician, who for some time
scarcely quitted his bedside either night or day.   While
I was in momentary dread of a relapse, with a confession
from his physician that such a relapse must be fatal, you
will feel that I was much more to be pitied than my
friend.   At length, art or nature triumphed over the
enemy of life.   I was soon assured that all immediate
danger was past: and now for many days I have had the
satisfaction of seeing him recover, though by slow degrees,
his health and strength, his sleep and appetite.   He now
walks about the garden, and receives his particular
friends, but has not yet gone abroad.   His future health
will depend very much upon his own prudence; but, at
all events, this has been a very serious warning; and the
slightest indisposition will hereafter assume a very formidable aspect.   But let us turn from this melancholy
subject.—The Man of the People escaped from the
tumult, the bloody tumult of the Westminster election, to
the lakes and mountains of Switzerland, and I was
informed that he was arrived at the Lion d'Or.   I sent a
compliment; he answered it in person, and settled at my

house for the remainder of the day. I have ate and drank, and conversed and sat up all night with Fox in England; but it never has happened, perhaps it never can happen again, that I should enjoy him as I did that day, alone, from ten in the morning till ten at night. Poor Deyverdun, before his accident, wanted spirits to appear, and has regretted it since. Our conversation never flagged a moment; and he seemed thoroughly pleased with the place and with his company. We had little politics; though he gave me, in a few words, such a character of Pitt, as one great man should give of another his rival: much of books, from my own, on which he flattered me very pleasantly, to Homer and the Arabian Nights; much about the country, my garden (which he understands far better than I do), and, upon the whole, I think he envies me, and would do so were he minister. The next morning I gave him a guide to walk him about the town and country, and invited some company to meet him at dinner. The following day he continued his journey to Berne and Zurich, and I have heard of him by various means. The people gaze on him as a prodigy, but he shows little inclination to converse with them. * * * *. Our friend Douglas has been curious, attentive, agreeable; and in every place where he has resided some days, he has left acquaintance who esteem and regret him: I never knew so clear and general an impression.

After this long letter I have yet many things to say, though none of any pressing consequence. I hope you are not idle in the deliverance of Beriton, though the late events and edicts in France begin to reconcile me to the possession of dirty acres. What think you of Necker and the States General? Are not the public expectations too sanguine? Adieu, I will write soon to my lady separately, though I have not any particular subject for her ear. Ever yours.

Lausanne, Nov. 29, 1788.

As I have no correspondents but yourself, I should have been reduced to the stale and stupid communications of the newspapers, if you had not dispatched me an excellent sketch of the extraordinary state of things. In so new a case the *salus populi* must be the first law; and any extraordinary acts of the two remaining branches of the legislature must be excused by necessity, and ratified by general consent. * * * * * *. Till things are settled, I expect a regular journal.

From kingdoms I descend to farms. * * * * *. Adieu.

Lausanne, Dec. 13, 1788.

* * * * * *. Of public affairs I can only hear with curiosity and wonder: careless as you may think me, I feel deeply interested. You must now write often; make Miss Firth copy any curious fragments; and stir up any of my well-informed acquaintance, Batt, Douglas, Adam, perhaps Lord Loughborough, to correspond with me; I *will* answer them.

We are now cold and gay at Lausanne. The Severys came to town yesterday, I saw a good deal of Lords Malmsbury and Beauchamp and their ladies; Ellis, of the Rolliad, was with them; I like him much: I gave them a dinner.

Adieu for the present. Deyverdun is not worse.

Lausanne, April 25, 1789.

Before your letter, which I received yesterday, I was in the anxious situation of a king, who hourly expects a courier from his general, with the news of a decisive engagement. I had abstained from writing, for fear of dropping a word, or betraying a feeling, which might render you too cautious or too bold. On the famous 8th of April, between twelve and two, I reflected that the business was determined; and each succeeding day I computed the speedy approach of your messenger, with favourable or melancholy tidings. When I broke the seal I expected to read, " What a d——d unlucky fellow you are! Nothing tolerable was offered, and I indignantly withdrew the estate." I *did* remember the fate of poor Lenborough, and I was afraid of your magnanimity, &c. It is whimsical enough, but it is human nature, that I now began to think of the deep-rooted foundations of land, and the airy fabric of the funds. I not only consent, but even wish to have eight or ten thousand pounds on a good mortgage. The pipe of wine you sent me was seized, and would have been confiscated, if the government of Berne had not treated me with the most flattering and distinguished civility: they not only released the wine, but they paid out of their own pockets the shares to which the bailiff and the informer were entitled by law. I should not forget that the bailiff refused to accept of his part. Poor Deyverdun's constitution is quite broken; he has had two or three attacks, not so violent as the first: every time the door is hastily opened, I expect to hear of some fatal accident: the best or worst hopes of the physicians are only that he may linger some

time longer; but, if he lives till the summer, they propose sending him to some mineral waters at Aix, in
Savoy.   You will be.glad to hear that I am now assured
of possessing, during my life, this delighful house and
garden.   The act has been lately executed in the best
form, and the handsomest manner.   I know not what to
say of your miracles at home : we rejoice in the king's
recovery, and its ministerial consequences; and I cannot
be insensible to the hope, at least the chance, of seeing in
this country a first lord of trade, or secretary at war.   In
your answer, which I shall impatiently expect, you will
give me a full and true account of your designs, which
by this time must have dropped, or be determined at
least, for the present year.   If you come, it is high time
that we should look out for a house—a task much less
easy than you may possibly imagine.   Among new
books, I recommend to you the Count de Mirabeau's
great work, Sur la Monarchie Prussienne; it is in your
own way, and gives a very just and complete idea of
that wonderful machine.   His Correspondance Secrette
is diabolically good.   Adieu.   Ever yours.

Lausanne, June 13, 1789.

You are in truth a wise, active, indefatigable, and inestimable friend ; and as our virtues are often connected
with our faults, if you were more tame and placid, you
would be perhaps of less use and value.   A very important and difficult transaction seems to be nearly terminated with success and mutual satisfaction : we seem
to run before the wind with a prosperous gale ; and, unless we should strike on some secret rocks, which I do

not foresee, shall, on or before the 31st July, enter the harbour of Content; though I cannot pursue the metaphor by adding we shall *land,* since our operation is of a very opposite tendency. I could not easily forgive myself for shutting you up in a dark room with parchments and attorneys, did I not reflect that this probably is the last material trouble that you will ever have on my account; and that after the labours and delays of twenty years, I shall at last attain what I have always sighed for, a clear and competent income, above my wants, and equal to my wishes. In this contemplation you will be sufficiently rewarded. I hope **** will be content with our title-deeds, for I cannot furnish another shred of parchment. Mrs. Gibbon's jointure is secured on the Beriton estate, and her legal consent is requisite for the sale. Again and again I must repeat my hope that she is perfectly satisfied, and that the close of her life may not be embittered by suspicion, or fear, or discontent. What new security does she prefer,—the funds, the mortgage, or your land? At all events she must be made easy. I wrote to her again some time ago, and begged that if she were too weak to write, she would desire Mrs. Gould or Mrs. Holroyd to give me a line concerning her state of health. To this no answer; I am afraid she is displeased.

Now for the disposal of the money: I approve of the £8000 mortgage on Beriton; and honour your prudence in not showing by the comparison of the rent and interest, how foolish it is to purchase land. * * * *
* * * * * * * * * *. There is a chance of my drawing a considerable sum into this country, for

an arrangement which you yourself must approve, but which I have not time to explain at present. For the sake of dispatching, by this evening's post, an answer to your letter which arrived this morning, I confine myself to the *needful*, but in the course of a few days I will send a more familiar epistle. Adieu. Ever yours,

Lausanne, July 14, 1789.

Poor Deyverdun is no more: he expired Saturday the 4th instant: and in his unfortunate situation, death could only be viewed by himself, and his friends, in the light of a consummation devoutly to be wished. Since September he has had a dozen apoplectic strokes, more or less violent: in the intervals between them his strength gradually decayed; every principle of life was exhausted; and had he continued to drag a miserable existence, he must probably have survived the loss of his faculties. Of all misfortunes this was what he himself most apprehended: but his reason was clear and calm to the last; he beheld his approaching dissolution with the firmness of a philosopher. I fancied that time and reflection had prepared me for the event; but the habits of three-and-thirty year's friendship are not so easily broken. The first days, or more especially the first nights, were indeed painful. Last Wednesday and Saturday it would not have been in my power to write. I must now recollect myself, since it is necessary for me not only to impart the news, but to ask your opinion in a very serious and doubtful question, which must be decided without loss of time. I shall state the facts, but as I am on the spot, and as new lights may occur, I do not promise implicit obedience.

Had my poor friend died without a will, a female *first* cousin settled somewhere in the north of Germany, and whom I believe he had never seen, would have been his heir at law. In the next degree he had several cousins; and one of these an old companion, by name M. de Montagny, he has chosen for his heir. As this house and garden was the best and clearest part of poor Deyverdun's fortune; as there is a heavy duty or fine (what they call *lods*) on every change of property out of the legal descent; as Montagny has a small estate and a large family, it was necessary to make some provision in his favour. The will therefore leaves me the option of enjoying this place during my life, on paying the sum of £250 (I reckon in English money) at present and an annual rent of £30; or else of purchasing the house and garden for a sum which, including the duty, will amount to £2500. If I value the rent of £30 at twelve years' purchase, I may acquire my enjoyment for life at about the rate of £600; and the remaining £1900 will be the difference between that tenure and absolute perpetual property. As you have never accused me of too much zeal for the interest of posterity, you will easily guess which scale at first preponderated. I deeply felt the advantage of acquiring, for the smaller sum, every possible enjoyment, as long as I myself should be capable of enjoying: I rejected with scorn, the idea of giving £1900 for ideal posthumous property; and I deemed it of little moment whose name, after my death should be inscribed on my house and garden at Lausanne. How often did I repeat to myself the philosopical lines of Pope, which seemed to determine the question:

Pray Heaven, cries Swift, it last as you go on ;
I wish to God this house had been your own.
Pity to build without or son or wife:
Why, you'll enjoy it *only* all your life.
Well, if the use be mine, does it concern one,
Whether the name belong to Pope or Vernon ?

In this state of self-satisfaction I was not much disturbed by all my real or nominal friends, who exhort me to prefer the right of purchase: among such friends, some are careless and some are ignorant ; and the judgment of those, who are able and willing to form an opinion, is often biassed by some selfish or social affection, by some visible or invisible interest. But my own reflections have gradually and forcibly driven me from my first propensity ; and these reflections I will now proceed to enumerate:

1. I can make this purchase with ease and prudence. As I have had the pleasure of *not* hearing from you very lately, I flatter myself that you advance on a carpet road, and that almost by the receipt of this letter (July 31st) the acres of Beriton will be transmuted into sixteen thousand pounds: if the payment be not absolutely completed on that day, **** will not scruple, I suppose, depositing the £2600 at Gosling's, to meet my draft. Should he hesitate, I can desire Darell to sell *quantum sufficit* of my short annuities. As soon as the new settlement of my affairs is made, I shall be able, after deducting this sum, to square my expense to my income, &c.

2. On mature consideration, I am perhaps less selfish and less philosophical than I appear at first sight : indeed, were I not so, it would now be in my power to turn my for-

tune into life-annuities, and let the devil take the hindmost.
I feel, (perhaps it is foolish,) but I feel that this little
paradise will please me still more when it is absolutely
my own; and that I shall be encouraged in every improvement of use or beauty, by the prospect that, after
my departure, it will be enjoyed by some person of my
own choice. I sometimes reflect with pleasure that my
writings will survive me: and that idea is at least as
vain and chimerical.

3. The heir, M. de Montagny, is an old acquaintance.
My situation of a life-holder is rather new and singular
in this country: the laws have not provided for many nice
cases which may arise between the landlord and tenant:
some I can forsee, others have been suggested, many
more I might feel when it would be too late. His right
of property might plague and confine me: he might
forbid my lending to a friend, inspect my conduct, check
my improvements, call for securities, repairs, &c. But
if I purchase, I walk on my own terrace, fierce and erect,
the free master of one of the most delicious spots on the
globe.

Should I ever migrate homewards, (you stare, but such
an event is less improbable than I could have thought it
two years ago,) this place would be disputed by strangers
and natives.

Weigh these reasons, and send me without delay a
rational explicit opinion, to which I shall pay such regard
as the nature of circumstances will allow. But, alas!
when all is determined, I shall possess this house, by
whatsoever tenure, without friendship or domestic society.
I did not imagine, six years ago, that a plan of life so

congenial to my wishes, would so speedily vanish.   I
cannot write upon any other subject.   Adieu, yours
ever.

Lausanne, August, 1789.

After receiving and dispatching the power of attorney,
last Wednesday, I opened with some palpitation, the unexpected missive which arrived this morning.   The
perusal of the contents spoiled my breakfast.   They are
disagreeable in themselves, alarming in their consequences, and peculiarly unpleasant at the present moment,
when I hoped to have formed and secured the arrangements of my future life.   I do not perfectly understand what are these deeds which are so inflexibly required : the wills and marriage-settlements I have sufficiently answered.   But your arguments do not convince
****, and I have very little hope from the Lenborough
search?   What will be the event?   If his objections are
only the result of legal scrupulosity, surely they might
be removed, and every chink might be filled, by a general
bond of indemnity, in which I boldly ask you to join, as
it will be a substantial important act of friendship, without any possible risk to yourself or your successors.
Should he still remain obdurate, I must believe what I
already suspect, that **** repents of his purchase, and
wishes to elude the conclusion.   Our case would be then
hopeless, *ibi omnis effusus labor*, and the estate would be
returned on our hands with the taint of a bad title.   The
refusal of mortgage does not please me ; but surely our
offer shows some confidence in the goodness of my title.
If he will not take eight thousand pounds at *four per cent.*
we must look out elsewhere ; new doubts and delays

will arise, and I am persuaded that you will not place an implicit confidence in any attorney. I know not as yet your opinion about my Lausanne purchase. If you are against it, the present position of affairs gives you great advantage, &c., &c. The Severys are all well; an uncommon circumstance for the four persons of the family at once. They are now at Mex, a country-house six miles from hence, which I visit to-morrow for two or three days. They often come to town, and we shall contrive to pass a part of the autumn together at Rolle. I want to change the scene; and beautiful as the garden and prospect must appear to every eye, I feel that the state of my own mind casts a gloom over them; every spot, every walk, every bench, recals the memory of those hours, of those conversations, which will return no more. But I tear myself from the subject. I could not help writing to-day, though I do not find I have said anything very material. As you must be conscious that you have agitated me, you will not postpone any agreeable, or even *decisive* intelligence. I almost hesitate, whether I shall run over to England, to consult with you on the spot, and to fly from poor Deyverdun's shade, which meets me at every turn. I did not expect to have felt his loss so sharply. But six hundred miles! Why are we so far off?

Once more, What is the difficulty with the title? Will men of sense, in a sensible country, never get rid of the tyranny of lawyers? more oppressive and ridiculous than even the old yoke of the clergy. Is not a term of seventy or eighty years, nearly twenty in my own person, sufficient to prove our legal possession? Will not the records of fines and recoveries attest that *I* am free from any bar of entails and settlements? Consult some sage of the law, whether their present demand be necessary and legal. If your ground be firm, force them to execute the agreement or forfeit the deposit. But if, as I much fear, they have a right, and a wish, to elude the consummation, would it not be better to release them at once, than to be hung up for five years, as in the case of Lovegrove, which cost me in the end four or five thousand pounds? You are bold, you are wise; consult, resolve, act. In my penultimate letter I dropped a strange hint, that a migration homeward was not impossible. I know not what to say; my mind is all afloat; yet you will not reproach me with caprice or inconsistency. How many years did you d—n my scheme of retiring to Lausanne! I executed that plan; I found as much happiness as is compatible with human nature, and during four years (1783 1787) I never breathed a sigh of repentance. On my return from England the scene was changed: I found only a faint semblance of Deyverdun, and that semblance was each day fading from my sight. I have passed an anxious year, my anxiety is now at an end, and the prospect before me is a melancholy solitude. I am still deeply rooted in this country; the possession of this paradise, the friendship of the Severy's, a mode of society suited to my taste, and the enormous trouble and *expense* of a migration. Yet in England (when the present clouds are dispelled) I could form a very comfortable establishment in London, or rather at Bath; and I have a very noble country-seat at about ten miles from East Grin-

stead in Sussex.* That spot is dearer to me than the
rest of the three kingdoms; and I have sometimes wondered how two men, so opposite in their tempers and
pursuits, should have imbibed so long and lively a propensity for each other. Sir Stanier Porten is just dead.
He has left his widow with a moderate pension, and two
children, my nearest relations: the eldest, Charlotte, is
about Louisa's age, and also a most amiable, sensible
young creature. I have conceived a romantic idea of
educating and adopting her; as we descend into the vale
of years, our infirmities require some domestic female
society: Charlotte would be the comfort of my age, and
I could reward her care and tenderness with a decent
fortune. A thousand difficulties oppose the execution of
the plan, which I have never opened but to you; yet it
would be less impracticable in England than in Switzerland. Adieu. I am wounded, pour some oil into my
wounds: yet I am less unhappy since I have thrown my
mind upon paper.

Are you not amazed at the French revolution? They
have the power, will they have the moderation, to estab-
lish a good constitution? Adieu, ever yours.

Lausanne Sept. 9. 1789.

Within an hour after the reception of your last, I drew
my pen for the purpose of a reply, and my exordium ran
in the following words: "I find by experience, that it is
much more rational, as well as easy, to answer a letter of
real business by the return of the post." This important

---

* Alluding to Sheffield-place.

truth is again verified by my own example. After writing three pages I was called away by a very rational motive, and the post departed before I could return to the conclusion. A second delay was coloured by some decent pretence. Three weeks have slipped away, and I now force myself on a task, which I should have despatched without an effort on the first summons. My only excuse is, that I had little to write about English business, and that I could write nothing definite about my Swiss affairs. And first, as Aristotle says, of the first,

1. I was indeed in low spirits when I sent what you so justly style my dismal letter; but I do assure you, that my own feelings contributed much more to sink me, than any events or terrors relative to the sale of Beriton. But I again hope and trust, from your consolatory epistle, that, &c. &c.

2. My Swiss transaction has suffered a great alteration. I shall not become the proprietor of my house and garden at Lausanne, and I relinquish the phantom with more regret than you could easily imagine. But I have been determined by a difficulty, which at first appeared of little moment, but which has gradually swelled to an alarming magnitude. There is a law in this country, as well as in some provinces of France, which is styled "le droit de retrait, le retrait lignagere" (Lord Lough-bourough must have heard of it), by which the relations of the deceased are entitled to redeem a house or estate at the price for which it has been sold; and as the sum fixed by poor Deyverdun is much below its known value, a crowd of competitors are beginning to start. The best opinions (for they are divided) are in my favour,

that I am not subject to "le droit de retrait," since I take not as a purchaser, but as a legatee. But the words of the will somewhat ambiguous, the event of law is always uncertain, the administration of justice at Berne (the last appeal) depends too much on favour and intrigue; and it is very doubtful whether I could revert to the life-holding, after having chosen and lost the property. These considerations engaged me to open negotiations with M. de Montagny, through the medium of my friend the judge; and as he most ardently wishes to keep the house, he consented, though with some reluctance, to my proposals. Yesterday he signed a covenant in the most regular and binding form, by which he allows my power of transferring my interest, interprets in the most ample sense my right of making alterations, and expressly renounces all claim, as landlord, of visiting or inspecting the premises. I have promised to lend him twelve thousand livres, (between seven and eight hundred pounds), secured on the house and land. The mortgage is four times its value; the interest of four pounds per cent. will be anually discharged by the rent of thirty guineas. So that I am now tranquil on that score for the remainder of my days. I hope that time will gradually reconcile me to the place which I have inhabited with my poor friend; for in spite of the *cream* of London, I am still persuaded that no other place is so well adapted to my taste and habits of studious and social life.

Far from delighting in the whirl of a metropolis, my only complaint against Lausanne is the great number of strangers, always of English, and now of French, by whom we are infested in summer. Yet we have escaped the *d——d* great ones, the Count d'Artois, the Polignacs, &c. who slip by us to Turin.   What a scene is France! While the assembly is voting abstract propositions, Paris is an independent republic; the provinces have neither authority nor freedom, and poor Necker declares that credit is no more, and that the people refuse to pay taxes. Yet I think you must be séduced by the abolition of tithes.   If Eden goes to Paris you may have some curious information.   Give me some account of Mr. and Mrs. Douglas.   Do they live with Lord North?   1 hope they do.   When will parliament be dissolved?   Are you still Covéntry mad?   I embrace my lady, the sprightly Maria, and the smiling Louisa.   Alas! alas! you will never come to Switzerland.   Adieu, ever yours.

Lausanne, Sept. 25th, 1789.

Alas! what perils do environ
The man who meddles with cold iron.

Alas! what delays and difficulties do attend the man who meddles with legal and landed business! yet if it be only to disappoint your expectation, I am not so very nervous at this new provoking obstacle.   I had totally forgotten the deed in question, which was contrived in the last year of my father's life, to tie his hands and regulate the disorders of his affairs; and which might have been so easily cancelled by Sir Stanier, who had not the smallest interest in it, either for himself or his family. The amicable suit which is now become necessary must, I think, be short and unambiguous, yet I cannot help dreading the crotchets that lurk under the chancellor's great wig; and, at all events, I forsee some additional delay and expense. The golden pill of the £2000 has soothed my discontent; and if it be safely lodged with the Goslings, I agree with you in considering it as an unequivocal pledge of a fair and willing purchaser. It is, indeed, chiefly in that light I now rejoice in so large a deposit, which is no longer necessary in its full extent. You are apprised by my last letter that I have reduced myself to the life enjoyment of the house and garden. And, in spite of my feelings, I am every day more convinced that I have chosen the safer side. I believe my cause to have been good, but it was doubtful. Law in this country is not so expensive as in England, but it is more troublesome. I must have gone to Berne, have solicited my judges in person—a vile custom! the event was uncertain; and during at least two years, I should have been in a state of suspense and anxiety: till the conclusion of which it would have been madness to have attempted any alteration or improvement. According to my present arrangement I shall want no more than £1100 of the £2000, and I suppose you will direct Gosling to lay out the remainder in India bonds, that it may not lie quite dead, while I am accountable to **** for the interest. The elderly lady in a male habit, who informed me that Yorkshire is a register county, is a certain judge, one Sir William Blackstone, whose name you may possibly have heard. After stating the danger of purchasers and creditors, with regard to the title of estates on which they lay out or lend their money, he thus continues: "In Scotland every act and event regarding the transmission of property is regularly entered on record; and some of our own provincial divisions, particularly the extended county of York and the populous county of Middlesex, have prevailed with the legislature to erect such registers within their respective districts." (Blackstone's Commentaries, vol. ii. p. 343, edition of 1774, in quarto.) If I am mistaken, it is in pretty good company; but I suspect that we are all right, and that the register is confined to one or two ridings. As we have, alas! two or three months before us, I should hope that your prudent sagacity will discover some sound land, in case you should not have time to arrange another mortgage. I now write in a hurry, as I am just setting out for Rolle, where I shall be settled with cook and servants in a pleasant apartment till the middle of November. The Severys have a house there, where they pass the autumn. I am not sorry to vary the scene for a few weeks, and I wish to be absent while some alterations are making in my house at Lausanne. I wish the change of air may be of service to Severy the father, but we do not at all like his present state of health. How completely, alas, how completely! could I now lodge you: but your firm resolve of making me a visit seems to have vanished like a dream. Next summer you will not find five hundred pounds for a rational friendly expedition; and should parliament be dissolved, you will perhaps find five thousand for ****. I cannot think of it with patience. Pray take serious strenuous measures for sending me a pipe of excellent Madeira in cask, with some dozens of Malmsey Madeira. It should be consigned to Messrs. Romberg, voituriers, at Ostend, and I must have timely notice of its march. We have so much to say about

France, that I suppose we shall never say anything. That country is now in a state of dissolution. Adieu.

Lausanne, December 15th, 1789.

You have often reason to accuse my strange silence and neglect in the most important of *my own* affairs; for I will presume to assert, that in a business of yours of equal consequence, you should not find me cold or careless.   But on the present occasion my silence is, perhaps, the highest compliment I ever paid you.   You remember the answer of Philip of Macedon: "Philip may sleep while he knows that Parmenio is awake." I expected, and, to say the truth, I wished that my Parmenio would have decided and acted, without expecting my dilatory answer, and in his decision I should have acquiesced with implicit confidence.   But since you will have my opinion, let us consider the present state of my affairs.   In the course of my life I have often known, and sometimes felt, the difficulty of getting money, but I now find myself involved in a more singular distress, the difficulty of placing it, and if it continues much longer, I shall almost wish for my land again.

I perfectly agree with you, that it is bad management to purchase in the funds when they do not yield four pounds per cent. * * *. Some of this money I can place safely, by means of my banker here; and I shall possess, what I have always desired, a command of cash, which I cannot abuse to my prejudice, since I have it in my power to supply with my pen any extraordinary or fanciful indulgence of expense.   And so much—much, indeed—for pecuniary matters.   What would you have

me say on the affairs of France?   We are too near, and
too remote, to form an accurate judgment of that wonderful scene.   The abuses of the court and government
called aloud for reformation; and it has happened, as it
will always happen, that an innocent, well-disposed
prince has paid the forfeit of the sins of his predecessors;
of the ambition of Louis XIV., of the profusion of Louis
XV.   The French nation had a glorious opportunity, but
they have abused, and may lose their advantages.   It
they had been content with a liberal translation of our
system, if they had respected the prerogatives of the
crown, and the privileges of the nobles, they might have
raised a solid fabric, on the only true foundation, the
natural aristocracy of a great country.   How different is
the prospect!   Their king brought a captive to Paris,
after his palace had been stained with the blood of his
guards; the nobles in exile; the clergy plundered in a
way which strikes at the root of all property: the capital
an independent republic; the union of the provinces dissolved; the flames of discord kindled by the worst of
men; (in that light I consider Mirabeau;) and the honest-
est of the assembly a set of wild visionaries, (like our Dr.
Price,) who gravely debate, and dream about the estab-
blishment of a pure and perfect democracy of five-and-
twenty millions, the virtues of the golden age, and the
primitive rights and equality of mankind, which would
lead, in fair reasoning, to an equal partition of lands and
money.   How many years must elapse before France
can recover any vigour, or resume her station among
the powers of Europe!   As yet, there is no symptom of

a great man, a Richelieu or a Cromwell, arising, either to restore the monarchy, or to lead the commonwealth. The weight of Paris, more deeply engaged in the funds than *all* the rest of the kingdom, will long delay a bankruptcy; and if it should happen, it will be, both in the cause and the effect, a measure of weakness rather than of strength. You send me to Chamberry, to see a prince and an archbishop. Alas! we have exiles enough here, with the Marshall de Castries and the Duke de Guignes at their head: and this inundation of strangers, which used to be confined to the summer, will now stagnate all the winter. The only ones whom I have seen with pleasure are M. Mounier, the late president of the national assembly, and the Count de Lally; they have both dined with me. Mounier, who is a serious dry politician, is returned to Dauphiné. Lally is an amiable man of the world, and a poet: he passes the winter here. You know how much I prefer a quiet select society to a crowd of names and titles, and that I always seek conversation with a view to amusement rather than information. What happy countries are England and Switzerland, if they know and preserve their happiness.

I have a thousand things to say to my lady, Maria, and Louisa, but I can add only a short postscript about the the Madeira. Good Madeira is now become essential to my health and reputation. May your hogshead prove as good as the last; may it not be intercepted by the rebels or the Austrians. What a scene again in that country! Happy England! Happy Switzerland! I again repeat. Adieu.

Lausanne, January 27th, 1790.

Your two last epistles of the 7th and 11th instant, were somewhat delayed on the road; they arrived within two days of each other, the last this morning, (the 27th): so that I answer by the first, or at least by the second post. Upon the whole, your French method, though sometimes more rapid, appears to me less sure and steady than the old German highway, &c., &c. *   *   *   *   *

But enough of this. A new and brighter prospect seems to be breaking upon ns, and few events of *that kind* have ever given me more pleasure than your successful negotiation and ****'s satisfactory answer. The agreement is, indeed, equally convenient for both parties: no time or expense will be wasted in scrutinizing the title of the estate; the interest will be secured by the clause of five per cent., and I lament with you, that no larger sum than £8000 can be placed on Beriton, without asking (what might be somewhat impudent) a collateral security, &c., &c. *   *   *   *   * But I wish you to choose and execute one or the other of these arrangements with sage discretion and absolute power. I shorten my letter, that I may dispatch it by this post. I see the time, and I shall rejoice to see it at the end of twenty years, when my cares will be at an end, and our friendly pages will no longer be sullied with the repetition of dirty land and vile money: when we may expatiate on the politics of the world and our personal sentiments. Without expecting your answer of business, I mean to write soon in a purer style, and I wish to lay open to my friend the state of my mind, which (exclusive of all worldly concerns) is not perfectly at ease. In the meanwhile, I must add two or three short articles. 1. I am astonished at Elmsly's silence, and the immobility of your picture. Mine should have departed long since, could I have found a sure opportunity, &c., &c. Adieu, yours.

Lausanne, May 15th, 1790.

Since the first origin (*ab ovo*) of our connexion and correspondence, so long an interval of silence has not intervened, as far as I remember, between us, &c., &c.

From my silence you conclude that the moral complaint, which I had insinuated in my last, is either insignificant or fanciful. The conclusion is rash. But the complaint in question is of the nature of a slow lingering disease, which is not attended with any immediate danger. As I have not leisure to expatiate, take the idea in three words: "Since the loss of poor Deyverdun, I am *alone*; and even in Paradise, solitude is painful to a social mind. When I was a dozen years younger, I *scarcely* felt the weight of a single existence amidst the crowds of London, of parliament, of clubs; but it will press more heavily upon me in this tranquil land, in the decline of life, and with the increase of infirmities. Some expedient, even the most desperate, must be embraced, to secure the domestic society of a male or female companion. But I am not in a hurry; there is time for reflection and advice." During this winter such finer feelings have been suspended by the grosser evil of bodily pain. On the ninth of February I was seized by such a fit of the gout as I had never known, though I must be thankful that its dire effects have been confined to the feet and knees without ascending to the more noble parts.   With some viscissitudes of better and worse, I have groaned between two and three months: the debility has survived the pain, and though now easy, I am carried about in my chair, without any power, and with a very distant chance, of supporting myself, from the extreme weakness and contraction of the joints of my knees.   Yet I am happy in a skilful physician, and kind assiduous friends ; every evening, during more than three months, has been enlivened (excepting when I have been forced to receive them) by some cheerful visits, and very often by a chosen party of both sexes.   How different is such society from the solitary evenings which I have passed in the tumult of London !   It is not worth while fighting about a shadow, but should I ever return to England, Bath, not the metropolis, would be my last retreat.

Your portrait is at last arrived in perfect condition, and now occupies a conspicuous place over the chimney-glass in my library.   It is the object of general admiration ; good judges (the few) applaud the work ; the name of Reynolds opens the eyes and mouths of the many ; and were not I afraid of making you vain, I would inform you that the original is not allowed to be more than five-and-thirty.   In spite of private reluctance and public discontent, I have honourably dismissed *myself*.*   I shall arrive at Sir Joshua's before the end of the month: he will give me a look, and perhaps a touch; and you will be indebted to the president one guinea for the carriage. Do not be nervous, I am not rolled up ; had I been so, you might have gazed on my charms four months ago.   I

* His portrait.

want some account of yourself, of my lady, (shall we never directly correspond?) of Louisa, and of Maria. How has the latter since her launch supported a quiet winter in Sussex? I so much rejoice in your divorce from that b—— Kitty Coventry, that I care not what marriage you contract. A great city would suit your dignity, and the duties which would kill me in the first session, would supply your activity with a constant fund of amusement. But tread softly and surely; the ice is deceitful, the water is deep, and you may be soused over head and ears before you are aware. Why did not you or Elmsly send me the African pamphlet* by the post? it would not have cost much. You have such a knack of turning a nation, that I am afraid you will triumph (perhaps by the force of argument) over justice and humanity. But do you not expect to work at Beelzebub's sugar plantations in the infernal regions, under the tender government of a negro driver? I should suppose both my lady and Miss Firth very angry with you.

As to the bill for prints, which has been too long neglected, why will you not exercise the power, which I have never revoked, over all my cash at the Goslings? The Severy family has passed a very favourable winter; the young man is impatient to hear from a family which he places above all others: yet he will generously write next week, and send you a drawivg of the alterations in the house. Do not raise your ideas; you know *I* am satisfied with convenience in architecture, and some elegance in furniture. I admire the coolness with which

* Observations on the project for abolishing the Slave Trade, by Lord Sheffield.

you ask me to epistolize Reynal and Elmsly, as if a letter were so easy and pleasant a task; it appears less so to me every day.

1790.

Your indignation will melt into pity, when you hear that for several weeks past I have been again confined to my chamber and my chair. Yet I must hasten, generously hasten, to exculpate the gout, my old enemy, from the curses which you already pour on his head. He is not the cause of this disorder, although the consequences have been somewhat similar. I am satisfied that this effort of nature has saved me from a very dangerous, perhaps a fatal, crisis; and l listen to the flattering hope that it may tend to keep the gout at a more respectful distance, &c. &c. &c.

The whole sheet has been filled with dry selfish business; but I must and will reserve some lines of the cover for a little friendly conversation. I passed four days at the castle of Coppet with Necker; and could have wished to have shown him, as a warning to any aspiring youth possessed with the demon of ambition. With all the means of private happiness in his power, he is the most miserable of human beings: the past, the present, and the future are equally odious to him. When I suggested some domestic amusement of books, building, &c. he answered, with a deep tone of despair, " In the state in which I now am, I can feel only the blast that has overthrown me." How different from the careless cheerfulness with which our poor friend Lord North supported his fall! Madame Necker maintains more external composure, *mais le diable n'y perd rien.* It is true that

Necker wished to be carried into the closet like old Pitt, on the shoulders of the people; and that he has been ruined by the democracy which he had raised. I believe him to be an able financier, and know him to be an honest man; too honest, perhaps, for a minister. His rival Colonne has passed through Lausanne, in his way from Turin; and was soon followed by the Prince of Condé, with his son and grandson; but I was too much indisposed to see them. They have, or have had, some wild projects of a counter-revolution: horses have been bought, men levied: such foolish attempts must end in the ruin of the party. Burke's book is a most admirable medicine against the French disease, which has made too much progress even in this happy country. I admire his eloquence, I approve his politics, I adore his chivalry, and I can forgive even his superstition. The primitive church, which I have treated with some freedom, was itself at that time an innovation, and I was attached to the old pagan establishment. The French spread so many lies about the sentiments of the English nation, that I wish the most considerable men of all parties and descriptions would join in some public act, declaring themselves satisfied and resolved to support our present constitution. Such a declaration would have a wonderful effect in Europe; and, were I thought worthy, I myself would be proud to subscribe to it. I have a great mind to send you something of a sketch, such as all thinking men might adopt.

I have intelligence of the approach of my Madeira. I accept with equal pleasure the second pipe, now in the torrid zone. Send me some pleasant details of your domestic state, of Maria, &c. If my lady thinks that my silence is a mark of indifference, my lady is a goose. I *must* have you all at Lausanne next summer.

Lausanne, August 7, 1790.

I answer at once your two letters ; and I should probably have taken earlier notice of the first, had I not been in daily expectation of the second. I must begin on the subject of what really interests me the most, your glorious election for Bristol. Most sincerely do I congratulate your exchange of a cursed expensive jilt, who deserted you for a rich Jew, for an honourable connexion with a chaste and virtuous matron, who will probably be as constant as she is disinterested. In the whole range of election from Caithness to St. Ives, I much doubt whether there be a single choice so truly honourable to the member and the constituents. The second commercial city invites, from a distant province, an independent gentleman, known only by his active spirit, and his writings on the subject of trade ; and names him, without intrigue or expense, for her representative: even the voice of party is silenced, while factions strive which shall applaud the most.

You are now sure, for seven years to come, of never wanting food—I mean business ; what a crowd of suitors or complainants will besiege your door! what a load of letters and memorials will be heaped on your table! I much question whether even you will not sometimes exclaim, *Ohe! jam satis est!* but that is your affair. Of the excursion to Coventry I cannot decide, but I hear it is pretty generally blamed: but, however, I love grati-

tude to an old friend; and shall not be very angry if you
d——d them with a farewell to all eternity.   But I cannot repress my indignation at the use of those foolish, obsolete, odious words, Whig and Tory.   In the American
war they might have some meaning; and then your lordship was a Tory, although you supposed yourself a Whig:
since the coalition all general principles have been con-
founded, and if there ever was an opposition to men, not
measures, it is the present.   Luckily, both the leaders are
great men; and, whatever happens, the country must
fall upon its legs.   What a strange mist of peace and war
seems to hang over the ocean!   We can perceive nothing but secrecy and vigour: but those are excellent
qualities in a minister.   From yourself and politics I now
return to my private concerns, which I shall methodi-
cally consider under the three great articles of mind,
body, and estate.

1. I am not absolutely displeased with your firing so
hastily at the hint, a tremendous hint, in my last letter.
But the danger is not so serious or imminent as you seem
to suspect; and I give you my word, that, before I take
the slightest step which can bind me either in law, conscience, or honour, I will faithfully communicate, and we
will freely discuss, the whole state of the business.   But
at present there is not any thing to communicate or discuss; I do assure you that I have not any particular object
in view: I am not in love with any of the hyænas of
Lausanne, though there are some who keep their claws
tolerably well pared.   Sometimes, in a solitary mood, I
have fancied myself married to one or other of these
whose society and conversation are the most pleasing to

me; but when I have painted in my fancy all the probable consequences of such an union, I have started from my dream, rejoiced in my escape, and ejaculated a thanksgiving that I was still in possession of my natural freedom. Yet I feel, and shall continue to feel, that domestic solitude, however it may be alleviated by the world, by study, and even by friendship, is a comfortless state, which will grow more painful as I descend into the vale of years. At present my situation is very tolerable; and if at dinner-time, or at my return home in the evening, I sometimes sigh for a companion, there are many hours and many occasions, in which I enjoy the superior blessing of being sole master of my own house. But your plan, though less dangerous, is still more absurd than mine: such a couple as you describe could not be found; and, if found, would not answer my purpose: their rank and position would be awkward and ambiguous to myself and my acquaintance; and the agreement of three persons of three characters would be still more impracticable. My plan of Charlotte Porten is undoubtedly the most desirable; and she might either remain a spinster (the case is not without example,) or marry some Swiss of my choice, who would increase and enliven our society; and both would have the strongest motives for kind and dutiful behaviour. But the mother has been indirectly sounded; and will not hear of such a proposal for some years. On my side, I would not take her, but as a piece of soft wax which I could model to the language and manners of the country: I must therefore be patient.

Young Severy's letter, which may be now in your hands, and which, for these three or four last posts, has furnished my indolence with a new pretence for delay, has already informed you of the means and circumstances of my resurrection. Tedious indeed was my confinement, since I was not able to move from my house or chair, from the ninth of February to the first of July, very nearly five months. The first weeks were accompanied with more pain than I have ever known in the gout, with anxious days and sleepless nights; and when that pain subsided, it left a weakness in my knees which seemed to have no end. My confinement was however softened by books, by the possession of every comfort and convenience, by a succession each evening of agreeable company, and by a flow of equal spirits and general good health. During the last weeks I descended to the ground floor, poor Deyverdun's apartment, and constructed a chair like Merlin's, in which I could wheel myself in the house and on the terrace. My patience has been universally admired; yet how many thousands have passed those five months less easily than myself. I remember making a remark perfectly simple, and perfectly true: "At present," I said to Madame de Severy, "I am not positively miserable, and I may reasonably hope a daily or weekly improvement, till sooner or later in the summer I shall recover new limbs, and new pleasures, which I do not now possess; have any of you such a prospect?" The prediction has been accomplished, and I have arrived to my present condition of strength, or rather of feebleness: I now can walk with tolerable ease in my garden and smooth places; but on the rough pavement of the town I use, and perhaps shall use, a sedan chair. The Pyrmont waters have performed wonders; and my physician (not Tissot, but a very sensible man) allows me to hope, that the term of the interval will be in proportion to that of the fit.

Have you read in the English papers that the government of Berne is overturned, and that we are divided into three democratical leagues? true as what I have read in the French papers, that the English have cut off Pitt's head, and abolished the House of Lords. The people of this country are happy; and in spite of some miscreants, and more foreign emissaries, they are sensible of their happiness.

Finally—Inform my lady, that I am indignant at a false and heretical assertion in her last letter to Severy, "that friends at a distance cannot love each other if they do not write." I love her better than any woman in the world; indeed I do; and yet I do not write. And she herself—but I am calm. We have now nearly one hundred French exiles, some of them worth being acquainted with; particularly a Count de Schomberg, who is become almost my friend; he is a man of the world, of letters, and of sufficient age, since in 1753 he succeeded to Marshal Saxe's regiment of dragoons. As to the rest, I entertain them, and they flatter me: but I wish we were reduced to our Lausanne Society. Poor France! the state is dissolved, the nation is mad! Adieu.

Lausanne, April 9th, 1791.

First, of my health; it is now tolerably restored: my legs are still weak, but the animal in general is in sound and lively condition; and we have great hopes from the fine weather and the Pyrmont waters. I most sincerely

wished for the presence of Maria, to embellish a ball
which I gave the 29th of last month to all the best company, natives and foreigners, of Lausanne, with the aid of
the Severys, especially of the mother and son, who
directed the œconomy, and performed the honours of the
fête. It opened about seven in the evening; the assembly of men and women was pleased and pleasing, the
music good, the illumination splendid, the refreshments
profuse: at twelve, one hundred and thirty persons sat
down to a very good supper; at two, I stole away to
bed, in a snug corner; and I was informed at breakfast,
that the remains of the veteran and young troops, with
Severy and his sister at their head, had concluded the
last dance about a quarter before seven. This magnificent entertainment has gained me great credit; and the
expense was more reasonable than you can easily
imagine. This was an extraordinary event, but I give
frequent dinners; and in the summer I have an assembly
every Sunday evening. What a wicked wretch! says
my lady.

I cannot pity you for the accumulation of business, as
you ought not to pity me, if I complained of tranquility of
Lausanne: we suffer or enjoy the effects of our own
choice. Perhaps you will mutter something of our not
being born for ourselves, of public spirit (I have formerly read of such a thing), of private friendship, for
which I give you full and ample credit, &c. But your
parliamentary operations, at least, will probably expire in
the month of June; and I shall refuse to sign the New-
haven conveyance, unless I am satisfied that you will
execute the Lausanne visit this summer. On the 15th of

June, suppose lord, lady, Maria, and maid, (poor Louisa!) in a post coach, with Etienne on horseback, set out from Downing-street, or Sheffield-place, cross the channel from Brighton to Dieppe, visit the national assembly, buy caps at Paris, examine the ruins of Versailles, and arrive at Lausanne, without danger or fatigue, the second week in July; you will be lodged pleasantly and comfortably, and will not perhaps despise my situation. A couple of months will roll, alas! too hastily away: you will all be amused by new scenes, new people; and whenever Maria and you, with Severy, mount on horseback to visit the country, the glaciers, &c., my lady and myself shall form a very quiet tête-à-tête at home. In September, if you are tired, you may return by a direct or indirect way; but I only desire that you will not make the plan impracticable by grasping at too much. In return, I promise you a visit of three or four months in the autumn of ninety-two: you and my booksellers are now my principal attractions in England. You had some right to growl at hearing of my supplement in the papers: but Cadell's indiscretion was founded on a hint which I had thrown out in a letter, and which in all probability will never be executed. Yet I am not totally idle. Adieu.

Lausanne, May 18th, 1791.

I write a short letter, on small paper, to inform you, that the various deeds, which arrived safe and in good condition, have this morning been sealed, signed, and delivered, in the presence of respectable and well known English witnesses. To have read the aforesaid acts, would have been difficult ; to have understood them, impracticable. I therefore signed them with my eyes shut, and in that implicit confidence, which we freemen and Britons are humbly content to yield to our lawyers and ministers. I hope, however, most seriously hope, that every thing has been carefully examined, and that I am not totally ruined. It is not without much impatience that I expect an account of the payment and investment of the purchase-money. It was my intention to have added a new edition of my will : but I have an unexpected call to go to Geneva to-morrow with the Severys, and must defer that business a few days, till after my return. On my return I may possibly find a letter from you, and will write more fully in answer : my posthumous work, contained in a single sheet, will not ruin you in postage. In the meanwhile, let me desire you either never to talk of Lausanne, or to execute the journey this summer ; after the despatch of public and *private* business, there can be no real obstacle but in yourself. Pray do not go to war with Russia : it is very foolish : I am quite angry with Pitt. Adieu.

Lausanne, May 31st, 1791.

At length I see a ray of sunshine breaking from a dark cloud. Your epistle of the 13th arrived this morning, the 25th instant, the day after my return from Geneva ; it has been communicated to Severy. We now believe that you intend to visit Lausanne this summer, and we hope that you will execute that intention. If you are a man of honour, you shall find me one ; and, on the day of your arrival at Lausanne, I will ratify my engagement of visiting the British isle before the end of the year 1792, excepting only the fair and foul exception of the gout. You rejoice me, by proposing the addition of dear Louisa; it was not without a bitter pang that I threw her overboard, to lighten the vessel and secure the voyage: I was fearful of the governess, a second carriage, and a long train of difficulty and expense, which might have ended in blowing up the whole scheme. But if you can bodkin the sweet creature into the coach, she will find an easy welcome at Lausanne. The first arrangements which I must make before your arrival, may be altered by your own taste, on a survey of the premises, and you will all be commodiously and pleasantly lodged. You have heard a great deal of the beauty of my house, garden, and situation: but such are their intrinsic value, that, unless I am much deceived, they will bear the test even of exaggerated praise. From my knowledge of your lordship, I have always entertained some doubt how you would get through the society of a Lausanne winter: but I am satisfied that, exclusive of friendship, your summer visits to the banks of the Leman Lake will long be remembered as one of the most agreeable periods of your life; and that you will scarcely regret the amusement of a Sussex committee of navigation in the dog days. You ask for details: what details? a map of France and a post-book are easy and infallible guides. If the ladies are not afraid of the ocean, you are not ignorant of the passage from Brighton to Dieppe: Paris will then be in your direct road; and even allowing you to look at the Pandæmonium, the ruins of Versailles, &c., a fortnight diligently employed will clear

you from Sheffield-Place to Gibbon Castle.   What can
I say more ?

As little have I to say on the subject of my worldly
matters, which seems now, Jupiter be praised, to be drawing to a final conclusion; since, when people part with
their money, they are indeed serious.   I do not perfectly
understand the ratio of the precise sum which you have
poured into Gosling's reservoir, but suppose it will be
explained in a general account.

You have been very dutiful in sending me, what I
have always desired, a cut Woodfall on a remarkable debate; a debate, indeed, most remarkable!   Poor
**** is the most eloquent and rational madman that I
ever knew.   I love Fox's feelings, but I detest the political principles of the man, and of the party.   Formerly
you detested them more strongly, during the American
war, than myself.   I am half afraid that you are corrupted
by your unfortunate connexions.   Should you admire
the national assembly, we shall have many an altercation,
for I am as high an aristocrat as Burke himself; and
he has truly observed, that it is impossible to debate with
temper on the subject of that cursed revolution.   In my
last excursion to Geneva I frequently saw the Neckers,
who by this time are returned to their summer residence
at Coppet.   He is much restored in health and spirits,
especially since the publication of his last book, which has
probably reached England.   Both parties who agree in
abusing him, agree likewise that he is a man of virtue
and genuis: but I much fear that the purest intentions
have been productive of the most baneful consequences.
Our military men, I mean the French, are leaving us

every day for the camp of the Princes at Worms, and support what is called ———— representation.   Their hopes are sanguine; I will not answer for their being well grounded: it is *certain*, however, that the emperor had an interview the 19th instant with the Count of Artois at Mantua: and the aristocrats talk in mysterious language of Spain, Sardinia, the empire, four or five armies, &c.   They will doubtless strike a blow this summer: may it not recoil on their own heads!   Adieu Embrace our female travellers.   A short delay.

Lausanne, June 12th, 1791.

I now begin to see you all in real motion, swimming from Brighton to Dieppe, according to my scheme, and afterwards treading the direct road which you cannot well avoid, to the turbulent capital of the late kingdom of France.   I know not what more to say, or what further instructions to send; they would indeed be useless, as you are travelling through a country which has been sometimes visited by Englishmen: only this let me say, that, in the midst of anarchy, the roads were never more secure than at present.   As you will wish to assist at the national assembly, you will act prudently in obtaining from the French in London a good recommendation to some leading member; Cazales, for instance, or the Abbé Maury.   I soon expect from Elmsly a cargo of books; but you may bring me any new pamphlet of exquisite flavour, particularly the last works of John Lord Sheffield,* which the dog has always neglected to

---

* Observations on the Corn Laws.

send. You will have time to write once more, and you must endeavour, as nearly as possible, to mark the day of your arrival. You may come either by Lyons and Geneva, by Dijon and Les Rousses, or by Dole and Pontarlière. The post will fail you on the edge of Switzerland, and must be supplied by hired horses. I wish you to make your last day's journey easy, so as to dine upon the road, and arrive by tea-time. The pulse of the counter revolution beats-high, but I cannot send you any certain facts. Adieu. I want to *hear* my lady abusing me for never writing. *All* the Severys are very impatient.

Notwitstanding the high premium, I do not absolutely wish you drowned. Besides all other cares, I must marry and propagate, which would give me a great deal of trouble.

Lausanne, July 1st, 1791.

In obedience to your orders, I direct a flying shot to Paris, though I have not any thing particul ar to add, excepting our impatience is increased in the *inverse ratio* of time and space. Yet I almost doubt whether you have passed the sea. The news of the king of France's escape must have reached you before the 28th, the day of your departure, and the prospect of strange unknown disorder may well have suspended your firmest resolves. The royal animal is again caught, and all may probably be quiet. I was just going to exhort you to pass through Brussels and the confines of Germany ; a fair Irishism, since if you read this, you are already at Paris. The only reasonable advice which now remains, is to obtain, by means of Lord Gower, a sufficiency, or even superfluity, of forcible passports, such as leave no room for cavil on a jealous frontier.   The frequent intercourse with Paris has proved that the best and shortest road, instead of Besançon, is by Dijon, Dole, Les Rousses, and Nyon.   Adieu.   I warmly embrace the ladies.   It would be idle now to talk of business.

———————

It has appeared from the foregoing letters, that a visit from myself and family, to Mr. Gibbon at Lausanne, had been for some time in agitation.   This long-promised excursion took place in the month of June 1791, and occasioned a considerable cessation of our correspondence. I landed at Dieppe immediately after the flight from, and return to, Paris of the unfortunate Louis XVI.   During my stay in that capital, I had an opportunity of seeing the extraordinary ferment of men's minds, both in the national assembly, and in private societies, and also in my passage through France to Lausanne, where I recalled to my memory the interesting scenes I had witnessed, by frequent conversations with my deceased friend.   I might have wished to record his opinions on the subject of the French Revolution, if he had not expressed them so well in the annexed letters.   He seemed to suppose, as some of his letters hint, that I had a tendency to the now French opinions.   Never, indeed, I can with truth aver, was suspicion more unfounded; nor could it have been admitted into Mr. Gibbon's mind, but that his extreme friendship for me, and his utter abhorrence of these notions, made him anxious and even jealous, even to an excess that I should not entertain them. He was, however, soon undeceived; he found that I was as averse to them as himself. I had from the first expressed an opinion, that such a change as was aimed at in France, must derange all the regular governments in Europe, hazard the internal quiet and dearest interests of this country, and probably end in bringing on mankind a much greater portion of misery, than the most sanguine reformer had ever promised to himself or others to produce of benefit, by the visionary schemes of liberty and equality, with which the ignorant and vulgar were misled and abused.

Mr. Gibbon, at first, like many others, seemed pleased with the prospect of the reform of inveterate abuses; but he very soon discovered the mischief which was intended, the imbecility with which concessions were made, and the ruin that must arise from the want of resolution or conduct, in the administration of France. He lived to reprobate, in the strongest terms possible, the folly of the first reformers, and the something worse than the extravagance and ferocity of their successors. He saw the wild and mischievous tendency of those reformers, which, while they professed nothing but amendment, really meant destruction to all social order; and so strongly was his opinion fixed, as to the danger of hasty innovation, that he became a warm and zealous advocate for every sort of old establishment, which he marked in various ways, sometimes rather ludicrously; and I recollect, in a circle where French affairs were the topic, and some Portuguese present, he, seemingly with seriousness, argued in favour of the inquisition at Lisbon, and said he would not, at the present moment, give up even that old establishment.

It may, perhaps, not be quite uninteresting to the readers of these Memoirs, to know that I found Mr. Gibbon at Lausanne in possession of an excellent house; the view from which, and from the terrace, was so uncommonly beautiful, that even his own pen would with difficulty describe the scene which it commanded. This prospect comprehended every thing grand and magnificent, which could be furnished by the finest mountains among the Alps, the most extensive view of the Lake of Geneva, with a beautifully varied and cultivated country, adorned by numerous villas, and picturesque buildings, intermixed with beautiful masses of stately trees. Here my friend received us with an hospitality and kindness which I can never forget. The best apartments of the house were appropriated to our use; the choicest society of the place was sought for, to enliven our visit, and to render every day of it cheerful and agreeable. It was impossible for any man to be more esteemed and admired than Mr. Gibbon was at Lausanne. The preference he had given to that place in adopting it for a residence, rather than his own country, was felt and acknowledged by all the inhabitants; and he may have been said almost to have given the law to a set of as willing subjects as any man ever presided over. In return for the deference shown to him, he mixed, without any affectation, in all the society. I mean all the best society that Lausanne afforded; he could indeed command it, and was, perhaps, for that reason the more partial to it; for he often declared that he liked society more as a relaxation from study, than as expecting to derive from it amusement or instruction; that to books he looked for improvement, not to living persons. But this I considered partly as an answer to my expressions of wonder, that a man who might choose the most various and the most generally improved society in the world—namely, in England—should prefer the very limited circle of Lausanne, which he never deserted, but for an occasional visit to M. and Madame Necker. It must not, however, be understood, that in choosing Lausanne for his home, he was insensible to the merits of a residence in England: he was not in possession of an income which corresponded with his notions of ease and comfort in his own country. In Switzerland his fortune was ample. To this consideration of fortune may be added another, which also had its weight; from early youth Mr. Gibbon had contracted a partiality for foreign taste and foreign habits of life, which made him less a stranger abroad than he was, in some respects, in his native country. This arose, perhaps, from having been out of England from his sixteenth to his twenty-first year; yet when I came to Lausanne, I found him apparently without relish for French society. During the stay I made with him he renewed his intercourse with the principal French who were at Lausanne; of whom there happened to be a considerable number, distinguished for rank or talents: many indeed respectable for both.* During my stay in

* Marshal de Castries and several branches of his family, Duc de Guignes and daughters, Duc and Duchesse de Guiche, Madame de Grammont, Princesse d'Henin, Princesse de Bouillon, Duchesse de Biron, Prince de Salm, Compte de Schomberg, Count de Lally, Lally Tolendal, M. Mounier, Madame d'Aguesseau and family, M. de Malsherbes, &c. &c.

Switzerland, I was not absent from my friend's house, except during a short excursion that we made together to Mr. Necker's at Coppet, and a tour to Geneva, Chamouni, over the Col de Balme, to Martigny, St. Maurice, and round the Lake by Vevay to Lausanne. In the social and singularly pleasant months that I passed with Mr, Gibbon, he enjoyed his cheerfulness, with good health. Since he left England, in 1788, he had a severe attack, mentioned in one of the foregoing letters, of an erisipelas, which at last settled in one of his legs, and left something of a dropsical tendency; for at this time I first perceived a considerable degree of swelling about the ancle.

In the beginning of October I left this delightful residence; and some time after my return to England, our correspondence recommenced.

LETTERS

FROM

EDWARD GIBBON, ESQ.

TO

LORD SHEFFIELD AND OTHERS.

LETTERS FROM EDWARD GIBBON, ESQ. TO LORD
SHEFFIELD AND OTHERS.

EDWARD GIBBON, ESQ. TO THE HON. MISS HOLROYD.

Lausanne, Nov. 9th, 1791.

GULLIVER is made to say, in presenting his interpreter,
" My tongue is in the mouth of my friend."   Allow me
to say, with proper expressions and excuses, " My pen is
in the hand of my friend;" and the aforesaid friend begs
leave thus to continue.*

I remember to have read somewhere in Rousseau, of a
lover quitting very often his mistress, to have the pleasure of corresponding with her.   Though not absolutely
your lover, I am very much your admirer, and should be
extremely tempted to follow the same example.   The
spirit and reason which prevail in your conversation, appear to great advantage in your letters.   The three
which I have received from Berne, Coblentz, and Brussels
have given me much real pleasure : first, as a proof that
you are often thinking of me; secondly, as an evidence
that you are capable of keeping a resolution; and
thirdly, from their own intrinsic merit and entertainment.
The style, without any allowance for haste or hurry, is
perfectly correct; the manner is neither too light nor too

* The remainder of the letter was dictated by Mr. Gibbon, and written
by M. Wilh. de Severy.—S.

grave; the dimensions neither too long nor too short; they are such, in a word, as I should like to receive from the daughter of my best friend. I attend your lively journal, through bad roads and worse inns. Your description of men and manners conveys very satisfactory information; and I am particularly delighted with your remark concerning the irregular behaviour of the Rhine. But the Rhine, alas! after some temporary wanderings, will be content to flow in his old channel, while man— man is the greatest fool of the whole creation.

I direct this letter to Sheffield-place, where I suppose you arrived in health and safety. I congratulate my lady on her quiet establishment by her fireside; and hope you will be able, after all your excursions, to support the climate and manners of old England. Before this epistle reaches you, I hope to have received the two promised letters from Dover and Sheffield-place. If they should not meet with a proper return, you will pity and forgive me. I have not yet heard from Lord Sheffield, who seems to have devolved on his daughter the task which she has so gloriously executed. I shall probably not write to him, till I have received his first letter of business from England; but with regard to my lady I have most excellent intentions.

I never could understand how two persons of such superior merit, as Miss Holroyd and Miss Lausanne, could have so little relish for one another, as they appeared to have in the beginning; and it was with great pleasure that I observed the degrees of their growing intimacy, and the mutual regret of their separation. Whatever you may imagine, your friends at Lausanne

have been thinking as frequently of yourself and company, as you could possibly think of them: and you will
be very ungrateful if you do not seriously resolve to
make them a second visit under such name and title as
you may judge most agreeable. None of the Severy
family, except perhaps my secretary, are inclined to forget you; and I am continually asked for some account of
your health, motions and amusements. Since your
departure, no great events have occurred. I have made
a short excursion to Geneva and Coppet, and found M.
Necker in much better spirits than when you saw him.
They pressed me to pass some weeks this winter in
their house at Geneva; and I may possibly comply, at
least in part, with their invitation. The aspect of Lausanne is peaceful and placid; and you have no hopes of
a revolution driving me out of this country. We hear
nothing of the proceedings of the commission,* except
by playing at cards every evening with Monsieur
Fischer, who often speaks of Lord Sheffield with esteem
and respect. There is no appearance of Rosset and La

---

* A commission at the head of which was Monsieur Fischer, one of the
principal members of the government of Berne, a very active and intelli-
gent man, who would have distinguished himself in the administration of
any country. This commission, which was accompanied by two or three
thousand of the best of the German militia of the canton of Berne, was sent
for the purpose of examining into some attempts to introduce the French
revolutionary principles into the Pays de Vaud. Several persons were
seized; the greater part were released; the examination was secret, but
Rosset and La Motte were confined in the Castle of Chillon; and being
afterwards condemned, for correspondence with the French, to a long imprisonment, were transferred to the castle of Arbourg, from whence they
escaped.

Motte being brought to a speedy trial, and they still remain in the castle of Chillon, which (according to the
geography of the national assembly) is washed by the
sea.   Our winter begins with great severity; and we
shall not probably have many balls, which, as you may
imagine, I lament much.   Angletine does not consider
two French words as a letter.   Montrond sighs and
blushes whenever Louisa's name is mentioned: Phillip-
pine wishes to converse with her on men and manners.
The French ladies are settled in town for the winter, and
they form, with Mrs. Trevor, a very agreeable addition
to our society.   It is now enlivened by a visit of the
Chevalier de Boufflers, one of the most accomplished men
of the *ci-devant* kingdom of France.

As Mrs. Wood,* who has miscarried, is about to leave
us, I must either cure or die; and, upon the whole, I
believe the former will be most expedient.   You will see
her in London, with dear Corea, next winter.   My rival
magnificently presents me with a hogshead of Madeira;
so that in honour I could not supplant him: yet I do
assure you, from my heart, that another departure is
much more painful to me.   The apartment† below is shut
up, and I know not when I shall again visit it with pleasure.
Adieu.   Believe me, one and all, most affectionately yours.

EDWARD GIBBON, ESQ. TO THE RIGHT HON. LORD SHEFFIELD.

Lausanne, December 28, 1791.

Alas! alas! the demon of procrastination has again
possessed me.   Three months have nearly rolled away

* Madame de Silva.

† The apartment principally inhabited during the residence of my family
at Lausanne.—S.

since your departure; and seven letters, five from the most valuable Maria, and two from yourself, have extorted from me only a single epistle, which, perhaps, would never have been written, had I not used the permission of employing my own tongue and the hand of a secretary. Shall I tell you, that for these last six weeks, the eve of every day has witnessed a *firm* resolution, and the day itself has furnished some ingenious delay? This morning, for instance, I determined to invade you as soon as the breakfast things should be removed: they were removed; but I had something to read, to write, to meditate, and there was time enough before me. Hour after hour has stolen away, and I finally begin my letter at two o'clock, evidently too late for the post, as I must dress, dine, go abroad, &c. A foundation, however, *shall be* laid, which will stare me in the face; and next Saturday I shall probably be roused by the awful reflection that it is the last day in the year.

After realizing this summer an event which I had long considered as a dream of fancy, I know not whether I should rejoice or grieve at your visit to Lausanne. While I possessed the family, the sentiment of pleasure highly predominated; when, just as we had subsided in a regular, easy, comfortable plan of life, the last trump sounded, and, without speaking of the pang of separation, you left me to one of the most gloomy, solitary months of October, which I have ever passed. For yourself and daughters, however, you have contrived to snatch some of the most interesting scenes of this world. Paris, at such a moment, Switzerland, and the Rhine, Strasburg, Coblentz, have suggested a train of lively images and useful ideas, which will not be speedily erased. The mind of the young damsel, more especially, will be enlarged and enlightened in every sense. In four months she has lived many years; and she will much deceive and displease me, if she does not review and methodize her journal, in such a manner as she is capable of performing, for the amusement of her particular friends. Another benefit which will redound from your recent view is, that every place, person, and object, about Lausanne, are now become familiar and interesting to you. In our future correspondence (do I dare pronounce the word correspondence?) I can talk to you as freely of every circumstance as if it were actually before your eyes. And first, of my own improvements.—All those venerable piles of ancient verdure which you *admired*, have been eradicated in one fatal day. Your faithful substitutes, William de Severy and Levade, have never ceased to persecute me, till I signed their death warrant. Their place is now supplied by a number of picturesque naked poles, the foster fathers of as many twigs of platanuses, which may afford a grateful but distant shade to the founder, or to his " seris nepotibus." In the meanwhile, I must confess that the terrace appears broader, and that I discover a much larger quantity of snow than I should otherwise do. The workmen admire your ingenious plan for cutting out a new bed-chamber and bookroom; but, on mature consideration, we all unanimously prefer the old scheme of adding a third room on the terrace beyond the library, with two spacious windows, and a fire-place between. It will be larger (28 feet by 21), and pleasanter, and warmer: the difference of expense

will be much less considerable than I imagined : the door
of communication with the library will be artfully buried
in the wainscot ; and, unless it be opened by my own
choice, may always remain a profound secret. Such is
the design ; but as it will not be executed before next
summer, you have time and liberty to state your objec-
jections. I am much colder about the staircase, but it
may be finished, according to your idea, for thirty pounds;
and I feel they will persuade me. Am I not a very rich man?
When these alterations are completed, few authors of six
volumes in quarto will be more agreeably lodged than
myself. Lausanne is now full and lively ; all our native
families are returned from the country ; and, praised be
the Lord, we are infested with few foreigners, either
French or English. Even our democrats are more reasonable or more discreet ; it is agreed to waive the subject of politics, and all seem happy and cordial, I have
a grand dinner this week, a supper of thirty or forty
people on twelfth-day, &c. ; some concerts have taken
place, some balls are talked of ; and even Maria
would allow (yet it is ungenerous to say even Maria) that
the winter scene in Lausanne is tolerably gay and active.
I say nothing of the Severys, as Angletine has epistolized
Maria last post. She has probably hinted that her brother meditates a short excursion to Turin ; that worthy
fellow Trevor has given him a pressing invitation to his
own house. In the beginning of February I propose
going to Geneva for three or four weeks. I shall lodge
and eat with the Neckers ; my mornings will be my own,
and I shall spend my evenings in the society of the place,
where I have many acquaintance. This short absence

will agitate my stagnant life, and restore me with fresh
appetite to my house, my library, and my friends. Before that time (the end of February) what events may
happen, or be ready to happen! The national assembly
(compared to which the former was a senate of heroes
and demi-gods) seem resolved to attack Germany "avec
quatre millions de bayonettes libres;" the army of the
princes must soon either fight, or starve, or conquer.
Will Sweden draw his sword? will Russia draw her
purse? an empty purse! All is darkness and anarchy:
neither party is strong enough to oppose a settlement; and
I cannot see a possibility of an amicable arrangement,
where there are no heads (in any sense of the word) who
can answer for the multitude. Send me your ideas, and
those of Lord Guildford, Lord Loughborough, Fox, &c.

Before I conclude, a word of my vexatious affairs.—
Shall I never sail on the smooth stream of good security
and half-yearly interest? Will every body refuse my
money? I had already written to Darell and Gosling to
obey your commands, and was in hopes that you had
already made large and salutary evacuations. During
your absence I never expected much effect from the cold indifference of agents; but you are now in England—you
will be speedily in London; set all your setting dogs to
beat the field, hunt, enquire.—why should you not adver-
tise? Yet I am almost ashamed to complain of some
stagnation of interest, when I am witness to the natural
and acquired philosophy of so many French, who are
reduced from riches, not to indigence but to absolute
want and beggary. A Count Argout has just left us,
who possessed ten thousand a-year in the island of St.

Domingo ; he is utterly burned and ruined ; and a brother, whom he tenderly loved, has been murdered by the negroes. These are real misfortunes. I have much revolved the plan of the Memoirs I once mentioned ; and, as you do not think it ridiculous, I believe I shall make an attempt: if I can please myself, I am confident of not displeasing ; but let this be a profound secret between us: people must not be prepared to laugh ; they must be taken by surprise. Have you looked over your, or rather my letters? Surely in the course of the year, you may find a safe and cheap occasion of sending me a parcel ; they may assist me. Adieu. I embrace my lady: send me a favourable account of her health. I kiss the Marmaille. By an amazing push of remorse and diligence I have finished my letter (three pages and a half) this same day since dinner; but I have not time to read it. Ever yours.

Half-past six.

TO THE SAME.

Lausanne, December 31st, 1792.
To-morrow a new year, *multos et felices.*

I now most sincerely repent of my late repentance, and do almost swear never to renounce the amiable and useful practice of procrastination. Had I delayed, as I was strongly tempted, another post, your missive of the 13th, which did not reach me till this morning (three mails were due), would have arrived in time, and I might have avoided this second Herculean labour. It will be, however, no more than an infant Hercules. The topics of conversation have been fully discussed, and I shall now confine myself to the needful of the new busi-

ness. *Felix faustumque fit!* may no untoward accident
disarrange your Yorkshire mortgage; the conclusion of
which will place me in a clear and easy state, such as I
have never known since the first hour of property. * * * *

The three per cents are so high, and the country is in
such a d——d state of prosperity under that fellow Pitt,
that it goes against me to purchase at such low interest.
In my visit to England next autumn, or in the spring following, (alas you *must* acquiesce in the alternative,) I
· hope to be armed with sufficient materials to draw a sum,
which may be employed as taste or fancy shall dictate,
in the improvement of my library, a service of plate, &c.
I am not very sanguine, but surely this is no uncomfortable prospect. This pecuniary detail, which has not indeed been so unpleasant as it used formerly to be, has
carried me farther than I expected. Let us now drink
and be merry. I flatter myself that your Madeira, improved by its travels, will set forwards for Messrs. Romberg, at Ostend, early in the spring: and I should be
very well pleased if you could add a hogshead of excellent claret, for which we should be entitled to the draw-
back: they must halt at Basle, and send notice to me for
a safe conduct. Have you had any intelligence from
Lord Auckland about the wine which he was to order
from Bordeaux, by Marseilles and the Rhone? The
one need not impede the other: I wish to have a large
stock. Corea has promised me a hogshead of his native
Madeira, for which I am to give him an order on Cadell
for a copy of the Decline and Fall: he vanished without
notice, and is now at Paris. Could you not fish out his
direction by Mrs. Wood, who by this time is in England?

I rejoice in Lally's prosperity. Have you reconsidered my proposal of a declaration of constitutional principles from the heads of the party? I think a foolish address from a body of Whigs to the national assembly renders it still more incumbent on you. Achieve my worldly concerns, *et eris mihi magnus Apollo.* Adieu, ever yours.

TO THE SAME.

Lausanne, April 4th, 1794.

For fear you should abuse me, as usual, I will begin the attack, and scold you, for not having yet sent me the long-expected intelligence of the completion of my mortgage. You had positively assured me that the second of February would terminate my worldly cares, by a consummation so devoutly to be wished. The news, therefore, might reach me about the eighteenth; and I argued with the gentle logic of laziness, that it was perfectly idle to answer your letter, till I could chant a thanksgiving song of gratitude and praise. As every post disappointed my hopes, the same argument was repeated for the next; and twenty empty handed postilions have blown their insignificant horns, till I am provoked at last to write by sheer impatience and vexation. *Facit indignatio versum. Cospetto di Baccho;* for I must ease myself by swearing a little. What is the cause, the meaning, the pretence, of this delay? Are the Yorkshire mortgagors inconstant in their wishes? Are the London lawyers constant in their procrastination? Is a letter on the road, to inform me that all is concluded, or to tell me that all is broken to pieces? Had the money been placed in the three per cents last May, besides the annual interest it would have

gained by the rise of stock nearly twenty per cent.   Your
lordship is a wise man, a successful writer, and a useful
senator: you understand America and Ireland, corn and
slaves, but your prejudice against the funds,* in which I
am often tempted to join, makes you a little blind to their
increasing value in the hands of our virtuous and excellent minister.   But our regret is vain: one pull more and
we reach the shore; and our future correspondence will
be no longer tainted with business.   Shall I then be more
diligent and regular?   I hope and believe so; for now
that I have got over this article of worldly interest, my
letter seems to be almost finished.   *A propos* of letters,
am I not a sad dog to forget my Lady and Maria?
Alas! the dual number has been prejudicial to both.
"How happy could I be with either, were t'other dear
charmer away."   I am like the ass of famous memory;
I cannot tell which way to turn first, and there I stand
mute and immovable.   The baronial and maternal dignity of my lady, supported by twenty years' friendship,
may claim the preference.   But the five incomparable
letters of Maria!—Next week, however.—Am I not
ashamed to talk of next week?

I have most successfully, and most agreeably, executed my plan of spending the month of March at Geneva,
in the Necker house, and every circumstance that I had
arranged turned out beyond my expectation; the freedom
of the morning, the society of the table and drawing-
room, half an hour past two till six or seven; an evening
assembly and card-party, in a round of the best company,

* It would be more correct if he had only stated, my preference of land to
all other property.

and, excepting one day in the week, a private supper of free and friendly conversation. You would like Geneva better than Lausanne; there is much more information to be got among the men; but though I found some agreeable women, their manners and style of life are, upon the whole, less easy and pleasant than our own. I was much pleased with Necker's brother, M. de Germany, a good-humoured, polite, sensible man, without the genius and fame of the statesman, but much more adapted for private and ordinary happiness. Madame de Stael is expected in a few weeks at Coppet, where they receive her, and where, " to dumb forgetfulness a prey," she will have leisure to regret " the pleasing anxious being," which she enjoyed amidst the storms of Paris. But what can the poor creature do? her husband is in Sweden, her lover is no longer secretary at war, and her father's house is the only place where she can reside with the least degree of prudence and decency. Of that father I have really a much higher idea than I ever had before; in our domestic intimacy he cast away his gloom and reserve; I saw a great deal of his mind, and all that I saw is fair and worthy. He was overwhelmed by the hurricane, he mistook his way in the fog, but in such a perilous situation, I much doubt whether any mortal could have seen or stood. In the meanwhile, he is abused by all parties, and none of the French in Geneva will set their foot in his house. He remembers Lord Sheffield with esteem; his health is good, and he would be tranquil in his private life, were not his spirits continually wounded by the arrival of every letter and every newspaper. His sympathy is deeply interested by the fatal consequences

of a revolution, in which he had acted so leading a part;
and he feels as a friend for the danger of M. de Lessart,
who may be guilty in the eyes of the Jacobins, or even
of his judges, by those very actions and dispatches
which would be most approved by all the lovers of his
country. What a momentous event is the emperor's
death? In the forms of a new reign, and of the imperial
election, the democrats have at least gained time, if they
knew how to use it. But the new monarch, though of a
weak complexion, is of a martial temper; he loves the
soldiers, and is beloved by them; and the slow, fluctu-
ating politics of his uncle may be succeeded by a direct
line of march to the gates of Strasburg and Paris. It is
the opinion of the master movers in France, (I know it
most certainly,) that their troops will not fight, that the
people have lost all sense of patriotism, and that on the
first discharge of an Austrian cannon the game is up.
But what occasion for Austrians or Spaniards? the
French are themselves their greatest enemies; four
thousand Marseillais are marched against Arles and
Avignon, the *troupes de ligne* are divided between the
two parties, and the flame of civil war will soon extend
over the southern provinces. You have heard of the unworthy treatment of the Swiss regiment of Ernst. The
canton of Berne has bravely recalled them, with a stout
letter to the king of France, which must be inserted in
all the papers. I now come to the most unpleasant article, our home politics. Rosset and La Motte are condemned to fine and twenty years imprisonment in the
fortress of Arbourg. We have not yet received their
official sentence, nor is it believed that the proofs and

proceedings against them will be published ; an awkward
circumstance, which it does not seem easy to justify.
Some (though none of note) are taken up, several are fled,
many more are suspected and suspicious.   All are silent,
but it is the silence of fear and discontent ; and the secret
hatred which rankled against government begins to point
against the few who are known to be well affected.   I
never knew any place so much changed as Lausanne,
even since last year ; and though you will not be much
obliged to me for the motive, I begin very seriously to
think of visiting Sheffield-place by the month of September next.   Yet here again I am frightened, by the dan-
gers of a French, and the difficulties of a German, route.
You must send me an account of the passage from Dieppe
to Brighton, with an itinerary of the Rhine, distances,
expenses, &c.   As usual, I just save the post, nor have I
time to read my letter, which after wasting the morning
in deliberation, has been struck off in a heat since dinner.
No news of the Madeira.   The views of Sheffield-place
are just received ; they are admired, and shall be
framed. Severy has spent the carnival at Turin.   Trevor
is only the best man in the world.

TO THE SAME.

Lausanne, May 30th, 1792.

After the receipt of your *penultimate*, eight days ago,
I expected with much impatience, the arrival of your
next-promised epistle.   It arrived this morning, but has
not completely answered my expectations.   I wanted,
and I hoped for a full and fair picture of the present and
probable aspect of your political world, with which, at

this distance, I seem every day less satisfied. In the slave question you triumphed last session, in this you have been defeated. What is the cause of this alteration? If it proceeded only from an impulse of humanity, I cannot be displeased, even with an error; since it is very likely that my own vote (had I possessed one) would have been added to the majority. But in this rage against slavery, in the numerous petitions against the slave-trade, was there no leaven of new democratical principles? no wild ideas of the rights and natural equality of man? It is these I fear. Some articles in newspapers, some pamphlets of the year, the Jockey Club, have fallen into my hands. I do not infer much from such publications; yet I have never known them of so black and malignant a cast. I shuddered at Grey's motion; disliked the half-support of Fox, admired the firmness of Pitt's declaration, and excused the usual intemperance of Burke. Surely such men as ****, ********, ******, have talents for mischief. I see a club of reform which contains some respectable names. Inform me of the professions, the principles, the plans, the resources, of these reformers. Will they heat the minds of the people? Does the French democracy gain no ground? Will the bulk of your party stand firm to their own interest, and that of their country? Will you not take some active measures to declare your sound opinions, and separate yourselves from your rotten members? or if you allow them to perplex government, if you trample with this solemn business, if you do not resist the spirit of innovation in the first attempt, if you admit the smallest and most specious change in our parliamentary system, you are lost. You will be driven from one step to another; from principles just in theory, to consequences most pernicious in practice; and your first concessions will be productive of every subsequent mischief, for which you will be answerable to your country and to posterity. Do not suffer yourselves to be lulled into a false security; re-member the proud fabric of the French monarchy. Not four years ago it stood founded, as it might seem, on the rock of time, force, and opinion, supported by the triple aristocracy of the church, the nobility, and the parliaments. They are crumbled into dust; they are vanished from the earth. If this tremendous warning has no effect on the men of property in England; if it does not open every eye, and raise every arm, you will deserve your fate. If I am too precipitate, enlighten; if I am too desponding, encourage me.

My pen has run into this argument; for, as much a foreigner as you think me, on this momentous subject, I feel myself an Englishman.

The pleasure of residing at Sheffield-place is, after all, the first and the ultimate object of my visit to my native country. But when or how will that visit be effected? Clouds and whirlwinds, Austrian Croats, and Gallic can-nibals, seem on every side to impede my passage. You appear to apprehend the perils or difficulties of the Ger-man road, and French peace is more sanguinary than civilized war. I must pass through, perhaps, a thousand republics or municipalities, which neither obey nor are obeyed. The strictness of passports, and the popular ferment, are much increased since last summer: aristo-crat is in every mouth, lanterns hang in every street, and an hasty word or a casual resemblance may be fatal. Yet, on the other hand, it is probable that many English, men, women, and children, will traverse the country without any accident before next September; and I am sensible that many things appear more formidable at a distance than on a nearer approach. Without any absolute determination, we must see what the events of the next three or four months will produce. In the mean while, I shall expect with impatience your next letter: let it be speedy; my answer shall be prompt.

You will be glad, or sorry, to learn that my gloomy apprehensions are much abated, and that my departure, whenever it takes place, will be an act of choice, rather than of necessity. I do not pretend to affirm, that secret discontent, dark suspicion, private animosity, are very materially assuaged; but we have not experience, nor do we now apprehend, any dangerous acts of violence, which may compel me to seek a refuge among the friendly Bears,* and to abandon my library to the mercy of the democrats. The firmness and vigour of government have crushed, at least for a time, the spirit of innovation; and I do not believe that the body of the people, especially the peasants, are disposed for a revolution. From France, praised be the demon of anarchy! the insurgents of the Pays de Vaud could not at present have much to hope; and should the *gardes nationales*, of which there is little appearance, attempt an incursion, the country is armed and prepared, and they would be resisted with equal numbers and superior discipline. The Gallic wolves that prowled round Geneva are drawn away,

* Berne.

some to the south and some to the north, and the late
events in Flanders seem to have diffused a general contempt, as well as abhorrence, for the lawless savages,
who fly before the enemy, hang their prisoners, and
murder their officers. The brave and patient regiment
of Ernest is expected home every day, and as Berne will
take them into present pay, that veteran and regular
corps will add to the security of our frontier.

I rejoice that you have so little to say on that subject
of worldly affairs.* * * * This summer we are
threatened with an inundation, besides many nameless
English and Irish; but I am anxious for the Duchess of
Devonshire and the Lady Elisabeth Foster, who are
on their march. Lord Malmsbury, the *audacieux* Harris,
will inform you that he has seen me: *him* I would have
consented to keep.

One word more before we part; call upon Mr. John
Nicols, bookseller and printer, at Cicero's Head, Red-
Lion-passage, Fleet-street, and ask him whether he did
not, about the beginning of March, receive a very polite
letter from Mr. Gibbon of Lausanne? To which, either
as a man of business or a civil gentleman, he should have
returned an answer. My application related to a domestic article in the Gentleman's Magazine of August, 1788,
(p. 698,) which had lately fallen into my hands, and concerning which I requested some farther lights. Mrs.
Moss delivered the letters* into my hands, but I doubt
whether they will be of much service to me; the work
appears far more difficult in the execution than in the

* His letters to me for a certain period, which he desired me to send, to
assist him in writing his Memoirs.—S.

idèa, and as I am now taking my leave for some time of the library, I shall not make much progress in the memoirs of P. P. till I am on English ground. But is it indeed true, that I shall eat my Sussex pheasants this autumn? The event is in the book of Fate, and I cannot unroll the leaves of September and October. Should I reach Sheffield-place, I hope to find the whole family in a perfect state of existence, except a certain Maria Holroyd, my fair and *generous* correspondent, whose annihilation on proper terms I most fervently desire. I must receive a copious answer before the end of next month, June, and again call upon you for a map of your political world. The chancellor roars; does he break his chain? *Vale.*

TO THE SAME.

Lausanne, August 23rd, 1792.

When I inform you that the design of my English expedition is at last postponed till another year, you will not be much surprised. The public obstacles, the danger of one road, and the difficulties of another, would alone be sufficient to arrest so unwieldy and inactive a being; and these obstacles on the side of France, are growing every day more insuperable. On the other hand, the terrors, which might have driven me from hence, have, in a great measure, subsided; our state prisoners are forgotten: the country begins to recover its old good humour and unsuspecting confidence, and the last revolution of Paris appears to have convinced almost every body of the fatal consequences of democratical principles, which lead by a path of flowers into the abyss of hell. I may

therefore wait with patience and tranquillity till the Duke
of Brunswick shall have opened the French road.   But
if I am not driven from Lausanne, you will ask, I hope
with some indignation, whether I am not drawn to England, and more especially to Sheffield-place?   The desire
of embracing you and yours is now the strongest, and
must gradually become the sole, inducement that can
force me from my library and garden, over seas and
mountains.   The English world will forget and be forgotten, and every year will deprive me of some acquaintance, who by courtesy are styled friends: Lord
Guildford and Sir Joshua Reynolds! two of the men,
and two of the houses in London, on whom I the most
relied for the comforts of society.

September 12th, 1792.

Thus far had I written in the full confidence of finishing and sending my letter the next post; but six post-
days have unaccountably slipped away, and were you
not accustomed to my silence, you would almost begin to
think me on the road.   How dreadfully, since my last
date, has the French road been polluted with blood! and
what horrid scenes may be acting at this moment, and
may still be aggravated, till the Duke of Brunswick is
master of Paris!   On every rational principle of calculation he must succeed; yet sometimes, when my spirits
are low, I dread the blind efforts of mad and desperate
multitudes fighting on their own ground.   A few days or
weeks must decide the military operations of this year,
and perhaps for ever; but on the fairest supposition, I
cannot look forwards to any firm settlement, either of a
legal or an absolute government.   I cannot pretend to

give you any Paris news. Should I inform you, as we
believe, that *Lally is still among the cannibals*, you would
possibly answer, that he is now sitting in the library at
Sheffield.   Madame de Stael, after miraculously escaping
through pikes and poniard, has reached the castle of Coppet, where I shall see her before the end of the week.
If any thing can provoke the King of Sardinia and the
Swiss, it must be the foul destruction of *his* cousin Madame de Lamballe, and of *their* regiment of guards.   An
extraordinary counsel is summoned at Berne,*but resentment
may be checked by prudence.*   In spite of Maria's laughter,
I applaud your moderation, and sigh for a hearty union of
all the sense and property of the country.   The times
require it; but your last political letter was a cordial to
my spirits.   The Duchess of D. rather dislikes a coalition: amiable creature!   The Eliza is furious against you
for not writing.   We shall lose them in a few days; but
the motions of Eliza and the Duchess for Italy or England, are doubtful.   Ladies Spencer and Duncannon certainly pass the Alps. I live with them. Adieu. Since
I do not appear in person, I feel the absolute propriety of
writing to my lady and Maria; but there is far from the
knowledge to the performance of a duty. Ever yours.

TO THE SAME.

Lausanne, October 5th, 1792.

As our English newspapers must have informed you
of the invasion of Savoy by the French, and as it is possible that you may have some trifling apprehensions of my
being killed and eaten by those cannibals, it has appeared
to me that a short extraordinary dispatch might not be

unacceptable on this occasion. It is indeed true, that about ten days ago the French army of the South, under the command of M. de Montesquiou, (if any French army can be said to be under any command,) has entered Savoy, and possessed themselves of Chamberry, Mont-melian, and several other places. It has always been the practice of the King of Sardinia to abandon his Trans-alpine dominions ; but on this occasion the court of Turin appears to have been surprised by the strange eccentric motions of a democracy, which always acts from the passion of the moment; and their inferior troops have retreated, with some loss and disgrace, into the passes of the Alps. Mount Cenis is now impervious, and our English travellers who are bound for Italy, the Duchess of Devonshire, Ancaster, &c. will be forced to explore a long and circuitous road through the Tyrol. But the Chablais is yet intact, nor can our telescope discover the tricolor banners on the other side of the lake. Our ac-counts of the French numbers seem to vary from fifteen to thirty thousand men; the regulars are few, but they are followed by a rabble rout, which must soon, however, melt away, as they will find no plunder, and scanty sub-sistence, in the poverty and barrenness of Savoy. N. B. I have just seen a letter from M. de Montesquiou, who boasts that at his first entrance into Savoy he had only twelve battalions. Our intelligence is far from correct.

The magistrates of Geneva were alarmed by this dan-gerous neighborhood, and more especially by the well-know animosity of an exiled citizen, Claviere, who is one of the six ministers of the French republic. It was carried by a small majority in the general council, to call in the succour of three thousand Swiss, which is stipulated by ancient treaty. The strongest reason or pretence of the minority, was founded on the danger of provoking the French, and they seemed to have been justified by the event; since the complaint of the French resident amounts to a declaration of war. The fortifications of Geneva are not contemptible, especially on the side of Savoy; and it is much doubted whether M. de Montesquiou is prepared for a regular siege; but the malcontents are numerous within the walls, and I question whether the spirit of the citizens will hold out against a bombardment. In the meanwhile the diet has declared, that the first cannon fired against Geneva will be considered as an act of hostility against the whole Helvetic body. Berne, as the nearest and most powerful canton, has taken the lead with great vigour and vigilance; the road is filled with the perpetual succession of troops and artillery; and, if some dissatisfaction lurks in the towns, the peasants, especially the Germans, are inflamed with a strong desire of encountering the murderers of their countrymen. Mr. de Watteville, with whom you dined at my house last year, refused to accept the command of the Swiss succour of Geneva, till it was made his first instruction that he should never, in any case, surrender himself prisoner of war.

In this situation, you may suppose that we have some fears. I have great dependence, however, on the many chances in our favour, the valour of the Swiss, the return of the Piedmontèse with their Austrian allies, eight or ten thousand men from the Milanese, a diversion from

Spain, the great events (how slowly they proceed) on the side of Paris, the inconstancy and want of discipline of the French, and the near approach of the winter season. I am not nervous, but I will not be rash. It will be painful to abandon my house and library; but if the danger should approach, I will retreat before it, first to Berne, and gradually to the North. Should I even be forced to take refuge in England (a violent measure so late in the year) you would perhaps receive me as kindly as you did the French priests—a noble act of hospitality. Could I have foreseen this storm, I would have been there six weeks ago; but who can foresee the wild measures of the savages of Gaul? We thought ourselves perfectly out of the hurricane latitudes. Adieu. I am going to bed, and must rise early to visit the Neckers at Rolle, whither they have retired, from the frontier situation of Coppet. Severy is on horseback, with his gragoons: his poor father is dangerously ill. It will be shocking if it should be found necessary to remove him. While we are in this very awkward crisis, I will write at least every week. Ever yours. Write instantly, and remember all my commissions.

TO THE SAME.

I will keep my promise of sending you a weekly journal of our troubles, that, when the piping times of peace are restored, I may sleep in long and irreproachable silence; but I shall use a smaller paper, as our military exploits will seldom be sufficient to fill the ample size of our English quarto.

October 13th, 1792.

Since my last of the 6th, our attack is not more eminent, and our defence is most assuredly stronger, two
very important circumstances, at a time when every day
is leading us, though not so fast as our impatience could
wish, towards the unwarlike month of November; and
we observe with pleasure that the troops of M. de Montesquiou, which are chiefly from the southern provinces,
will not cheerfully entertain the rigour of an Alpine
winter. The 7th instant, M. de Chateauneuf, the French
resident, took his leave with an haughty mandate, commanding the Genevais, as they valued their safety and
the friendship of the republic, to dismiss their Swiss allies,
and to punish the magistrates who had traitorously proposed the calling in these foreign troops. It is precisely
the fable of the wolves, who offered to make peace with
the sheep, provided they would send away their dogs.
You know what became of the sheep. This demand appears to have kindled a just and general indignation,
since it announced an edict of proscription; and must
lead to a democratical revolution, which would probably
renew the horrid scenes of Paris and Avianon. A general assembly of the citizens was convened, the message
was read, speeches were made, oaths were taken, and it
was resolved, with only three dissentient voices, to live
and die in the defence of their country. The Genevais
muster above three thousand well-armed citizens; and
the Swiss, who may easily be increased, in a few hours,
to an equal number, add spirit to the timorous, and confidence to the well-affected: their arsenals are filled with

arms, their magazines with ammunition, and their grana-
ries with corn.   But their fortifications are extensive and
imperfect, they are commanded from two adjacent hills;
a French faction lurks in the city, the character of the
Genevais is rather commercial than military; and their
behaviour, lofty promise, and base surrender, in the year
1782, is fresh in our memories.   In the meanwhile, 4000
French at the most are arrived in the neighboring camp,
nor is there yet any appearance of mortars or heavy
artillery.   Perhaps a haughty menace may be repelled
by a firm countenance.   If it were worth while talking
of justice, what a shameful attack of a feeble unoffending
state!   On the news of their danger, all Switzerland,
from Schaffhausen to the Pays de Vaud, has risen in
arms; and a French resident, who has passed through
the country, in his way from Ratisbon, declares his intention of informing and admonishing the national convention.   About eleven thousand Bernais are already posted
in the neighbourhood of Coppet and Nyon; and new
reinforcements of men, artillery, &c. arrive every day.
Another army is drawn together to oppose M. de Fer-
rieres, on the side of Bienne and the bishopric of Basle;
and the Austrians in Swabia would be easily persuaded
to cross the Rhine in our defence.   But we are yet ignorant whether our sovereigns mean to wage offensive or
defensive war.   If the latter, which is more likely, will
the French begin the attack?   Should Geneva yield to
fear or force, this country is open to an invasion; and
though our men are brave, we want generals; and I
despise the French much less than I did two months ago.
It should seem that our hopes from the King of Sardinia

and the Austrians of Milan are faint and distant; Spain sleeps, and the Duke of Brunswick (amazement!) seems to have failed in his great project. For my part, till Geneva falls, I do not think of a retreat; but, at all events, I am provided with two strong horses, and a hundred louis in gold. Zürich would be probably my winter quarters, and the society of the Neckers would make any place agreeable. Their situation is worse than mine: I have no daughter ready to lie in; nor do I fear the French aristocrats on the road. Adieu. Keep my letters; excuse contradictions and repetitions. The Duchess of Devonshire leaves us next week. Lady Elizabeth abhors you. Ever yours.

TO THE SAME.

October 20th, 1792.

Since my last, our affairs take a more pacific turn; but I will not venture to affirm that our peace will be either safe or honourable. M. de Montesquiou and three of the commissioners of the convention, who are at Carrouge, have had frequent conferences with the magistrates of Geneva; several expresses have been dispatched to and from Paris, and every step of the negotiation, is communicated to the deputies of Berne and Zurich. The French troops observe a very tolerable degree of order and discipline: and no act of hostility has yet been committed on the territory of Geneva.

October 27.

My usual temper very readily admitted the excuse, that it would be better to wait another week, till the final settlement of our affairs. The treaty is signed be-

tween France and Geneva; and the ratification of the
convention is looked upon as assured, if any thing can be
assured in that wild democracy. On condition that the
Swiss garrison, with the approbation of Berne and Zurich,
be recalled before the first of December, it is stipulated that
the independence of Geneva shall be preserved inviolate;
that M. de Montesquiou shall immediately send away his
heavy artillery; and that no French troops shall approach
within ten leagues of the city. As the Swiss have acted
only as auxiliaries, they have no occasion for a direct
treaty; but they cannot prudently disarm, till they are
satisfied of the pacific intentions of France; and no such
satisfaction can be given till they have acknowledged the
new republic, which they will probably do in a few days,
with a deep groan of indignation and sorrow; it has
been cemented with the blood of their countrymen! But
when the emperor, the King of Prussia, the, first general,
and the first army in Europe have failed, less powerful
states may acquiesce, without dishonour, in the determination of fortune. Do you understand this most unexpected failure? I will allow an ample share to the bad-
ness of the roads and the weather, to famine and disease,
to the skill of Dumourier, a heaven-born general, and to
the enthusiastic ardour of the new Romans; but still,
still there must be some secret shameful cause at the
bottom of this strange retreat. We are now delivered
from the impending terrors of siege and invasion. The
Geneva *emigrés*, particularly the Neckers, are hastening
to their homes; and I shall not be reduced to the hard
necessity of seeking a winter asylum at Zurich or Con-
stance: but I am not pleased with our future prospects.

It is much to be feared that the present government of Geneva will be soon modelled after the French fashion; the new republic of Savoy is forming on the opposite bank of the Lake; the Jacobin missionaries are powerful and zealous; and malcontents of this country who begin again to rear their heads, will be surrounded with temptations, and examples, and allies. I know not whether the Pays de Vaud will long adhere to the dominion of Berne; or whether I shall be permitted to end my days in this little paradise which I have so happily suited to my taste and circumstances.

Last Monday only I received your letter, which had strangely loitered on the road since its date of the 29th of September. There must surely be some disorder in the posts, since the Eliza departed indignant at never having heard from you.

The case of my wine I think peculiarly hard; to lose my Madeira, and to be scolded for losing it. I am much indebted to Mr. Nichols for his genealogical communications, which I am impatient to receive; but I do not understand why so civil a gentleman could not favour me, in six months, with an answer by the post: since he entrusts me with these valuable papers, you have not I presume informed him of my negligence and awkwardness in regard to manuscripts. Your reproach rather surprises men, as I suppose I am much the same as I have been for these last twenty years. Should you hold your resolution of writing only such things as may be published at Charing-cross, our future correspondence would not be very interesting. But I expect and require, at this important crisis, a full and confident account of your views concerning England, Ireland, and France. You have a strong and clear eye; and your pen is, perhaps, the most useful quill that ever has been plucked from a goose. Your protection of the French refugees is highly applauded. Rosset and La Motte have escaped from Arbourg, perhaps with connivance to avoid disagreeable demands from the republic. Adieu. Ever yours.

TO THE SAME.

November 10th, 1792.

Received this day, November 9th, a most amiable dispatch from the too humble secretary* of the family of Epsee,† dated October 24th, which I answer the same day. It will be acknowledged, that I have fulfilled my engagements with as much accuracy as our uncertain state and the fragility of human nature would allow. I resume my narrative. At the time when we imagined that all was settled by an equal treaty between two such unequal powers as the Geneva Flea and the Leviathan France, we were thunderstruck with the intelligence that the ministers of the republic refused to ratify the conditions; and they were indignant, with some colour of reason, at the hard obligation of withdrawing their troops to the distance of ten leagues, and of consequently leaving the Pays de Gex naked, and exposed to the Swiss, who had assembled 15,000 men on the frontier, and with whom they had not made any agreement. The messenger who was sent last Sunday from Geneva is not yet returned; and many persons are afraid of some design

* Miss Holroyd. † Meaning Sheffield-place.

and danger in this delay. Montesquiou has acted with politeness, moderation and apparent sincerity; but he may resign, he may be superseded, his place may be occupied by an *enragé*, by Servan, or Prince Charles of Hesse, who would aspire to imitate the predatory fame of Custine in Germany. In the meanwhile, the general holds a wolf by the ears; an officer who has seen his troops, about 18,000 men (with a tremendous train of artillery), represents them as a black, daring, desperate crew of buccaneers, rather shocking than contemptible; the officers (scarcely a gentleman among them), without servants, or horses, or baggage, lying *higgledy piggledy* on the ground with the common men, yet maintaining a rough kind of discipline over them. They already begin to accuse and even to suspect their general, and call aloud for blood and plunder: could they have an opportunity of squeezing some of the rich citizens, Geneva would cut up as fat as most towns in Europe. During this suspension of hostilities they are permitted to visit the city without arms, sometimes three or four hundred at a time; and the magistrates, as well as the Swiss commander, are by no means pleased with this dangerous intercourse, which they dare not prohibit. Such are our fears; yet it should seem on the other side, that the French affect a kind of magnanimous justice towards their little neighbour, and that they are not ambitious of an unprofitable contest with the poor and hardy Swiss. The Swiss are not equal to a long and expensive war; and as most of our militia have families and trades, the country already sighs for their return. Whatever can be yielded without absolute danger or disgrace, will doubtless be granted; and the business will probably end in our owning the sovereignty, and trusting to the good faith of the republic of France: how that word would have sounded four years ago! The measure is humiliating; but after the retreat of the Duke of Brunswick, and the failure of the Austrians, the smaller powers may acquiesce without dishonour. Every dog has his day; and these Gallic dogs have their day, at least, of most insolent prosperity. After forcing or tempting the Prussians to evacuate their country, they conquer Savoy, pillage Germany, threaten Spain: the Low Countries are ere now invaded; Rome and Italy tremble; they scour the Mediterranean, and talk of sending a squadron into the South Sea. The whole horizon is so black, that I begin to feel some anxiety for England, the last refuge of liberty and law; and the more so, as I perceive from Lord Sheffield's last epistle that his firm nerves are a little shaken; but of this more in my next, for I want to unburthen my conscience. If England, with the experience of our happiness and French calamities, should now be seduced to eat the apple of false freedom, we should indeed deserve to be driven from the paradise which we enjoy. I turn aside from the horrid and improbable, (yet not impossible) supposition, that, in three or four year's time, myself and my best friends may be reduced to the deplorable state of the French emigrants: they thought it as impossible three or four years ago. Never did a revolution affect. to such a degree, the private existence of such numbers of the first people of a great country: your examples of misery I could easily match with similar examples in this country and the neighbourhood; and our sympathy is the deeper as we do not possess, like you, the means of alleviating, in some degree, the misfortunes of the fugitives. But I must have, from the very excellent pen of the Maria, the tragedy of the Archbishop of Arles; and the longer the better. Madame de Biron has probably been tempted by some faint and (I fear) fallacious promises of clemency to the women, and which have likewise engaged Madame d'Aguesseau and her two daughters to revisit France. Madame de Bouillon stands her ground, and her situation as a foreign princess is less exposed. As Lord Sheffield has assumed the glorious character of protector of the distressed, his name is pronounced with gratitude and re- spect. The D. of Richmond is praised on Madame de Biron's account. To the Princess d'Henin and Lally, I wish to be remembered. The Neckers cannot venture into Ge- neva, and Madame de Stael will probably lie in at Rolle. He is printing a defence of the King, &c. against their re- publican judges; but the name of Necker is unpopular to all parties, and I much fear that the guillotine will be more speedy than the press. It will, however, be an eloquent performance; and, if I find an opportunity, I am to send you one, to you Lord Sheffield by his particular desire: he wishes likewise to convey some copies with speed to our principal people, Pitt, Fox, Lord Stormont, &c. But such is the rapid succession of events, that it will appear like the Pouvoir Executif, his best work, after the whole scene has been totally changed. Ever yours.

P. S. The revolution of France, and my triple despatch by the same post to Sheffield-place, are, in my opinion, the two most singular events in the eighteenth century. I found the task so easy and pleasant, that I had some thoughts of adding a letter to the gentle Louisa. I am this moment informed, that our troops on the frontier are beginning to move, on their return home; yet we hear nothing of the treaty's being concluded.

EDWARD GIBBON, ESQ., TO THE HON. MISS HOLROYD.

Lausanne, Nov. 10th, 1792.

In dispatching the weekly political journal to Lord S. my conscience (for I have some remains of conscience) most powerfully urges me to salute, with some lines of friendship and gratitude, the amiable secretary, who might save herself the trouble of a modest apology. I have not yet forgotten our different behaviour after the much lamented *separation* of October the 4th, 1791, your meritorious punctuality, and my unworthy silence. I have still before me that entertaining narrative, which would have interested me, not only in the progress of the *carissima familia*, but in the motions of a Tartar camp, or the march of a caravan of Arabs: the mixture of just observation and lively imagery, the strong sense of a man expressed with the easy elegance of a female. I still recollect with pleasure the happy comparison of the Rhine, who had heard so much of liberty on both his banks, that he wandered with mischievous licentiousness over all the adjacent meadows.* The inundation, alas! has now spread much wider; and it is sadly to be feared that the Elbe, the Po, and the Danube, may imitate the

* Mr. Gibbon alludes to letters written to him by Miss Holroyd, when she was returning from Switzerland, along the Rhine, to England.

vile example of the Rhine : I shall be content, however, if our own Thames still preserves his fair character, of

Strong without rage, without o'erflowing full.

The agreeable epistle of Maria produced only some dumb intentions, and some barren remorse; nor have I deigned, except by a brief missive from my chancellor, to express how much I loved the author, and how much I was pleased with the composition. That amiable author I have known and loved from the first dawning of her life and *coquetry* to the present maturity of her talents ; and as long as I remain on this planet, I shall pursue, with the same tender and even anxious concern, the future steps of her establishment and life. That establishment must be splendid ; that life must be happy. She is endowed with every gift of nature and fortune; but the advantage which she will derive from them, depends almost entirely on herself. You must not, you shall not, think yourself unworthy to write to any man : there is none whom your correspondence would not amuse and satisfy. I will not undertake a task, which my taste would adopt, and my indolence would too soon relinquish ; but I am really curious, from the best motives, to have a particular account of your own studies and daily occupation. What books do you read? and how do you employ your time and your pen? Except some professed scholars, I have often observed that women in general read much more than men; but, for want of a plan, a method, a fixed object, their reading is of little benefit to themselves, or others. If you will inform me of the species of reading to which you have the most propensity, I shall be happy to

contribute my share of advice or assistance. I lament
that you have not left me some monument of your pencil.
Lady Elizabeth Foster has executed a very pretty drawing, taken from the door of the green-house where we
dined last summer, and including the poor acacia (now
recovered from the cruel shears of the gardener), the end
of the terrace, the front of the pavilion, and a distant view
of the country, lake, and mountains. I am almost reconciled to D'Apples' house, which is nearly finished. Instead of the monsters which Lord Hercules Sheffield
extirpated, the terrace is already shaded with the new
acacias and plantains; and although the uncertainty of
possession restrains me from building, I myself have
planted a bosquet at the bottom of the garden, with such
admirable skill that it affords shade without intercepting
prospect. The society of the aforesaid Eliza, of the
Duchess of D. &c. has been very interesting; but they
are now flown beyond the Alps, and pass the winter at
Pisa. The Legards, who have long since left this place,
should be at present in Italy; but I believe Mrs. Grim-
stone and her daughter returned to England. The Le-
vades are highly flattered by your remembrance. Since
you still retain some attachment to this delightful country,
and it is indeed delightful, why should you despair of
seeing it once more? The happy peer or commoner,
whose name you may assume, is still concealed in the
book of fate; but whosoever he may be, he will cheerfully obey your commands, of leading you from————
Castle to Lausanne, and from Lausanne to Rome and
Naples. Before that event takes place, I may possibly
see you in Sussex; and, whether as a visitor or as a fugi-

tive, I hope to be welcomed with a friendly embrace.
The delay of this year was truly painful, but it was inevitable; and individuals must submit to those storms
which have overturned the thrones of the earth. The
tragic story of the Archbishop of Arles I have now somewhat a better right to require at your hands. I wish to
have it in all its horrid details;* and as you are now so

* The answer to Mr. Gibbon's letter is annexed, as the best account I
have seen of the barbarous transaction alluded to.—S.

"Sheffield-place, November, 1791.

"Your three letters received yesterday caused the most sincere pleasure
to each individual of this family; to none more than myself. Praise, (I
fear, beyond my deserts,) from one whose opinion I so highly value, and
whose esteem I so much wish to preserve, is more pleasing than I can describe. I had not neglected to make the collection of facts which you
recommend, and which the great variety of unfortunate persons whom we
see, or with whom we correspond, enables me to make.

"As to that part of your letter which respects *my studies*, I can only
say, the slighest hint on that subject is always received with the greatest
gratitude, and attended to with the utmost punctuality; but I must decline
that topic for the present, to obey your commands, which require from me
the horrid account of the massacre aux Carmes.—Eight respectable ecclesiastics, landed, about the beginning of October, from an open boat at Sea-
ford, wet as the waves. The natives of the coast were endeavouring to get
from them what they had not, viz. money, when a gentleman of the neighbourhood came to their protection; and, finding they had nothing, showed
his good sense, by dispatching them to Milord Sheffield: they had been
pillaged, and with great difficulty had escaped from Paris. The reception
they met with at this house, seemed to make the greatest impression
on them; they were in ecstacy on finding M. de Lally living: they gradually became cheerful, and enjoyed their dinner; they were greatly affected
as they recollected themselves, and found us attending on them. Having
dined, and drank a glass of wine, they began to discover the beauties of
the dining-room, and of the chateau: as they walked about, they were
overheard to express their admiration at the treatment they met, and *from
Protestants.* We then assembled in the library, formed a half circle round

much mingled with the French exiles, I am of opinion
that were you to keep a journal of all the authentic facts

the fire, M. de Lally and Milord occupying the hearth à l'Anglaise, and
questioned the priests concerning their escape. Thus we discovered that
two of these unfortunate men were in the Carmelite convent at the time of
the massacre of one hundred and twenty priests, and had most miraculously
escaped, by climbing trees in the garden, and from thence over the tops of
the buildings. One of them, a man of superior appearance, described in
the most pathetic manner, the death of the Archbishop of Arles, (and with
such simplicity and feeling, as to leave no doubt of the truth of all that he
said,) to the following purport.—On the second of September, about five
o'clock in the evening, at the time they were permitted to walk in the
garden, expecting every hour to be released, they expressed their surprise
at seeing several large pits, which had been digging for two days past:
they said, the day is almost spent; and yet Manuel told a person who
interceded for us last Thursday, that on the Sunday following not one
should remain in captivity; we are still prisoners. Soon after, they heard
shouts, and some musket shots. An ensign of the national guard, some
commissaries of the sections, and some Marseillais rushed in; the miserable
victims, who were dispersed in the garden, assembled under the walls of
the church, not daring to go in, lest it should be polluted with blood. One
man, who was behind the rest, was shot. 'Point de coup de fusils,' cried
one of the chiefs of the assassins, thinking that kind of death too easy.
'These well-trained fusileers went to the rear: les piques, les haches, les
poignards came forward. They demanded the Archbishop of Arles; he
was immediately surrounded by all the priests. The worthy prelate said to
his friends, 'Let me pass; if my blood will appease them, what signifies
it, if I die! Is it not my duty to preserve your lives at the expense of my
own?' He asked the eldest of the priests to give him absolution: he
knelt to receive it; and when he arose, forced himself from them,
advanced slowly, and with his arms crossed upon his breast, and his eyes
raised to heaven, said to the assassins, 'Je suis celui que vous cherchez.'
His appearance was so dignified and noble, that, during ten minutes, not
one of these wretches had courage to lift his hand against him; they
upbraided each other with cowardice, and advanced; one look from this
venerable man struck them with awe, and they retired. At last, one of
the miscreants struck off the cap of the archbishop with a pike; respect

which they relate, it would be an agreeable exercise at present, and a future source of entertainment and instruction.

I should be obliged to you, if you would make, or find, some excuse for my not answering a letter from your

once violated, their fury returned, and another from behind cut him through the skull with a sabre. He raised his right hand to his eyes; with another stroke they cut off his hand. The Archbishop said, ' Oh, mon Dieu !' and raised the other; a third stroke across the face left him sitting; the fourth extended him lifeless on the ground ; and then all pressed forward, and buried their pikes and poniards in the body. The priests all agreed, that he had been one of the most amiable men in France ; and that his only *crime* was, having, since the revolution, expended his private fortune, to support the necessitous clergy of the diocese. The second victim was the General des Benedictins. Then the national guards obliged the priests to go into the church, telling them, they should appear, one after another, before the commissaires du section. They had hardly entered, before the people impatiently called for them; upon which, all kneeling before the altar, the Bishop of Beauvais gave them absolution: they were then obliged to go out, two by two; they passed before a commissaire, who did not question, but only counted his victims;† they had in their sight the heaps of dead, to which they were going to add. Among the one hundred and twenty priests thus sacrificed, were the Bishops of Zaintes and Beauvais (both of the Rochefoucauld family.) I should not omit to remark, that one of the priests observed they were assassinated, because they would not swear to a constitution which their murderers had destroyed. We had to comfort us for this melancholy story the most grateful expressions of gratitude towards the English nation, from whom they did not do us the justice to expect such a reception.

" There can be no doubt that the whole business of the massacres was concerted at the Duke of Orleans' house. I shall make you as dismal as myself by this narration. I must change the style." * * * * * * * * * *

† * * * * Visum est lenti quæsisse nocentem
Innumerum paras magna perit.
                                    Lucan, lib. 2. v. 110.—8.

aunt, which was presented to me by Mr. Fowler. I showed him some civilities, but he is now a poor invalid, confined to his room. By her channel and yours I should be glad to have some information of the health, spirits, and situation of Mrs. Gibbon of Bath, whose alarms (if she has any) you may dispel. She is in my debt. Adieu, most truly yours.

EDWARD GIBBON, ESQ. TO THE RIGHT HON. LADY SHEFFIELD.

Lausanne, November 10, 1792.

I could never forgive myself, were I capable of writing by the same post, a political epistle to the father, and a friendly letter to the daughter, without sending any token of remembrance to the respectable matron, my dearest my lady, whom I have now loved as a sister for something better or worse than twenty years. No, indeed, the historian may be careless, he may be indolent, he may always intend and never execute, but he is neither a monster nor a statute; he has a memory, a conscience, a heart, and that heart is sincerely devoted to Lady S****. He must even acknowledge the fallacy of a sophism which he has sometimes used, and she has always and most truly denied; that, where the persons of a family are strictly united, the writing to one is in fact writing to all: and that consequently all his numerous letters to the husband, may be considered as equally addressed to his wife. He feels, on the contrary, that separate minds have their distinct ideas and sentiments, and that each character, either in speaking or writing, has its peculiar tone of conversation. He agrees with the maxim of Rousseau, that three friends who wish to disclose a common secret, will impart it only *deux à deux;* and he is satisfied that, on the present memorable occasion, each of the persons of the Sheffield family will claim a peculiar share in this triple missive, which will communicate, however, a triple satisfaction. The experience of what may be effected by vigorous resolution, encourages the historian to hope that he shall cast the skin of the old serpent, and hereafter show himself as a new creature.

I lament, on all our accounts, that the last year's expedition to Lausanne did not take place in a golden period of health and spirits. But we must reflect, that human felicity is seldom without alloy; and if we cannot indulge the hope of your making a second visit to Lausanne, we must look forwards to my residence next summer at Sheffield-place, where I must find you in the full bloom of health, spirits, and beauty. I can perceive, by all public and private intelligence, that your house has been the open hospitable asylum of French fugitives; and it is a sufficient proof of the firmness of your nerves, that you have not been overwhelmed or agitated by such a concourse of strangers. Curiosity and compassion may, in some degree, have supported you. Every day has presented to your view some new scene of that strange tragical romance, which occupies all Europe so infinitely beyond any event that has happened in our time, and you have the satisfaction of not being a mere spectator of the distress of so many victims of false liberty. The benevolent fame of Lord S. is widely diffused.

From Angletine's last letter to Maria, you have already some idea of the melancholy state of her poor father.

As long as Mr. de Severy allowed our hopes and fears
to fluctuate with the changes of his disorder, I was unwil-
wing to say anything on so painful a subject; and it is
with the deepest concern that I now confess our absolute
despair of his recovery. All his particular complaints
are now lost in a general dissolution of the whole frame:
every principle of life is exhausted, and as often as I am
admitted to his bed-side, though he still looks and smiles
with the patience of an angel, I have the heartfelt grief
of seeing him each day drawing nearer to the term of his
existence. A few weeks, possibly a few days, will deprive me of the most excellent friend, and break forever
the most perfect system of domestic happiness, in which I
had so large and intimate a share. Wilhelm (who has
obtained leave of absence from his military duty) and his
sister behave and feel like tender and dutiful children;
but they have a long gay prospect of life, and new connexions, new families will make them forget, in due time,
the common lot of mortality. But it is Madame de
Severy whom I truly pity; I dread the effects of the first
shock, and I dread still more the deep perpetual con-
suming affliction for a loss which can never be retrieved.
You will not wonder that such reflections sadden my
own mind, nor can I forget how much my situation is
altered since I retired, nine years ago, to the banks of the
Leman Lake. The death of poor Deyverdun first
deprived me of a domestic companion, who can never be
supplied; and your visit has only served to remind me
that man, however amused and occupied in his closet,
was not made to live alone. Severy will soon be no
more; his widow for a long time, perhaps for ever, will

be lost to herself and her friends, the son will travel, and I shall be left a stranger in the insipid circle of mere common acquaintance.   The revolution of France, which first embittered and divided the society of Lausanne, has opposed a barrier to my Sussex visit, and may finally expel me from the paradise which I inhabit.   Even that paradise, the expensive and delightful establishment of my house, library, and garden, almost becomes an incumbrance, by rendering it more difficult for me to relinquish my hold, or to form a new system of life in my native country, for which my income, though improved and improving, would be probably insufficient.   But every complaint should be silenced by the contemplation of the French; compared with whose cruel fate, all misery is relative happiness.   I perfectly concur in your partiality for Lally though Nature might forget some meaner ingredients, of prudence, economy, &c., she never formed a purer heart, or a brighter imagination.   If he be with you, I beg my kindest salutations to him.   I am every day more closely united with the Neckers.   Should France break, and this country be over-run, they would be reduced, in very humble circumstances, to seek a refuge; and where but in England?   Adieu, dear madam : there is, indeed, much pleasure in discharging one's heart to a real friend.   Ever yours.

EDWARD GIBBON, ESQ., TO THE RIGHT HON. LORD SHEFFIELD.

[Send me a list of these letters, with their respective dates.]

Lausanne, Nov. 25th, 1792.

After the triple labour of my last despatch, your experience of the creature might tempt you to suspect that it would again relapse into a long slumber. But, partly from the spirit of contradiction, (though I am not a lady,) and partly from the ease and pleasure which I now find in the task, you see me again alive, awake, and almost faithful to my hebdomidal promise. The last week has not, however, afforded any events deserving the notice of an historian. Our affairs are still floating on the waves of the convention, and the ratification of a corrected treaty, which had been fixed for the twentieth, is not yet arrived; but the report of the diplomatic committee has been favourable, and it is generally understood that the leaders of the French republic do not wish to quarrel with the Swiss. We are gradually withdrawing and disbanding our militia. Geneva will be left to sink or swim, according to the humour of the people; and our last hope appears to be, that by submission and good behaviour we shall avert for some time the impending storm. A few days ago, an odd incident happened in the French army; the desertion of the general. As the Neckers were sitting, about eight o'clock in the evening, in their drawing-room at Rolle,* the door flew open, and they were astounded by the servant's announcing Monsieur le General de Montesquiou! On the receipt of some secret intelligence of a *decret d'accusation*, and an order to arrest him, he had only time to get on horseback, to gallop through Geneva, to take boat for Coppet, and to escape from his pursuers, who were ordered to seize him alive or dead. He left the Neckers after supper, passed through Lausanne in the night, and proceeded to Berne and Basle, whence he intended to wind his way

* A considerable town between Lausanne and Geneva.

through Germany, amidst enemies of every description, and to seek a refuge in England, America, or the moon. He told Necker, that the sole remnant of his fortune consisted in a wretched sum of twenty thousand livres; but the public report, or suspicion, bespeaks him in much better circumstances. Besides the reproach of acting with too much tameness and delay, he is accused of making very foul and exhorbitant contracts: and it is certain that new Sparta is infected with this vice beyond the example of the most corrupt monarchy. Kellerman is arrived to take the command; and it is apprehended that on the first of December, after the departure of the Swiss, the French may *request* the permission of using Geneva, a friendly city, for their winter quarters. In that case, the democratical revolution, which we all foresee, will be very speedily effected.

I would ask you, whether you apprehend there was any treason in the Duke of Brunswick's retreat, and whether you have totally withdrawn your confidence and esteem from that once-famed general? Will it be possible for England to preserve her neutrality with any honour or safety? We are bound, as I understand, by treaty, to guarantee the dominions of the King of Sardinia and the Austrian provinces of the Netherlands. These countries are now invaded and over-run by the French. Can we refuse to fulfil our engagements, without exposing ourselves to all Europe as a perfidious or pusillanimous nation? Yet, on the other hand, can we assist those allies, without plunging headlong into an abyss, whose bottom no man can discover? But my only anxiety is for our domestic tranquillity; for I must

find a retreat in England, should I be driven from Lausanne. The idea of firm and honourable union of parties
pleases me much; but you must frankly unfold what
are the great difficulties that may impede so salutary a
measure: you write to a man discreet in speech, and
careful of papers. Yet what can such a coalition avail?
Where is the champion of the constitution? Alas, Lord
Guildford! I am much pleased with the Manchester ass.
The asses or wolves who sacrificed him have cast off the
mask too soon; and such a nonsensical act must open
the eyes of many simple patriots, who might have been
led astray by the specious name of reform. It should be
made as notorious as possible. Next winter may be the
crisis of our fate, and if you begin to improve the constitution, you may be driven step by step from the disfran-
chisement of Old Sarum to the king in Newgate; the
lords voted useless, the bishops abolished, and a house of
commons without articles (*sans culottes*). Necker has
ordered you a copy of his royal defence, which has met
with, and deserved univeral success. The pathetic and
argumentative parts are, in my opinion, equally good, and
his mild eloquence may persuade without irritating. I
have applied to this gentler tone some verses of Ovid,
(Metamorph. 1. iii. 302, &c.*) which you may read.
Madame de Stael has produced a second son. She talks
wildly enough of visiting England this winter. She is a

* Quà tamen usque potest, vires sibi demere tentat.
Nec, quo centimanum dejecerat igne Typhœa,
Nunc armatur eo : nimiùm ferritatis in illo.
Est aliud levius fulmen ; cui dextra Cyclopum
Sævitiæ, flammæque minus, minus addit iræ :
Tela secunda vocant Superi.

pleasant little woman.   Poor Severy's condition is hopeless.   Should he drag through the winter, Madame de
S. would scarcely survive him.   She kills herself with
grief and fatigue.   What a difference in Lausanne!   I
hope triple answers are on the road.   I must write soon;
the *times* will not allow me to read or think.   Ever yours.

TO THE SAME.

Lausanne, Dec. 14th, 1792.

Our little storm has now completely subsided, and we
are again spectators, though anxious spectators, of the
general tempest that invades or threatens almost every
country of Europe.   Our troops are every day disbanding and returning home, and the greatest part of the
French have evacuated the neighbourhood of Geneva.
Monsieur Barthelemy, whom you have seen secretary in
London, is most courteously entertained, as ambassador,
by the Helvetic body.   He is now at Berne, where a
diet will speedily be convened; the language on both
sides is now pacific, and even friendly, and some hopes
are given of a provision for the officers of the Swiss
guards who have survived the massacres of Paris.

January 1st, 1793.

With the return of peace I have relapsed into my
former indolence; but now awakening, after a fortnight's
slumber, I have little or nothing to add, with regard to
the internal state of this country, only the revolution of
Geneva has already taken place, as I announced, but
sooner than I expected.   The Swiss troops had no sooner
evacuated the place, than the *Egaliseurs,* as they are

called, assembled in arms; and as no resistance was made, no blood was shed on the occasion. They seized the gates, disarmed the garrison, imprisoned the magistrates, imparted the rights of citizens to all the rabble of the town and country, and proclaimed a *national* convention, which has not yet met. They are all for a pure and absolute democracy; but wish to remain a small independent state, whilst others aspire to become a part of the republic of France; and as the latter, though less numerous, are more violent and absurd than their adversaries, it is highly probable that they will succeed. The citizens of the best families and fortunes have retired from Geneva into the Pays de Vaud, but the French methods of recalling or proscribing emigrants will soon be adopted. You must have observed, that Savoy has now become "le department du Mont Blanc." I cannot satisfy myself whether the mass of the people is pleased or displeased with the change; but my noble scenery is clouded by the democratical aspect of twelve leagues of the opposite coast, which every morning obtrude themselves on my view. I here conclude the first part of the history of our Alpine troubles, and now consider myself as disengaged from all promises of periodical writing. Upon the whole, I kept it beyond our expectation; nor do I think that you have been sufficiently astonished by the wonderful effort of the triple dispatch.

You must now succeed to my task, and I shall expect, during the winter, a regular political journal of the events of your greater world. You are on the theatre, and may often be behind the scenes. You can always see, and may sometimes foresee. My own choice has indeed trans-

ported me into a foreign land ; but I am truly attached,
from interest and inclination, to my native country ; and
even as a citizen of the world, I wish the stability and
happiness of England, the sole great refuge of mankind
against the opposite mischiefs of despotism and democracy. I was indeed alarmed, and the more so, as I
saw that you were not without apprehension ; but I now
glory in the triumph of reason and genuine patriotism,
which seems to pervade the country ; nor do I dislike
some mixture of popular enthusiasm, which may be
requisite to encounter our mad or wicked enemies with
equal arms. The behaviour of Fox does not surprise me.
You may remember what I told you last year at Lausanne, when you attempted his defence, that * * * *
You have now crushed the daring subverters of the constitution ; but I now fear the moderate well-meaners—
reformers. Do not, I beseech you, tamper with parliamentary representation. The present house of commons
forms, in *practice*, a body of gentlemen, who must always
sympathise with the interests and opinions of the people ;
and the slightest innovation launches you, without rud-
der or compass, on a dark and dangerous ocean of theo-
retical experiment. On this subject I am indeed serious.

Upon the whole, I like the beginning of ninety-three
better than the end of ninety-two. The illusion seems
to break away throughout Europe. I think England and
Switzerland are safe. Brabant adheres to the old constitution. The Germans are disgusted with the rapine
and insolence of their deliverers. The pope is resolved
to head his armies, and the lazzaroni of Naples have
presented St. Januarius with a gold fuzee, to fire on

the brigands Français. So much for politics, which till
now never had such possession of my mind. Next post
I will write about myself and my own designs. Alas,
your poor eyes! make the Maria write; I will speedily
answer her. My lady is still dumb. The German posts
are now slow and irregular. You had better write by
the way of France, under cover. Direct to Le citoyen
Rebeur, à Pontalier, France.

Adieu; ever yours.

TO THE SAME.

Lausanne, Jan. 6th, 1793.

There was formerly a time when our correspondence
was a painful discussion of my private affairs; a vexatious
repetition of losses, of disappointments, of sales, &c.
These affairs are decently arranged: but public cares
have now succeeded to private anxiety, and our whole
attention is lately turned from Lenborough and Beriton,
to the political state of France and of Europe. From
these politics, however, one letter shall be free, while I
talk of myself and of my own plans; a subject most interesting to a friend, and only to a friend.

I know not whether I am sorry or glad that my expedition has been postponed to the present year. It is true,
that I now wish myself in England, and almost repent
that I did not grasp the opportunity when the obstacles
were comparatively smaller than they are now likely to
prove. Yet had I reached you last summer before the
month of August, a considerable portion of my time
would be now elapsed, and I should already begin to
think of my departure. If the gout should spare me this

winter, (and as yet I have not felt any symptom,) and if
the spring should make a soft and early appearance, it is
my intention to be with you in Downing-street before
the end of April, and thus to enjoy six weeks or two
months of the most agreeable season of London and the
neighbourhood, after the hurry of parliament is subsided,
and before the great rural dispersion·   As the banks of
the Rhine and the Belgic provinces are completely overspread with anarchy and war, I have made up my mind
to pass through the territories of the French republic.
From the best and most recent information, I am satisfied
that there is little or no real danger in the journey; and
I must arm myself with patience to support the vexatious
insolence of democratical tyranny.   I have even a sort
of curiosity to spend some days at Paris, to assist at the
debates of the Pandæmonium, to seek an introduction to
the principal devils, and to contemplate a new form of
public and private life, which never existed before, and
which I devoutly hope will not long continue to exist.
Should the obstacles of health or weather confine me at
Lausanne till the month of May, I shall scarcely be able
to resist the temptation of passing some part at least of
the summer in my own little paradise.   But all these
schemes must ultimately depend on the great question of
peace or war, which will indeed be speedily determined.
Should France become impervious to an English traveller, what must I do?   l shall not easily resolve to explore my way through the unknown language and abominable roads of the interior parts of Germany, to embark
in Holland, or perhaps at Hamburgh, and to be finally intercepted by a French privateer.   My stay in England

appears not less doubtful than the means of transporting myself. Should I arrive in the spring, it is possible, and barely possible, that I should return here in the autumn, it is much more probable that I shall pass the winter, and there may be even a chance of my giving my own country a longer trial. In my letter to my lady I fairly exposed the decline of Lausanne; but such an establishment as mine must not be lightly abandoned; nor can I discover what adequate mode of life my private circumstances, easy as they now are, could afford me in England. London and Bath have doubtless their respective merits, and I could wish to reside within a day's journey of Sheffield-place. But a state of perfect happiness is not to be found here below; and in the possession of my library, house, and garden, with the relics of our society, and a frequent intercourse with the Neckers, I may still be tolerably content. Among the disastrous changes of Lausanne, I must principally reckon the approaching dissolution of poor Severy and his family. He is still alive, but in such hopeless and painful decay, that we no longer conceal our wishes for his speedy release. I never loved nor esteemed him so much as in this last mortal disease, which he supports with a degree of energy, patience, and even cheerfulness, beyond all belief. His wife, whose whole time and soul are devoted to him, is almost sinking under her long anxiety. The children are most amiably assiduous to both their parents, and at all events, his filial duties and worldly cares must detain the son some time at home.

And now approach, and let me drop into your most

private ear, a literary secret. Of the Memoirs little has
been done, and with that little I am not satisfied. They
must be postponed till a mature season; and I much
doubt whether the book and the author can ever see the
light at the same time. But I have long revolved in my
mind another scheme of biographical writing: the lives,
or rather the characters, of the most eminent persons in
arts and arms, in church and state, who have flourished
in Britain from the reign of Henry VIII. to the present
age. This work, extensive as it may be, would be an
amusement rather than a toil; the materials are accessible in our own language, and for the most part ready to
my hands: but the subject, which would afford a rich
display of human nature and domestic history, would
powerfully address itself to the feelings of every Englishman. The taste or fashion of the times seems to delight
in picturesque decorations, and this series of British portraits might be aptly accompanied by the respective
heads, taken from originals, and engraved by the best
masters. Alderman Boydell, and his son-in-law, Mr.
George Nicoll, bookseller in Pallmall, are the great under-
takers in this line. On my arrival in England I shall be
free to consider, whether it may suit me to proceed in a
mere literary work without any other decorations than
those which it may derive from the pen of the author.
It is a serious truth, that I am no longer ambitious of
fame or money; that my habits of industry are much
impaired, and that I have reduced my studies to be the
loose amusement of my morning hours, the repetition of
which will insensibly lead me to the last term of

existence. And for this very reason I shall not be sorry to bind myself by a liberal engagement, from which I may not with honour recede.

Before I conclude, we must say a word or two of parliamentary and pecuniary concerns. 1. We all admire the generous spirit with which you d——d the assassins **. I hope that * * * * * The opinion of parliament in favour of Louis was declared in a manner worthy of the representatives of a great and wise nation. It will certainly have a powerful effect; and if the poor King be not already murdered, I am satisfied that his life is in safety: but is such a life worth his care? Our debates will now become every day more interesting; and as I expect from you only opinions and anecdotes, I most earnestly conjure you to send me Woodfall's Register as often (and that must be very often) as the occasion deserves it. I now spare no expense for news.

I want some account of Mrs. G.'s health. Will my lady never write? How can people be so indolent! I suppose this will find you at Sheffield-place during the recess, and that the heavy baggage will not move till after the birthday. Shall I be with you by the first of May? The Gods only know. I almost wish that I had accompanied Madame de Stael. Ever yours.

TO THE SAME.

Begun Feb. 9,—ended Feb. 18, 1793.

The struggle is at length over, and poor De Severy is no more! He expired about ten days ago, after every vital principle had been exhausted by a complication of disorders, which had lasted above five months: and a mortification in one of his legs, that gradually rose to the more noble parts, was the immediate cause of his death. His patience and even cheerfulness supported him to the fatal moment; and he enjoyed every comfort that could alleviate his situation, the skill of his physicians, the assiduous tenderness of his family, and the kind sympathy not only of his particular friends, but even of common acquaintance, and generally of the whole town. The stroke has been severely felt, yet I have the satisfaction to perceive that Madame de Severy's health is not affected; and we may hope that in time she will recover a tolerable share of composure and happiness. Her firmness was checked by the violent sallies of grief; her gentleness has preserved her from the worst of symptoms, a dry, silent despair. She loves to talk of her irreparable loss, she descants with pleasure on his virtues; her words are interrupted with tears, but those tears are her best relief; and her tender feelings will insensibly subside into an affectionate remembrance.*   Wilhelm is

---

* She is no more—that virtuous wife, that venerated mother, that sure and constant friend, whose value Mr. Gibbon so well appreciated, whom he speaks of with so much interest, with whom and whose worthy husband he passed, in the pleasure of intimate friendship, the last ten years of his life, and whose children were adopted by his heart.

Catherine Louise Jacqueline de Chandieu was born at Lausanne on the 3d of February, 1741. She had been endowed by nature with health and beauty, and a good education had added to these gifts the most agreeable and useful accomplishments, joined to the steady principles of an amiable and enlightened religion. Habitual association with those persons who were most distinguished by their merit, birth, or talents, had crowned the work of Nature and Education. In 1766 she married M. de Charière de Severy, and by these happy espousals insured that happiness which she had a right to expect. Without entering into the detail of her private and

much more deeply wounded than I could imagine, or than he expected himself; nor have I ever seen the affliction of a son more lively and sincere. Severy was indeed a very valuable man: without any shining qualifications, he was endowed in a high degree with good sense, honour, and benevolence; and few men have filled with

active virtues, we shall be contented with saying that Madame de Severy knew how to unite, during the course of her life, with a wisdom that was the fruit of reflection and piety, duties apparently the most opposite: that she was able to reconcile the faculty of pleasing with the most scrupulous reserve; to accept with discrimination the tributes paid to youth and beauty, and to preserve an angelic purity in an age of levity and folly.

Happy in the bosom of her family, yet at her estates, in the city, and in its most brilliant circles, she was everywhere in her appropriate place, and everywhere an object of consideration and respect. On the 29th of January, 1793, she was deprived, by a lingering malady, of a beloved husband. Her anxieties, watchings, and profound grief did not in the least abate her courage; she comforted and strengthened her children by inculcating into them the principles of a religion, which she had always looked on as her surest refuge in distress. She was still mourning in seclusion for the loss of her tenderly loved husband when the death of Mr. Gibbon called for renewed tears. Time had with difficulty begun to heal this double wound; she began again to adorn and animate society by her presence, her blooming beauty and noble carriage attracted every eye; she appeared and vanished. Her illness, which was of a complicated character, was neither long nor painful; and the serenity of a pure soul accompanied her, without anguish, into the bosom of eternal repose on the 17th of January, 1796.

Madame de Severy left two children, M. W. de Severy (whom Mr. Gibbon has sufficiently made known by these words inserted in his will, "whom I wish to style by the endearing name of son,") and M. Angletine de Severy, who vividly recalls to the mind the recollection of the graces and virtues of his mother. The happiness enjoyed by this family in intimate and continued intercourse with a mother who was their best friend, renders their loss irreparable, and their grief agonizing; they listen to no consolations but those offered by that pure religion whose cheering principles were implanted in their breasts by their virtuous mother.—S.

more propriety their circle in private life. For myself, I have had the misfortune of knowing him too late, and of losing him too soon. But enough of this melancholy subject.

The affairs of this theatre, which must always be minute, are now grown so tame and tranquil, that they no longer deserve the historian's pen. The new constitution of Geneva is slowly forming, without much noise or any bloodshed: and the patriots, who have staid in hopes of guiding or restraining the multitude, flatter themselves that they shall be able at least to prevent their mad countrymen from giving themselves to the French, the only mischief that would be absolutely irretrievable. The revolution of Geneva is of less consequence to us, however, than that of Savoy; but our fate will depend on the general event, rather than on these particular causes. In the meanwhile we hope to be quiet spectators of the struggle of this year; and we seem to have assurances that both the emperor and the French will compound for the neutrality of the Swiss. The Helvetic body does not acknowledge the republic of France; but Barthelemy, their ambassador, resides at Baden, and steals, like Chauvelin, into a kind of extra official negotiation. All spirit of opposition is quelled in the canton of Berne, and the perpetual banishment of the * * * * * * family has scarcely excited a murmur. It will probably be followed by that of * * * * * * * * * *: the crime alleged in their sentence is the having assisted at the federation dinner at Rolle two years ago; and as they are absent, I could almost wish that they had been summoned to appear, and heard in their own defence. To

the general supineness of the inhabitants of Lausanne
I must ascribe, that the death of Louis the Sixteenth has
been received with less horror and indignation than I
could have wished. I was much tempted to go into
mourning, and probably should, had the duchess been
still here; but as the only Englishman of any mark, I
was afraid of being singular; more especially as our
French emigrants, either from prudence or poverty, do
not wear black, nor do even the Neckers. Have you
read his discourse for the king? It might indeed super-
sede the necessity of mourning. I should judge from your
last letter, and from the diary, that the French declaration
of war must have rather surprised you. I wish, although
I know not how it could have been avoided, that we
might still have continued to enjoy our safe and prosperous neutrality. You will not doubt my best wishes for
the destruction of the miscreants; but I love England
still more than I hate France. All reasonable chances
are in favour of a confederacy, such as was never opposed to the ambition of Louis the Fourteenth; but, after
the experience of last year, I distrust reason, and confess
myself fearful for the event. The French are strong in
numbers, activity, enthusiasm; they are rich in rapine;
and although their strength may be only that of a
frenzy fever, they may do infinite mischief to their neighbours before they can be reduced to a strait waistcoat.
I dread the effects that may be produced on the minds
of the people by the increase of debt and taxes, probable
losses, and possible mismanagement. Our trade must
suffer; and though projects of invasion have been always

abortive, I cannot forget that the fleets and armies of Europe have failed before the towns in America, which have been taken and plundered by a handful of buccaneers. I know nothing of Pitt as a war minister; but it affords me much satisfaction that the intrepid wisdom of the new chancellor* is introduced into the cabinet. I wish, not merely on your own account, that you were placed in an active, useful station in government. I should not dislike you secretary at war.

I have little more to say of myself, or of my journey to England: you know my intentions, and the great events of Europe must determine whether they can be carried into execution this summer. If * * * * * has warmly adopted *your* idea, I shall speedily hear from him; but, in truth, I know not what will be my answer: I see difficulties which at first did not occur: I doubt my own perseverance, and my fancy begins to wander into new paths. The amusement of reading and thinking may perhaps satisfy a man who has paid his debt to the public; and there is more pleasure in building castles in the air than on the ground. I shall contrive some small assistance for your correspondent, though I cannot learn any thing that distinguishes him from many of his countrymen: we have had our full share of poor imigrants; but if you wish that any thing extraordinary should be done for this man, you must send me a measure. Adieu. I embrace my lady and Maria, as also Louisa. Perhaps I may soon write, without expecting an answer. Ever yours.

* Lord Loughborough.

TO THE SAME.

Lausanne, April 27, 1793.

My dearest friend, for such you most truly are, nor does there exist a person who obtains, or shall ever obtain a superior place in my esteem and affection.

After too long a silence I was sitting down to write, when, only yesterday morning (such is the irregular slowness of the English post) I was suddenly struck, indeed struck to the heart, by the fatal intelligence* from Sir Henry Clinton and M. de Lally. Alas! what is life, and what are our hopes and projects! When I embraced her at your departure from Lausanne, could I imagine that it was for the last time? When I postponed to another summer my journey to England, could I apprehend that I never, never should see her again? I always hoped that she would spin her feeble thread to a long duration, and that her delicate frame would survive (as is often the case) many constitutions of a stouter appearance. In four days! in your absence, in that of her children! But she is now at rest, and if there be a future life, her mild virtues have surely entitled her to the reward of pure and perfect felicity. It is for you that I feel; and I can judge of your sentiments by comparing them with my own. I have lost, it is true, an amiable and affectionate friend, whom I had known and loved above three and twenty years, and whom I often styled by the endearing name of sister. But you are deprived of the companion of your life, the wife of your choice, and the mother of your children—poor children! The

* The death of Lady Sheffield.

liveliness of Maria, and the softness of Louisa, render them almost equally the objects of my tenderest compassion. I do not wish to aggravate your grief; but, in the sincerity of friendship, I cannot hold a different language. I know the impotence of reason, and I much fear that the strength of your character will serve to make a sharper and more lasting impression.

The only consolation in these melancholy trials to which human life is exposed, the only one at least in which I have any confidence, is the presence of a real friend; and of that, as far as it depends on myself, you shall not be destitute. I regret the few days that must be lost in some necessary preparations; but I trust that to-morrow se'nnight (May the fifth) I shall be able to set forwards on my journey to England; and when this letter reaches you, I shall be considerably advanced on my way. As it is yet prudent to keep at a respectful distance from the banks of the French Rhine, I shall incline a little to the right, and proceed by Scaffhausen and Stutgard to Frankfort and Cologne: the Austrian Netherlands are now open and safe, and I am sure of being able at least to pass from Ostend to Dover; whence, without passing through London, I shall pursue the direct road to Sheffield-place. Unless I should meet with some unforeseen accidents and delays, I hope, before the end of the month, to share your solitude, and sympathise with your grief. All the difficulties of the journey, which my indolence had probably magnified, have now disappeared before a stronger passion; and you will not be sorry to hear, that, as far as Frankfort to Cologne, I shall enjoy the advantage of the society, the conversation, the

German language, and the active assistance of Severy.
His attachment to me is the sole motive which prompts
him to undertake this troublesome journey: and as soon
as he has seen me over the roughest ground, he will immediately return to Lausanne.   The poor young man
loved Lady S. as a mother, and the whole family is
deeply affected by an event which reminds them too
painfully of their own misfortune.   Adieu.   I could write
volumes, and shall therefore break off abruptly.   I shall
write on the road, and hope to find a few lines à poste
restante at Frankfort and Brussels.   Adieu; ever yours.

TO THE SAME.

Lausanne, May, 1793.

My dear Friend,—I must write a few lines before my
departure, though indeed I scarcely know what to say.
Nearly a fortnight has elapsed since the first melancholy
tidings, without my having received the slightest subsequent accounts of your health and situation.   Your own
silence announces too forcibly how much you are involved in your feelings; and I can but too easily conceive
that a letter to me would be more painful than to an indifferent person.   But that amiable man, Count Lally,
might surely have written a second time; but your sister,
who is probably with you; but Maria, alas! poor Maria!
I am left in a state of darkness to the workings of my own
fancy, which imagines every thing that is sad and shocking.   What can I think of for your relief and comfort?
I will not expatiate on those common-place topics, which
have never dried a single tear; but let me advise, let me
urge you to force yourself into business, as I would try

to force myself into study.   The mind must not be idle;
if it be not exercised on external objects, it will prey on
its own vitals.   A thousand little arrangements, which
must precede a long journey, have postponed my departure three or four days beyond the term which I had
first appointed; but all is now in order, and I set off to-
morrow, the ninth instant, with my valet de chambre, a
courier on horseback, and Severy, with his servant, as far
as Frankfort.   I calculate my arrival at Sheffield-place
(how I dread and desire to see that mansion!) for the
first week in June, soon after this letter; but I will try
to send you some later intelligence.   I never found myself stronger or in better health.   The German road is
now cleared, both of enemies and allies, and though I
must expect fatigue, I have not any apprehensions of
danger.   It is scarcely possible that you should meet me
at Frankfort, but I shall be much disappointed at not
finding a line at Brussels or Ostend.   Adieu.   If there
be any invisible guardians, may they watch over you
and yours!   Adieu.

TO THE SAME.

Frankfort, May 19th, 1793.

   And here I am, in good health and spirits, after one of
the easiest, safest, and pleasantest journies which I ever
performed in my whole life; not the appearance of an
enemy, and hardly the appearance of a war.   Yet I
hear, as I am writing, the cannon of the siege of Mayence, at the distance of twenty miles; and long, very
long, will it be heard.   It is confessed on all sides, that
the French fight with a courage worthy of a better cause.

The town of Mayence is strong, their artillery admirable; they are already reduced to horse-flesh, but they have still the resource of eating the inhabitants, and at last of eating one another; and, if that repast could be extended to Paris and the whole country, it might essentially contribute to the relief of mankind. Our operations are carried on with more than German slowness, and when the besieged are quiet, the besiegers are perfectly satisfied with their progress. A spirit of division undoubtedly prevails; and the character of the Prussians for courage and discipline is sunk lower than you can possibly imagine. Their glory has expired with Frederick. I am sorry to have missed Lord Elgin, who is beyond the Rhine with the King of Prussia. As I am impatient, I propose setting forwards to-morrow afternoon, and shall reach Ostend in less than eight days. The passage must depend on winds and packets; and I hope to find at Brussels or Dover a letter which will direct me to Sheffield-place or Downing-street. Severy goes back from hence. Adieu: I embrace the dear girls. Ever your.

TO THE SAME.

Brussels, May 27, 1793.

This day, between two and three o'clock in the after-noon, I arrived at this place in excellent preservation. My expedition, which is now drawing to a close, has been a journey of perseverance rather than speed, of some labour since Frankfort, but without the smallest degree of difficulty or danger. As I have every morning been seated in the chaise soon after sun-rise, I propose indulging to-morrow till eleven o'clock, and going that day no farther than Ghent. On Wednesday the 29th instant I shall reach Ostend in good time, just eight days, according to my former reckoning, from Frankfort. Beyond that I can say nothing positive; but should the winds be propitious, it is possible that I may appear next Saturday, June 1, in Downing-street. After that earliest date, you will expect me day by day till I arrive. Adieu. I embrace the dear girls, and salute Mrs. Holroyd. I rejoice that you have anticipated my advice by plunging into business; but I should now be sorry if that business, however important, detained us long in town. I do not wish to make a public exhibition, and only sigh to enjoy you and the precious remnant in the solitude of Sheffield-place. Ever yours.

If I am successful I may outstrip or accompany this letter. Yours and Maria's waited for me here, and over-paid the journey.

The preceding letters intimate that, in return for my visit to Lausanne in 1791, Mr. Gibbon engaged to pass a year with me in England: that the war having rendered travelling exceedingly inconvenient, especially to a person who, from his bodily infirmities, required every accommodation, prevented his undertaking so formidable a journey at the time he proposed.

The call of friendship, however, was sufficient to make him overlook every personal consideration, when he thought his presence might prove a consolation. I must ever regard it as the most endearing proof of his sensibility, and of his possessing the true spirit of friendship,

that after having relinquished the thought of his intended
visit, he hastened to England, in spite of increasing im-
pediments, to soothe me by the most generous sympathy,
and to alleviate my domestic affliction; neither his great
corpulency, nor his extraordinary bodily infirmities, nor
any other consideration, could prevent him a moment
from resolving on an undertading that might have de-
terred the most active young man. He, almost immediately, with alertness by no means natural to him,
undertook a great circuitous journey, along the frontiers
of an enemy, worse than savage, within the sound of
their cannon, within the range of the light troops of the
different armies, and through roads ruined by the enormous machinery of war.

The readiness with which he engaged in this kind
office of friendship, at a time when a selfish spirit might
have pleaded a thousand reasons for declining so hazard-
ous a journey, conspired, with the peculiar charms of his
society, to render his arrival a cordial to my mind. I
had the satisfaction of finding that his own delicate and
precarious health had not suffered in the service of his
friend. He arrived in the beginning of June at my
house in Downing-street, safe and in good health; and
after we had passed about a month together in London,
we settled at Sheffield-place for the summer; where his
wit, learning, and cheerful politeness delighted a great
variety of characters.

Although he was inclined to represent his health as
better than it really was, his habitual dislike to motion
appeared to increase; his inaptness to exercise confined
him to the library and dining-room, and there he joined

my friend Mr. Frederick North, in pleasant arguments against exercise in general.   He ridiculed the unsettled and restless disposition, that summer, the most uncomfortable, as he said, of all seasons, generally gives to those who have the use of their limbs.   Such arguments were little required to keep society within doors, when his company was only there to be enjoyed ; for neither the fineness of the season, nor the most promising parties of pleasure, could tempt the company of either sex to desert him.

Those who have enjoyed the society of Mr. Gibbon will agree with me, that his conversation was still more captivating than his writings.   Perhaps no man ever divided time more fairly between literary labour and social enjoyment; and hence, probably, he derived his peculiar excellence of making his very extensive knowledge contribute, in the highest degree, to the use or pleasure of those with whom he conversed.   He united, in the happiest manner imaginable, two characters which are not often found in the same person, the profound scholar and the fascinating companion.

It would be superfluous to attempt a very minute delineation of a character which is so distinctly marked in the Memoirs and Letters.   He has described himself without reserve, and with perfect sincerity.   The Letters, and especially the extracts from the Journal, which could not have been written with any purpose of being seen, will make the reader perfectly acquainted with the man.

Excepting a visit to Lord Egremont and Mr. Hayley, whom he very particularly esteemed, Mr. Gibbon was not absent from Sheffield-place till the beginning of October, when we were reluctantly obliged to part with him, that he might perform his engagement to Mrs. Gibbon at Bath, the widow of his father, who had early deserved, and invariably retained, his affection. From Bath he proceeded to Lord Spenser's at Althorp, a family which he always met with uncommon satisfaction. He continued in good health during the summer, and in excellent spirits (I never knew him enjoy better); and when he went from Sheffield-place, little did I imagine it would be the last time I should have the inexpressible pleasure of seeing him there in full possession of health.

The few following short letters, though not important in themselves, will fill up this part of the narrative better, and more agreeably, than any thing I can substitute in their place.

EDWARD GIBBON, ESQ. TO THE RIGHT HON. LORD SHEFFIELD.

October 2nd, 1793.

The Cork-street hotel has answered its recommendation; it is clean, convenient, and quiet. My first evening was passed at home in a very agreeable *tête-à-tête* with my friend Elmsley. Yesterday I dined at Craufurd's with an excellent set, in which were Pelham and Lord Egremont. I dine to-day with my Portuguese friend, Madame de Sylva, at Greniere's; most probably with Lady Webster, whom I met last night at Devonshire-house; a constant, though late, resort of society. The duchess is as good, and Lady Elizabeth as seducing, as ever. No news whatever. You will see in the papers Lord Hervey's memorial. I love vigour, but it is surely a strong a measure to tell a gentleman you have *resolved* to pass the winter in his house. London is not disagreeable; yet I shall probably leave it Saturday. If any thing should occur, I will write. Adieu; ever yours.

TO THE SAME.

Sunday afternoon I left London, and lay at Reading, and Monday in very good time I reached this place after a very pleasant airing; and am always so much delighted, and improved, with this union of ease and motion, that, were not the expense enormous, I would travel every year some hundred miles, more especially in England. I passed the day with Mrs. G. yesterday. In mind and conversation she is just the same as twenty years ago. She has spirits, appetite, legs, and eyes, and talks of living till ninety.* I can say from my heart, Amen. We dine at two, and remain together till nine; but, although we have much to say, I am not sorry that she talks of introducing a third or fourth actor. Lord Spenser expects me about the 20th; but if I can do it without offence, I shall steal away two or three days sooner, and you shall have advice of my motions. The troubles of Bristol have been serious and bloody. I know not who was in fault; but I do not like appeasing the mob by the extinction of the toll, and the removal of the Hereford militia, who had done their duty. Adieu. The girls must dance at Tunbridge. What would dear little aunt say if I was to answer her letter? Ever yours, &c.

York-house, Bath, October 9th, 1793.

* She was then in her eightieth year.

I still follow the old style, though the Convention has abolished the Christian era, with months, weeks, days, &c.

TO THE SAME.

York-house, Bath, October 13th, 1793.

I am as ignorant of Bath in general as if I were still at Sheffield. My impatience to get away makes me think it better to devote my whole time to Mrs. G.; and dear little aunt, whom I tenderly salute, will excuse me to her two friends, Mr. Hartley and Preston, if I make little or no use of their kind introduction. A *tête-à-tête* of eight or nine hours every day is rather difficult to support; yet I do assure you, that our conversation flows with more ease and spirit when we are alone, than when any auxiliaries are summoned to our aid. She is indeed a wonderful woman, and I think all her faculties of the mind stronger and more active than I have ever known them. I have settled, that ten full days may be sufficient for all the purposes of our interview. I should therefore depart next Friday, the 18th instant, and am indeed expected at Althorp on the 20th; but I may possibly reckon without my host, as I have not yet apprised Mrs. G. of the term of my visit; and will certainly not quarrel with her for a short delay. I must have some political speculations. The campaign, at least on our side, seems to be at an end. Ever yours.

TO THE SAME.

Althorp library, Tuesday, four o'clock.

We have so completely exhausted this morning among

the first editions of Cicero, that I can mention only my departure hence to-morrow, the sixth instant. I shall lie quietly at Woburn, and reach London in good time Thursday. By the following post I will write somewhat .more largely. My stay in London will depend, partly on my amusement, and your being fixed at Sheffieldplace; unless you think I can be comfortably arranged for a week or two with you at Brighton. The military remarks seem good; but now to what purpose! Adieu. I embrace and much rejoice in Louisa's improvement. Lord Ossory was from home at Farning-woods.

TO THE SAME.

London, Friday, Nov. 8th, four o'clock.

Walpole has just delivered yours, and I hasten to the direction, that you may not be at a loss. I will write to-morrow, but I am now fatigued, and rather unwell. Adieu. I have not seen a soul except Elmsley.

TO THE SAME.

St. James's Street, Nov. 9th, 1793.

As I dropt yesterday the word *unwell*, I flatter myself that the family would have been a little alarmed by my silence to-day. I am still awkward, though without any suspicions of gout, and have some idea of having recourse to medical advice. Yet I creep out to-day in a chair, to dine with Lord Lucan. But as it will be literally my first going down stairs, and as scarcely any one is apprised of my arrival, I know nothing, I have heard nothing, I have nothing to say. My present lodging, a house of Elmsley's, is cheerful, convenient, somewhat dear, but not so much as an hotel: a species of habitation for which I have not conceived any great affection. Had you been stationary at Sheffield, you would have seen me before the twentieth; for I am tired of rambling, and pant for my home; that is to say, for your house. But whether I shall have courage to brave * * * * and a bleak down, time only can discover. Adieu. I wish you back to Sheffield-place. The health of dear Louisa is doubtless the first object; but I did not expect Brighton after Tunbridge. Whenever dear little aunt is separate from you, I shall certainly write to her: but at present how is it possible? Ever yours.

TO THE SAME AT BRIGHTHELMSTONE.

St. James's Street, Nov. 11th, 1793.

I must at length withdraw the veil before my state of health, though the naked truth may alarm you more than a fit of the gout. Have you never observed, through my *inexpressibles*, a large prominency, which, as it was not at all painful, and very little troublesome, I had strangely neglected for many years? But since my departure from Sheffield-place it has increased, most stupenduously, is increasing, and ought to be diminished. Yesterday I sent for Farquhar, who is allowed to be a very skilful surgeon. After viewing and palping, he very seriously desired to call in assistance, and has examined it again to-day with Mr. Cline, a surgeon, as he says, of the first eminence. They both pronounce it a *hydrocele* (a collection of water), which must be let out by the operation of tapping; but from its magnitude and long neglect, they think it a most extraordinary case, and wish to have another surgeon, Dr. Bayley, present. If the business should go off smoothly, I shall be delivered from my burthen, (it is almost as big as a small child), and walk about in four or five days with a truss. But the medical gentlemen, who never speak quite plain, insinuate to me the possibility of an inflammation, of fever, &c. I am not appalled at the thoughts of the operation, which is fixed for Wednesday next, twelve o'clock; but it has occured to me that you might wish to be present, before and afterwards, till the crisis was past; and to give you that opportunity, I shall solicit a delay till Thursday, or even Friday. In the meanwhile, I crawl about with some labour, and much indecency, to Devonshire-house, where I left all the fine ladies making flannel waistcoats;* Lady Lucan's, &c. Adieu. Varnish the business for the ladies; yet I am afraid it will be public;—the advantage of being notorious. Ever yours.

IMMEDIATELY on receiving the last letter, I went the same day from Brighthelmstone to London, and was agreeably surprised to find that Mr. Gibbon had dined at Lord Lucan's, and did not return to his lodgings, where I waited for him till eleven o'clock at night. Those who have seen him within the last eight or ten years must be surprised to hear, that he could doubt whether his disorder was apparent. When he returned to England in 1787, I was greatly alarmed by a prodigious increase, which I always conceived to proceed from a rupture. I did not understand why he, who had talked with me on every

* For the soldiers in Flanders.

other subject relative to himself and his affairs without
reserve, should never in any shape hint at a malady so
troublesome; but on speaking to his valet de chambre,
he told me, Mr. Gibbon could not bear the least illusion
to that subject, and never would suffer him to notice it.
I consulted some medical persons, who with me supposing
it to be a rupture, were of opinion that nothing could
be done, and said that he surely must have had advice,
and of course had taken all necessary precautions. He
now talked freely with me about his disorder; which, he
said, began in the year 1761; that he then consulted Mr.
Hawkins, the surgeon, who did not decide whether it
was the beginning of a rupture, or an hydrocele; but he
desired to see Mr. Gibbon again when he came to town.
Mr. Gibbon not feeling any pain, nor suffering any inconvenience, as he said, never returned to Mr. Hawkins;
and although the disorder continued to increase gradually, and of late years very much indeed, he never mentioned it to any person, however incredible it may appear, from 1761 to November 1793. I told him, that I
had always supposed there was no doubt of its being a
rupture; his answer was, that he had never thought so,
and that he, and the physicians who attended him, were
of opinion that it was an hydrocele. It is now certain
that it was originally a rupture, and that an hydrocele
had lately taken place in the same part; and it is remarkable, that his legs, which had been swelled about
the ancle, particularly one of them, since he had the
erysipelas in 1790, recovered their former shape as soon
as the water appeared in another part, which did not
happen till between the time he left Sheffield-place, in

the beginning of October, and his arrival at Althorp, towards the latter end of that month. On the Thursday
following the date of his last letter, Mr. Gibbon was tap-
ped for the first time; four quarts of transparent watery
fluid were discharged by that operation. Neither inflammation nor fever ensued: the tumour was diminished to
nearly half its size; the remaining part was a soft irregular mass. I had been with him two days before, and I
continued with him above a week after the first tapping,
during which time he enjoyed his usual spirits; and the
three medical gentlemen who attended him will recollect
his pleasantry even during the operation. He was
abroad again in a few days, but the water evidently col-
lecting very fast, it was agreed that a second puncture
should be made a fortnight after the first. Knowing
that I should be wanted at a meeting in the country, he
pressed me to attend it; and promised that soon after
the second operation was performed he would follow me
to Sheffield-place: but before he arrived I received the
two following letters.   •

MR. GIBBON TO LORD SHEFFIELD AT BRIGHTON.

St. James's Street, Nov. 25th, 1793.

Though Farquhar has promised to write you a line,
I conceive you may not be sorry to hear directly from
me. The operation of yesterday was much longer, more
searching, and more painful than the former; but it has
eased and lightened me to a much greater degree.* No
inflammation, no fever, a delicious night, leave to go

* Three quarts of the same fluid as before were discharged.

abroad to morrow, and to go out of town when I please, *en attendant* the future measures of a radical cure. If you hold your intention of returning next Saturday to Sheffield-place, I shall probably join you about the Tuesday following, after having passed two nights at Beckenham.* The Devons are going to Bath, and the hospita-able Craufurd follows them. I passed a delightful day with Burke; an odd one with Monsignor Erskine, the Pope's Nuncio. Of public news, you and the papers know more than I do. We seem to have strong sea and land hopes, nor do I dislike the royalists having beaten the *sans cullottes* and taken Dol. How many minutes will it take to guillotine the seventy three new members of the Convention, who are now arrested? Adieu; ever yours.

MR. GIBBON TO LORD SHEFFIELD.

St. James's Street, Nov. 30th. 1793.

It will not be in my power to reach Sheffield-place quite so soon as I wished and expected. Lord Auckland informs me, that he shall be at Lambeth next week, Tuesday, Wednesday and Thursday. I have therefore agreed to dine at Beckenham on Friday. Saturday will be spent there; and unless some extraordinary temptation should detain me another day, you will see me by four o'clock Sunday the ninth of December. I dine to-morrow with the chancellor at Hampstead, and, what I do not like at this time of the year, without a proposal to stay all night. Yet I would not refuse, more especially as I had denied him on a former day. My health is good;

* Eden-farm.

but I shall have a final interview with Farquhar before
I leave town.   We are still in darkness about Lord
Howe and the French ships, but hope seems to prepon-
derate.   Adieu.   Nothing that relates to Louisa can be
forgotten.   Ever yours.

Mr. Gibbon generally took the opportunity of passing
a night or two with his friend Lord Auckland, at Eden-
farm, (ten miles from London) on his passage to Sheffield-
place ; and notwithstanding his indisposition, he had
lately made an excursion thither from London;
when he was much pleased by meeting the Archbishop of Canterbury, of whom he expressed a high
opinion.   He returned to London, to dine with Lord
Loughborough, to meet Mr. Burke, Mr. Windham, and
particularly Mr. Pitt, with whom he was not acquainted;
and in his last journey to Sussex, he revisited Eden-farm,
and was much gratified by the opportunity of again seeing, during a whole day, Mr. Pitt, who passed the night
there.   From Lord Auckland's, Mr. Gibbon proceeded
to Sheffield-place; and his discourse was never more
brilliant, nor more entertaining, than on his arrival.   The
parrallel he drew, and the comparisons he made, between
the leading men of this country, were sketched in his
best manner, and were infinitely interesting.   However,
this last visit to Sheffield-place became far different from
any he had ever made before.   That ready, cheerful,
various, and illuminating conversation, which we had
before admired in him was not always to be found in the
library or the dining-room.   He moved with difficulty,

and retired from company sooner than he had been used
to do. On the twenty-third of December, his appetite
began to fail him. He observed to me, that it. was a
very bad sign *with him* when he could not eat his
breakfast, which he had done at all times very heartily ;
and this seems to have been the strongest expression of
apprehension that he was ever observed to utter. A
considerable degree of fever now made its appearance.
Inflammation arose from the weight and bulk of the tumour. Water again collected very fast, and 'when the fever
went off, he never entirely recovered his appetite, even
for breakfast. I became very uneasy indeed at his situation towards the end of the month, and thought it necessary to advise him to set out for London. He had before settled his plan to arrive there about the middle of
January. 1 had company in the house, and we expected
one of his particular friends ; but he was obliged to
sacrifice all social pleasure to the immediate attention
which his health required. He went to London on the
seventh of January, and the next day 1 received the
following billet ; the last he ever wrote.

EDWARD GIBBON, ESQ. TO LORD SHEFFIELD.

St. James's Street, four o'clock, Tuesday.

'This date says every thing. I was almost killed
between Sheffield-place and East Grinstead, by hard,
frozen, long, and cross ruts, that would disgrace the
approach of an Indian wigwam. The rest was something less painful ; and I reached this place half dead,
ut not seriously feverish, or ill. I found a dinner invi-
ition from Lord Lucan ; but what are dinners to me?

I wish they did not know of my departure. I catch the flying post. What an effort! Adieu, till Thursday or Friday."

By his own desire, I did not follow him till Thursday the 9th. I then found him far from well. The tumour more distended than before, inflamed, and ulcerated in several places. Remedies were applied to abate the inflammation; but it was not thought proper to puncture the tumour for a third time, till Monday the 13th of January, when no less than six quarts of fluid were discharged. He seemed much relieved by the evacuation. His spirits continued good. He talked, as usual, of passing his time at houses which he had often frequented with great pleasure, the Duke of Devonshire's, Mr. Craufurd's, Lord Spencer's, Lord Lucan's, Sir Ralph Payne's, and Mr. Batt's; and when I told him that I should not return to the country, as I had intended, he pressed me to go; knowing I had an engagement there on public business, he said, "you may be back on Saturday, and I intend to go on Thursday to Devonshire-house." I had not any apprehension that his life was in danger, although I began to fear that he might not be restored to a comfortable state, and that motion would be very troublesome to him; but he talked of a radical cure. He said, that it was fortunate the disorder had shown itself while he was in England, where he might procure the best assistance; and if a radical cure could not be obtained before his return to Lausanne, there was an able surgeon at Geneva, who could come to tap him when it should be necessary.

On Tuesday the fourteenth, when the risk of inflammation and fever from the last operation was supposed to be
past, as the medical gentlemen who attended him expressed
no fears for his life, I went that afternoon part of the way
to Sussex, and the following day reached Sheffield-place.
The next morning, the sixteenth, I received by the post
a good account of Mr. Gibbon, which mentioned also that
he hourly gained strength.   In the evening came a letter
by express, dated noon that day, which acquainted me
that Mr. Gibbon had had a violent attack the preceding
night, and that it was not probable he should live till I
could come to him.   I reached his lodgings in St. James's
Street about midnight, and learned that my friend had
expired a quarter before one o'clock that day, the 16th
of January, 1794.

After I left him on Tuesday afternoon the fourteenth,
he saw some company, Lady Lucan and Lady Spenser,
and thought himself well enough at night to omit the
opium draught, which he had been used to take for some
time.   He slept very indifferently; before nine the next
morning he rose, but could not eat his breakfast.   However, he appeared tolerably well, yet complained at
times of a pain in his stomach.   At one o'clock, he received a visit of an hour from Madame de Sylva; and at
three, his friend, Mr. Craufurd, of Auchinames (whom
he always mentioned with particular regard) called, and
stayed with him till past five o'clock.   They talked, as
usual, on various subjects; and twenty hours before his
death, Mr. Gibbon happened to fall into a conversation,
not uncommon with him, on the probable duration of his
life.   He said, that he thought himself a good life for ten,

twelve, or perhaps twenty years. About six, he ate the
wing of a chicken, and drank three glasses of Madeira.
After dinner, he became very uneasy and impatient;
complained a good deal, and appeared so weak that his
servant was alarmed. Mr. Gibbon had sent to his friend
and relation, Mr. Robert Darell, whose house was not far
distant, desiring to see him, and adding that he had something particular to say. But, unfortunately, this desired
interview never took place.

During the evening, he complained very much of his
stomach, and of a disposition to vomit. Soon after nine,
he took his opium draught, and went to bed. About
ten, he complained of much pain, and desired that warm
napkins might be applied to his stomach. He almost
incessantly expressed a sense of pain till about four
o'clock in the morning, when he said he found his
stomach much easier. About seven, the servant asked,
whether he should send for Mr. Farquhar? He answered, no; that he was as well as he had been the day
before. At about half past eight, he got out of bed, and
said he was "plus adroit" than he had been for three
months past, and got into bed again, without assistance,
better than usual. About nine he said that he would
rise. The servant, however, persuaded him to remain in
bed till Mr. Farquhar, who was expected at eleven, should
come. Till about that hour, he spoke with great facility.
Mr. Farquhar came at the time appointed, and he was
then visibly dying. When the valet de chambre returned, after attending Mr. Farquhar out of the room,
Mr. Gibbon said, "Pourquoi est ce vouz me quittez?"
This was about half past eleven. At twelve, he drank

some brandy and water from a tea-pot, and desired his
favourite servant to stay with him. These were the last
words he pronounced articulately. To the last he preserved his senses; and when he could no longer
speak, his servant having asked a question, he made
a sign, to show that he understood him. He was quite
tranquil, and did not stir; his eyes half shut. About a
quarter before one, he ceased to breathe.*

* The body was not opened till the fifth day after his death. It was
then sound, except that a degree of mortification, not very considerable,
had taken place on a part of the colon: which, with the whole of the
omentum, of a very enlarged size, had descended into the scrotum, forming
a bag that hung down nearly as low as the knee. Since that part had been
inflamed and ulcerated, Mr. Gibbon could not bear a truss; and when the
last six quarts of fluid were discharged, the colon and omentum descending lower, they, by their weight, drew the mouth of the stomach down-
wards to the os pubis, and this probably was the immediate cause of his death.

The following is the account of the appearance of the body, given by an
eminent surgeon who opened it:

" Aperto tumore, qui ab inguine usque ad genu se extenderat, observatum
est partem ejus inferiorem constare ex tunicâ vaginali testis continenti
duas quasi libras liquoris serosi tincti sanguine. Ea autem fuit sacci illius
amplitudo ut portioni liquoris longè majori capiendæ sufficeret. In pos-
teriori parte hujus sacci testis situs fuit. Hunc ominò sanum invenimus.

" Partem tumoris superiorem occupaverant integrum ferè omentum et
major pars intestini coli. Hæ partes, sacco sibi proprio inclusæ, sibi invi-
cem et sacco suo adeò arctè adhæserunt ut coïvisse viderentur in massam
unam solidam et irregularem; cujus a tergo chorda spermatica sedem suam
obtinuerat.

" In omento et in intestino colo haud dubia recentis inflammationis signa
vidimus, necnon maculas nonnullas lividi coloris hinc inde sparsas.

" Aperto abdomine, ventriculum invenimus a naturali suo situ detractum
usque ad annulum musculi obliqui externi. Pylorum retrorsùm et quasi
sursùm a duodeno retractum. In hepate ingentum numerum parvorum tu
berculorum. Vesicam felleam bile admodùm distentam. In cæteris visceri
bus, examini anatomico subjectis, nulla morbi vestigia extiterunt."

The valet de chambre observed, that Mr. Gibbon did not, at any time, show the least sign of alarm, or apprehension of death; and it does not appear that he ever thought himself in danger, unless his desire to speak to Mr. Darell may be considered in that light.

Perhaps I dwell too long on these minute and melancholy circumstances. Yet the close of such a life can hardly fail to interest every reader; and I know that the public has received a very different and erroneous account of my friend's last hours.

I can never cease to feel regret that I was not by his side at this awful period: a regret so strong that I can express it only by borrowing (as the eloquent Mr. Mason has done on a similar occasion) the forcible language of Tacitus:—"Mihi præter acerbitatem amici erepti, auget mæstitiam quod assidere valetudini, fovere deficientem, satiari vultu, complexu non contigit." It is some consolation to me, that I have not, like Tacitus, by a long absence, anticipated the loss of my friend several years before his decease. Although I had not the mournful gratification of being near him on the day he expired, yet during his illness I had not failed to attend him, with that assiduity which his genius, his virtues, and, above all, our long, uninterrupted, and happy friendship demanded.

Postscript.—Mr. Gibbon's will is dated the 1st of Ocber, 1791, just before I left Lausanne; he distinguishes me, as usual, in the most flattering manner:

"I constitute and appoint the Right Honourable John Lord Sheffield, Edward Darell, Esquire, and John Thomas

Batt, Esquire, to be the executors of this my last will and testament; and as the execution of this trust will not be attended with much difficulty or trouble, I shall indulge these gentlemen in the pleasure of this last disinterested service, without wronging my feeling or oppressing my heir, by too light or too weighty a testimony of my gratitude. My obligations to the long and active friendship of Lord Sheffield, I could never sufficiently repay."

He then observes, that the Right Hon. Lady Eliot, of Port Eliot is his nearest relation on his father's side; but that her three sons are in such prosperous circumstances, that he may well be excused from making the two children of his late uncle, Sir Stanier Porten, his heirs, they being in a very different situation. He bequeathes annuities to two old servants: three thousand pounds, and his furniture, plate, &c. at Lausanne, to Mr. Wilhelm de Severy; one hundred pounds to the poor of Lausanne, and fifty guineas each to the following persons: Lady Sheffield and daughters, Maria and Louisa, Madame and Madamoiselle de Severy, the Count de Schomberg, Mademoiselle la Chanoinesse de Polier, and M. le Ministre Le Vade, for the purchase of some token which may remind them of a sincere friend. *The remains of Mr. Gibbon were deposited in Lord Sheffield's family burial-place in Sussex.*

FINIS.

Lightning Source UK Ltd.
Milton Keynes UK
01 November 2010

162210UK00008B/184/P

9 781148 969008